THE
END
OF THE
WORLD

'John Leslie is one of a very small group of philosophers thoroughly conversant with the latest ideas in physics and cosmology. Moreover, Leslie is able to write about these ideas with wit, clarity and penetrating insight. He has established himself as a thinker who is unafraid to tackle the great issues of existence, and able to sift discerningly through the competing – and frequently bizarre – concepts emanating from fundamental research in the physical sciences. Leslie is undoubtedly the world's expert on Brandon Carter's so-called Doomsday argument – a philosophical poser that is startling yet informative, seemingly outrageous yet intriguing, and ultimately both disturbing and illuminating. With his distinctive and highly readable style, combined with a bold and punchy treatment, Leslie offers a fascinating glimpse of the power of human reasoning to deduce our place in the universe.'

PAUL DAVIES, PROFESSOR OF NATURAL PHILOSOPHY, UNIVERSITY OF ADELAIDE, AND AUTHOR OF *THE LAST THREE MINUTES*

'This book is vintage John Leslie: it presents a bold and provocative thesis supported by a battery of arguments and references to the most recent advances in science. Leslie is one of the most original and interesting thinkers writing today. The subject matter of the book (the probability of the extinction of the human species in the near future) and Leslie's accessible writing style make this book of interest to readers in all academic fields as well as to the general public.

QUENTIN SMITH, PROFESSOR OF PHILOSOPHY, WESTERN MICHIGAN UNIVERSITY

'Leslie's graceful style and humour enliven this grim assessment of the odds against human survival, and the effort and restraint that will be needed to beat the odds.'

WERNER ISRAEL FRS, PROFESSOR OF PHYSICS, UNIVERSITY OF ALBERTA

JOHN LESLIE

THE
END
OF THE
WORLD

The SCIENCE and ETHICS
of HUMAN EXTINCTION

LONDON and NEW YORK

First published 1996
by Routledge
11 New Fetter Lane, London EC4P 4EE

Simultaneously published in the USA and Canada
by Routledge
29 West 35th Street, New York, NY 10001

© 1996 John Leslie

Typeset in Galliard by Florencetype Ltd, Stoodleigh, Devon
Printed and Bound in Great Britain by
Clays Ltd, St Ives plc

British Library Cataloguing in Publication Data
A catalogue record for this book is available from the British Library.

Library of Congress Cataloging in Publication Data
Leslie, John, 1940–
The end of the world:
the science and ethics of human extinction
John Leslie.
p. cm.
Includes bibliographical references and index.
1. End of the world – Moral and ethical aspects.
2. Extinction (Biology)
3. Man – Influence on nature. I. Title.
QB638.8.L47   1996
304.2–dc20   95–38891
CIP

ISBN 0–415–14043–9

CONTENTS

ACKNOWLEDGMENTS

Thanks are due to the editors of nine books and of the *American Philosophical Quarterly*, the *Bulletin of the Canadian Nuclear Society, Interchange*, the *Journal of Applied Philosophy, The Mathematical Intelligencer, Mind, Philosophia, The Philosophical Quarterly, Philosophy, Religious Studies* and other journals, for making space available for testing this book's ideas. Also to my wife Jill, for constant encouragement; to the Research School of Social Sciences of the Australian National University for a visiting fellowship during which work was begun on the central theme; to the Social Sciences and Humanities Research Council of Canada for a research grant, and for airfares allowing me to attend conferences in Leningrad, Tartu and San Francisco; to various departments of philosophy, physics, astrophysics and applied mathematics, for inviting lectures and paying travel and other costs; to Belgium's Fonds National de la Recherche Scientifique for funding a term's visitorship at the Institut d'Astrophysique, Université de Liège; and to everyone at Routledge, particularly Adrian Driscoll, Pauline Marsh and Michael Leiser, for their enthusiasm, professionalism and speediness.

Over a hundred people wrote useful letters – often very long ones – discussing the book's arguments and above all the Carter–Leslie 'doomsday argument'. I am particularly grateful for the letters and encouragement of J. D. Barrow, A. H. Batten, B. J. Carr, B. Carter, S. R. L. Clark, P. C. W. Davies, C. Davis, J.-P. Delahaye and all those who wrote to me in reaction to his discussion of my ideas in *Pour la science* (the French version of *Scientific American*), J. Demaret, G. F. R. Ellis, J. Ellis, G. Gale, J. R. Gott, A. Grünbaum, W. Israel, R. L. Jaffe, D. Lewis, A. D. Linde, M. Lockwood, B. McCusker, D. Mosey, G. Nerlich, C. Normore, D. Page, D. Parfit, P. J. E. Peebles, J. C. Polkinghorne,

ACKNOWLEDGMENTS

M. J. Rees, N. Rescher, J. J. C. Smart, R. Sylvan, F. J. Tipler, S. Weinberg and P. S. Wesson. Several of these also helped in the writing of my *Universes*, in which the doomsday argument appeared briefly (on p. 214). None of them can be held responsible for the defects of the present book. With any luck, the human race will exist for at least a few more years so that a hundred better ones will be covering the same wide ground.

Richard Gott's article in *Nature*, May 27, 1993, 'Implications of the Copernican principle for our future prospects', argues that, prima facie, humankind would seem unlikely to survive for very long, for if it did then you and I would have been very extraordinarily early in human population history. This disturbing theme, first developed by Brandon Carter, casts its shadow over all my pages, which warn of what may well happen unless we make strenuous efforts. Paul Davies defends the theme in his recently published *About Time*, also describing the lecture in which Carter first introduced it (to the Royal Society in 1983, with the comment that nuclear submarine commanders should reflect on it). It comes as a shock to many people. They can react aggressively. I am grateful above all to David Lewis for insisting that it needs to be taken seriously, to R. M. Sainsbury (an expert on puzzles and paradoxes who edits *Mind*) for agreeing with him, and to both of them for helping me to whip my treatment of it into shape.

Let's hope that John Mortimer was wrong in the words he gave to his most famous character: 'However forward-looking we may all pretend to be, humanity is far more interested in its past than the future. Tell a man like Claude Erskine-Brown that the planet earth will be burnt to a cinder a hundred years after his death and his eyes will glaze over and he'll change the subject to his past triumphs in motoring cases at Acton.'

The book is dedicated to the memory of my friend Ifan Morris.

INTRODUCTION
The risk of extinction
—— •◆• ——

Will the human race become extinct fairly shortly? Have the dangers been underestimated, and ought we to care?

The Introduction will give the book's main arguments, particularly a 'doomsday argument' originated by the cosmologist Brandon Carter. *We ought to have some reluctance to believe that we are very exceptionally early, for instance in the earliest 0.001 per cent, among all humans who will ever have lived.* This would be some reason for thinking that humankind will not survive for many more centuries, let alone colonize the galaxy.

Taken just by itself, the doomsday argument could do little to tell us how long humankind will survive. What it might indicate, though, is that the likelihood of Doom Soon is greater than we would otherwise think. Here, 'otherwise-thinking' involves taking account of well-recognized dangers like those of pollution and nuclear war.

There are also many other hazards which are seldom considered: for example, the risk that physicists of the future, experimenting at immensely high energies, will upset a space-filling 'scalar field' and destroy the world, a possibility taken seriously by some leading theorists.

There are even risks coming from philosophical arguments. There is the following argument, for example: that any possible humans of the future couldn't be missing any benefits if they were never in fact born, because you have to be born before you can really miss things.

1

CARTER'S DOOMSDAY ARGUMENT

Imagine a scene from the late twenty-first century. Twelve billion humans walk the Earth, but all are about to die. It might be through loss of the ozone layer, or poisoning by pollution, or nuclear war, but let us instead say that it is through germ warfare. The fatal virus had a long latency period in which it produced no symptoms so that it spread everywhere without being detected. The aggressor nation's vaccines to protect itself have failed.

One of the doomed humans complains of his remarkable bad luck in being born so late. 'There have been upward of fifteen thousand generations since the start of human history – yet here I am, in the one and only generation which will have no successors!' Isn't there an absurdity in his reasoning? If Doom were to strike in about AD 2090, then, because of population growth, perhaps a tenth of all humans who had ever lived would still be alive when it struck. Well, there can be nothing very remarkable in living at a time occupied by about one in ten humans.

Now consider the 'doomsday argument'.[1] Suppose that many thousand intelligent races, all of about the same size, had been more or less bound to evolve in our universe. We couldn't at all expect to be *in the very earliest*, could we? Very similarly, it can seem, you and I couldn't at all expect to find ourselves *among the very first* of many hundred billion humans – or of the many trillions in a human race which colonized its galaxy. *We couldn't at all expect to be in the first 0.1 per cent, let alone the first 0.001 per cent, of all humans who would ever have observed their positions in time.*

While technological advances encourage huge population explosions, they also bring new risks of sudden population collapse through nuclear war, industrial pollution, etc. If the human race came to an end soon after learning a little physics and chemistry, what would be remarkable in that? Suppose we were extremely confident that humans will have a long future. You and I would then simply have to accept that we were exceptionally early among all humans who would ever have been born. But mightn't it make more sense to think of ourselves as living at the same time as, say, 10 per cent of all humans? And shouldn't this consideration magnify any fears which we had for humanity's future, making our risk-estimates rather more pessimistic?

The doomsday argument aims to show that we ought to feel *some* reluctance to accept any theory which made us very exceptionally early among all humans who would ever have been born. The sheer fact that such a theory made us very exceptionally early would at least strengthen any reasons we had for rejecting it. Just how much would it strengthen them? The answer would depend on just how strong the competing reasons were – the reasons for thinking that the human race would survive for many more centuries, perhaps colonizing the whole of its galaxy. The competition between reasons might even be modelled mathematically. And in fact the doomsday argument first appeared in about 1980 in the mind of the Cambridge cosmologist Brandon Carter, elected a Fellow of the Royal Society in recognition of his research in applied mathematics.

What we must bear in mind is that Carter's doomsday argument doesn't generate any risk-estimates just by itself. It is an argument for *revising* the estimates which we generate when we consider various possible dangers. We should therefore consider some of them now, returning to this important argument only towards the end of the Introduction.

THREATS TO THE SURVIVAL OF THE HUMAN RACE

Estimating the probability that the human race will soon become extinct has become quite a popular activity. Many writers have considered such things as the dangers of nuclear war or of pollution. This book will make few claims to expertise about the details of such highly complex matters. What it will claim instead is that *even non-experts can see that the risks aren't negligible.* In view of how much is at stake, we have no right to disregard them.[2] Besides, even if the 'total risk' (obtained by combining the individual risks) appeared to be fairly small, Carter's doomsday argument could suggest that it should be re-evaluated as large. To get it to look small once more, we should then need to make vigorous risk-reduction efforts.

All the same, the book will in due course settle down to some fairly detailed discussion of risks, particularly those which our efforts might reduce. For the moment let us simply list a large variety of them, with a few quick comments.

Risks already well recognized

1   *Nuclear war.* Knowledge of how to build nuclear bombs cannot be eradicated. Small nations, terrorists and rich criminals wanting to become still richer by holding the world to ransom can already afford very destructive bombs. Production costs are falling and the world has many multi-billionaires. The effects of large-scale nuclear destruction are largely unknown. Radiation poisoning of the entire globe? 'Nuclear winter' in which dust and soot block sunlight, so that temperatures everywhere fall very sharply? Death of trees and grasses? Of oceanic plankton?

2   *Biological warfare* or terrorism or criminality. Biological weapons could actually be more dangerous than nuclear ones: less costly, and with a field of destruction harder to limit because the weapons were self-reproducing organisms.

3   *Chemical warfare* or terrorism or criminality.

4   *Destruction of the ozone layer* by chlorofluorocarbons or other things. Massive increase in the amount of ultraviolet light reaching the Earth's surface. Cancer runs riot? Death of trees, grasses, plankton?

5   *'Greenhouse effect'*: a rise in Earth's surface temperature because incoming radiation is less easily re-radiated into space, owing to build-up of atmospheric carbon dioxide, methane and other gases. The effect might conceivably be a runaway one because of positive feedback: for example, frozen arctic soils melt and become wetlands, emitting much carbon dioxide and methane and so helping to melt more soils, which leads to still greater emissions. After an increase – usually thought very unlikely – to a carbon dioxide level of 1 per cent, Earth could soon become rather like its neighbour Venus. On Venus, greenhouse-effect temperatures are sufficient to melt lead. On Earth they might approach the boiling point of water.

6 *Poisoning by pollution.* Already widespread, for instance in the form of acid rain, which can eat holes in clothing. Hundreds of new chemicals enter the environment each year. Their effects are often hard to predict. Who would have thought that the insecticide DDT would need to be banned or that spraying deodorant at your armpits could help destroy the ozone layer? Pollution could particularly affect sperm or produce cancers, from which many lake fish already suffer. Once again there is the danger of positive feedback: the rotting of a poisoned environment generates more poisons. And, at least in the short term, severe pollution seems almost inevitable when uncontrolled population growth is combined with demands for an acceptable standard of living.

7 *Disease.* As was shown by the Black Death of the Middle Ages, diseases can wipe out very large proportions of those exposed to them. They can now spread world wide very quickly, thanks to air travel. Many remain incurable. Tuberculosis, already killing about three million people annually, has recently developed strains resistant to all known drugs, and antibiotics are useless against viral diseases.

Risks often unrecognized

Group 1: Natural disasters

1 *Volcanic eruptions.* Sometimes blamed for the death of the dinosaurs. Eruption clouds might produce 'volcanic winter' instead of warfare's 'nuclear winter'.

2 *Hits by asteroids and comets.* The death of the dinosaurs was very probably caused by an asteroid. You may be far more likely to be killed by a continent-destroying impact than to win a major lottery: your chances of dying like this have been estimated as 1 in 20,000. If there are many life-bearing planets in the universe, perhaps most of them suffer disastrous impacts before intelligent living beings can evolve on them.

3 *An extreme ice age due to passage through an interstellar cloud?* Not likely in the next few hundred thousand years, despite the

point that changes to the 'solar wind' of charged particles might have drastic climatic effects, even at cloud densities far too small to produce much direct reduction of the sunlight reaching Earth's surface.[3]

4 *A nearby supernova* – a stellar explosion perhaps equivalent to that of a one-hundred-thousand-trillion-trillion-megaton H-bomb.

5 *Other massive astronomical explosions* produced when black holes complete their evaporation (a phenomenon discovered by Stephen Hawking's theoretical studies) or by the merger of two black holes or two neutron stars, or of a black hole and a neutron star.

6 *Essentially unpredictable breakdown of a complex system,* as investigated by 'chaos theory'. The system in question might be Earth's biosphere: its air, its soil, its water and its living things interact in highly intricate ways. On a very long timescale it might be the solar system itself, because planetary motions could be chaotic.[4]

7 *Something-we-know-not-what.* It would be foolish to think we had foreseen all possible natural disasters.

Group 2: Man-made disasters

1 *Unwillingness to rear children?* Although sometimes mentioned as a danger to the human race, it may be hard to take seriously. If only ten thousand people wanted children, their descendants could soon crowd the globe. Still, some of the rich nations are experiencing population shrinkage at present.

2 *A disaster from genetic engineering.* Perhaps a 'green scum' disaster in which a genetically engineered organism reproduces itself with immense efficiency, smothering everything? Or one involving organisms which invade the human body? On November 2, 1993, Toronto's *The Globe and Mail* reported on its front page – but without any mention of possible accidents – genetic alteration of salmonella bacteria at Washington

6

University in St Louis so as to cause 'a harmless, temporary infection in the intestine that triggers antibodies against genetic components of sperm that have been spliced into the bacteria', making the recipient woman infertile. A single dose of this 'birth control vaccine', taken orally, 'might prevent conception for several months or longer'. The effect 'would be reversible': 'you don't get your booster, and within a year or so you can conceive again', the Washington University researcher was reported as saying. But what if one did get one's booster – or one's first dose – by being infected by other people? After all, salmonella bacteria are a major source of infection globally. Perhaps the original genetically altered bacteria couldn't cause this kind of problem, but what if they underwent evolutionary change? And what if any major proportion of the world's women then became permanently infected, through constantly reinfecting one another?

3 *A disaster from nanotechnology.* Very tiny self-reproducing machines – they could be developed fairly soon through research inspired by Richard Feynman – might perhaps spread world wide within a month in a 'gray goo' calamity.

4 *Disasters associated with computers.* Computer-initiated nuclear war is the one most often discussed, but there might instead be breakdown of a computer network which had become vital to humanity's day-to-day survival. And, very speculatively, several writers have described computers replacing us, either (a) as an unintended result of competition between nation-states whose methods of production had become more and more computer-controlled; or (b) again unintendedly, after the task of designing computers had been given to computers themselves; or finally (c) through deliberate planning by scientists who viewed the life and intelligence of advanced computers as superior – possibly because death could be delayed for indefinitely long – to the life and intelligence of humans. (Whether the third of these possibilities would be 'a disaster' would depend, of course, on whether those scientists were correct. Whether it should count as 'the extinction of humankind' might itself be controversial if advanced computers inherited many human characteristics, maybe after an initial

period during which brains and computers worked in close association.)

5 *Some other disaster in a branch of technology, perhaps just agricultural, which had become crucial to human survival.* Modern agriculture is dangerously dependent on polluting fertilizers and pesticides, and on progressively fewer genetic varieties. Chaos theory warns us that any very complicated system, and in particular a system involving new technologies interacting in a complex manner, might break down in an essentially unpredictable fashion. Blackouts – failures of electrical power – and communication system failures in large regions of the United States have helped to illustrate the point.

6 *Production of a new Big Bang in the laboratory?* Physicists have investigated this possibility. It is commonly claimed that about twenty kilograms of matter – or its equivalent in energy – would need to be compressed into an impracticably small volume, but the cosmologist Andrei Linde has written to me that the correct figure is instead a hundred thousandth of a gram. Still, the compression would indeed have to be tremendous, and a Bang engineered in this fashion would very probably expand into a space of its own. To us, what we had produced would then look like nothing but a tiny black hole.

7 *The possibility of producing an all-destroying phase transition,* comparable to turning water into ice, could be much graver. In 1984, Edward Farhi and Robert Jaffe suggested that physicists might produce 'strange-quark matter' of a kind which attracted ordinary matter, changing it into more of itself until the entire Earth had been converted ('eaten'). It is thought, however, that strange-quark matter would instead repel ordinary matter. In contrast, there might be a very real *vacuum metastability danger* associated with experiments at extremely high energies. The space in which we live may be in a 'false vacuum' state, filled with a force field – technically speaking, it would be a scalar field – which is like a statue balancing upright: stable against small jolts but upsettable by large ones. If the jolt of a high-energy experiment produced a bubble of 'true vacuum', this would then expand at nearly the speed of light, destroying

everything, rather as when a tiny ice crystal changes a large volume of supercooled water into more ice crystals. We might be safe only so long as our experiments kept below the energies already reached by colliding cosmic rays. Many people think such energies will never be attained by us. But David Schramm and Leon Lederman, Nobel-prizewinning former Director of the National Accelerator Laboratory in Chicago, wrote in 1989 that we might reach them as early as the year 2100 with radically new technology.

8   *Annihilation by extraterrestrials*, either deliberately or through the kind of vacuum metastability disaster discussed a moment ago, a disaster produced by their high-energy experiments? We haven't yet discovered a single extraterrestrial, but our searches up to date have been so primitive that we'd have had no great chance of finding a civilization like Earth's, not even if it existed among the nearest stars. Still, in attempting to explain the 'Great Silence', the failure to detect broadcasts even from the enormously powerful transmitters of very advanced civilizations, several scientists have suggested that everyone is listening and nobody broadcasting, for fear of attracting hostile attention. Extraterrestrials might view us as a threat – for instance if there seemed a risk that we'd be the ones producing the vacuum metastability disaster. They might first become aware of our presence through detecting the impulses transmitted by the Arecibo radio telescope, which will reach sixty million stars during the next four thousand years, or those of our military early-warning radars. Perhaps, though, extraterrestrial intelligence evolves only very seldom, almost always then destroying itself quickly. (Note that there simply cannot have been, right out to as far as our telescopes can probe, any beings whose high-energy experiments had upset a metastable vacuum. Not, at any rate, unless this was so recently that light rays hadn't yet had time to carry the news to us, because all life would end when the news reached it.)

9   *Something-we-know-not-what.* We cannot possibly imagine every single danger which technological advances might bring with them.

Obviously many of the above-listed dangers are ones for which there is nothing like firm evidence. On the other hand, we can also lack firm evidence that they are absent. With respect to most of these matters we are just groping in the dark.

Risks from philosophy

Various risks in this category will be discussed in chapters 4 and 7.

1 *Threats associated with religions* can often count as 'threats based on philosophy', although sometimes it is very poor philosophy. It could be dangerous, for example, to choose as Secretary for the Environment some politician convinced that, no matter what anyone did, the world would end soon with a Day of Judgement. It could be just as bad to choose somebody who felt that God would keep the world safe for us for ever, or else would create any number of other worlds to replace ours if we destroyed it.

This isn't an outright attack on religious world-models or on the idea that there exist numerous other worlds, otherwise called 'universes'. My *Value and Existence* was a lengthy defence of a neoplatonic picture of God as an abstract creative force, or perhaps a world-creating person whose own reason for existence was neoplatonic. Such a person would then exist because he ought to exist, i.e. because the divine existence possessed what can be called *creative ethical requiredness*. Alternatively, it would be the world itself which possessed such requiredness. *Universes* and other writings of mine[5] defended these ideas once again, together with the notion that there exist many worlds, perhaps through divine action or perhaps because of blind physical mechanisms. Still, theories about God or about multiple worlds cannot be known to be right. We can't be at all sure that there would be other worlds to compensate for the mess we had made of ours.

2 *Schopenhauerian pessimism.* In attacking religion, many writers put such emphasis on the Problem of Evil – the existence of poisonous snakes, earthquakes, plagues, cancer, Nazi death

camps, and so on – that they in effect agree with Schopenhauer, who wrote that it would have been better if our planet had remained like the moon, a lifeless mass. It is then only a short step to thinking that we ought to make it lifeless.

3 *Ethical relativism, emotivism, prescriptivism and other doctrines* deny that anything is really worth struggling for, in the sense of 'really' in which two and two really make four or in which Africa really is larger than Iceland. (a) *Relativism* maintains that, for example, burning people alive for fun is only bad relative to particular moral codes, somewhat as putting out your tongue is a polite greeting in Tibet but rude elsewhere. (b) *Emotivism* holds that to call burning people 'really bad' describes no fact about the practice of people-burning. Instead, it merely expresses real disgust. (c) *Prescriptivism* again agrees that it describes no fact. 'It's a fact that burning people is bad' just means 'I hereby prescribe that nobody is to burn anybody.' (d) A popular doctrine, recently, has been that the feeling of duty not to burn people results from *'internalizing' a system of socially prescribed rules.* (Think of the Englishman who changes into a dinner-jacket for a solitary meal in the jungle.) Typically, the rules in such a system are ones which you hope others will obey during dealings with yourself. If you don't genuinely internalize the system, making it control your behaviour through actual preference, then your fellow humans will detect your lack of enthusiasm for it, shunning you. Once again it is standardly denied that there is a fact of the matter, 'out there in the world' regardless of whether anyone could prove it, *that burning people really is wrong.*

Might these be only caricatures of various philosophical doctrines? I am afraid not. They are the actual doctrines, very widely defended. True, their defenders are often enthusiastically kind individuals. (There is no psychological rule stating that people can be enthusiastic about a way of behaving only if they think it *really good as a matter of fact:* fact as much 'out there in the world' as the fact that two and two make four.) Yet if you accepted any of these doctrines, then it could be hard to say why you should endure mental or physical anguish, possibly resisting torture or great temptation, in order to remain a kind individual. For if you sent ten million people to their deaths to make your torments stop, what would be really wrong in that? *Really wrong* in the ordinary sense, instead of in such senses as 'being really of a sort whose avoidance I hereby prescribe'?

Notice that the 'contractarian' position which stresses tit-for-tat internalization – you internalize such and such a code of behaviour in your dealings with me, and I'll do the same in my dealings with you – could seem in trouble when faced with a question asked by Robert Heilbroner,[6] 'What have people of the far future ever done *to benefit me*?'

4   *'Negative utilitarianism'* is concerned mainly or entirely with reducing evils rather than with maximizing goods. Now, there will be at least one miserable person per century, virtually inevitably, if the human race continues. It could seem noble to declare that such a person's sufferings 'shouldn't be used to buy happiness for others' – and to draw the conclusion that the moral thing would be to stop producing children. Much of the danger of this way of thinking may come from the impossibility of actually proving its wrongness.

5   *Some philosophers attach ethical weight only to people who are already alive* or whose births are more or less inevitable. So (a) it wouldn't be a duty to keep the human race in existence if having children were found troublesome, and (b) there would actually seem to be a moral need to let the race become extinct – because the duty not to produce miserable children couldn't now be counterbalanced by any duty to produce happy ones. 'Nobody', it is said, 'is being treated unfairly by being left unborn.'

6   *Some philosophers speak of 'inalienable rights'* which must always be respected, though this makes the heavens fall (the right, perhaps, for parents to have as many children as they want, regardless of whether overpopulation threatens to render the atmosphere unbreathable).

7   *Prisoner's dilemma.* Many seem to place too much confidence in a particular way of treating this dilemma, which you can meet when asking yourself whether to rely on somebody else's

co-operation. (On the brink of nuclear war, for example, two nations may need to trust each other to remain inactive instead of striking first.) It has become fairly standard among philosophers to say that the advantages of uncooperative behaviour should always dominate the reasoning of anyone who had no inclination to be self-sacrificing.

8 *'Avenging justice' or 'Rational consistency'.* Some philosophers argue that carrying out a threat of revenge, for instance for a nuclear attack, could be appropriate regardless of whether anyone could benefit from it.

It is sometimes suggested that the annihilation of all life on Earth would be no great tragedy. Other intelligent beings would soon evolve somewhere, it is said, and these would then spread throughout the galaxy. But this overlooks the fact that we have precious little idea of how often intelligent life could be expected to evolve, even on ideally suitable planets. Perhaps not just the Milky Way but the entire universe would be for ever afterwards lifeless, if life on Earth came to an end soon.

It can seem unlikely that our galaxy already contains many technological civilizations, for, as Enrico Fermi noted, we could in that case have expected definite signs of their presence, if not through their radio signals then through Earth's actually being colonized by them. After all, it could well be that in a few million years the human race will have colonized the entire galaxy, if it survives.[7]

Notice that *observational selection effects* might help to explain our survival up to date. For instance, we couldn't observe that we were on a planet where disease or an asteroid impact had exterminated all intelligent life, even if such planets formed the vast majority of those on which such life had evolved. Intelligent living beings cannot find that they are in places devoid of living intelligence! Observational selection effects, of course, didn't *cause* us to be where we are. All the same, they could in a sense aid in accounting for it. They could make it unmysterious.

Now that we have seen what some of the risks might be, we can usefully return to Brandon Carter's 'doomsday argument' for thinking them *more dangerous than we'd otherwise have thought.* The doomsday argument, remember, is that we could hardly expect to be among the very earliest – among the first 0.01 per cent, for instance – of all humans who would ever have been born. On the other hand, it would be none too startling to be among something like the very last 10 per cent, which is where we'd be if the human race were to end shortly. (Of all humans who have yet been born, a fair proportion are alive at this very moment, thanks to recent population growth.) Now, suppose that you suddenly noticed all this. You should then be more inclined than before to forecast humankind's imminent extinction. This, at any rate, is what Carter is suggesting.

Suppose that millions of intelligent races will evolve during the history of our universe. Of all intelligent beings, might not a fair proportion find themselves in rapidly growing races which were about to become extinct through poisoning their environments with new chemicals, developing new forms of warfare, or otherwise misusing the science which had made the rapid growth possible? Carter's reasoning provides us with additional grounds for taking such scenarios seriously.

DOOMSDAY AND THE ANTHROPIC PRINCIPLE

Carter is particularly well known for his 'anthropic principle'. The principle reminds us that observers, for instance humans, can find themselves only at places and times where intelligent life is possible. Observers couldn't be at the center of the sun, presumably, or in the earliest few seconds of an immensely hot Big Bang. They might even be very unlikely to live before the universe had lasted for many billion years. Many billion years of evolution could be needed before intelligent life appeared.

As was illustrated by many examples in my *Universes* (1989) and as discussed by several contributors to my edited volume *Physical Cosmology and Philosophy* (1990), Carter's anthropic principle can often help to persuade us that our position in space and in time is in fact unusual:

14

(a) Suppose, for instance, that there were hardly any planets in our universe. You and I would still have to find that we were on a planet, or at least that our first ancestors had evolved on a planet, if intelligent life could arise only on planets and not inside stars or in interstellar space.

(b) Suppose that our universe, when it came to an end, would have included only a comparatively narrow 'window' of times when intelligent life was possible – perhaps because early times were too hot for life, while late ones were too cold. You and I could then have found ourselves only inside the narrow window.

(c) Again, what if the cosmos contained billions of huge domains, largely or entirely separate from one another and therefore perhaps deserving to be called 'universes'? What if only a half-dozen of these had properties permitting intelligent life to evolve? We should then have to be in one of the half-dozen. (Much of the interest of Carter's anthropic principle comes from three recent discoveries: *first*, that fairly plausible physical mechanisms could lead to the existence of numerous universes; *second*, that fundamental properties could well be expected to vary randomly from universe to universe; and *third*, that the actual properties of our universe seem impressively well suited – 'fine tuned' – for the evolution of intelligent life.)

We could, it seems, very reasonably believe that our actual place and time, and our universe as well, were of rather an unusual sort. If intelligent life can exist only in rare and unusual situations, then, Carter's anthropic principle reminds us, we oughtn't to be altogether surprised at finding ourselves in one of those situations. There would be nowhere else where we could possibly find ourselves.

Although, however, it can in this way encourage us to believe that our situation is rare and unusual, the anthropic principle can at the same time *discourage* the belief that it is *more rare and unusual than is needed* for the existence of life and intelligence. It can encourage us to think our situation fairly ordinary, at least among the situations in which intelligent observers can exist. Instead of considering what are (presumably) absolute preconditions of life and observership, such as the absence of billion-degree temperatures, users of 'anthropic' reasoning can well ask what an observer's situation *is at all likely to be.*

Imagine, for instance, that 99 per cent of all observers had body temperatures below the boiling point of water. You could then find it unsurprising that your own surroundings were below this temperature. Richard Gott speaks of the usefulness of a principle 'that the location of your birth in space and time in the Universe is privileged (or special) only to the extent implied by the fact that you are an intelligent observer'. If lacking evidence to the contrary, he says, you should assume 'that your location among intelligent observers is not special but rather picked at random'.[8] This line of thought led him to his own version of the doomsday argument, which he developed without any realization that Carter had got there first. It is no great surprise, though, that these two leading cosmologists should have arrived at the same idea independently. Cosmology is a discipline in which probabilistic arguments, and in particular ones concerned with the probable positions of observers, are often crucially important.

In the *New York Times*, July 27, 1993, Gott reacts to some pointlessly aggressive criticisms by Eric Lerner. Lerner had held that he himself, for example, couldn't usefully be treated as random. 'This is surprising', Gott comments, 'since my paper had made a number of predictions that, when applied to him, all turned out to be correct, namely that it was likely that he was (1) in the middle 95 percent of the phone book; (2) not born on Jan. 1; (3) born in a country with a population larger than 6.3 million, and most important (4) not born among the last 2.5 percent of all human beings who will ever live (this is true because of the number of people already born since his birth). Mr. Lerner may be more random than he thinks.'[9]

Recently the cosmologist Stephen Hawking pointed out the following intriguing fact. In any sufficiently gigantic universe, a few observers could exist without any evolutionary preliminaries. They might have no ancestors whatever. Why? The answer is that, as Hawking had shown, black holes aren't entirely black. Black holes radiate particles of all kinds, randomly. Sooner or later, therefore, in any large enough collection of black holes, some black hole or other would emit material particles which just chanced to

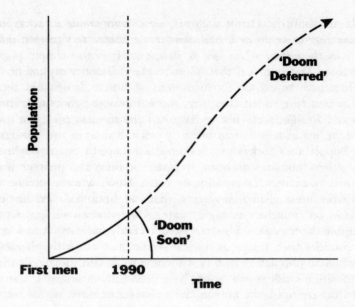

FIGURE 1 If the human race had been fated to last for many years and colonize the galaxy, could you at all have expected to find yourself as early as around AD 2000?

Source: Reprinted by permission of Springer-Verlag from J. Leslie, 'The Doomsday Argument', *The Mathematical Intelligencer*, Vol. 14, No. 2 (1992), pp. 48–51.

form a book, for example, or even any particular kind of book you cared to name – perhaps containing all the plays of Shakespeare. This is just a variant on the point that a monkey typing in a fully random fashion would sooner or later type a sonnet. Well, another thing which might conceivably be emitted by a black hole – and which actually would be emitted by a few black holes, if there were enough of them – would be a monkey, a rather primitive observer. There could even be nothing to stop a black hole from emitting an observer much like Shakespeare himself. Regardless, however, of how many black holes there are in our universe, *no observer should at all expect to find that he or she or it had come into existence in this curious way.*

Rather similarly, Carter suggests, *no observer should at all expect to find that he or she or it had come into existence very exceptionally early in the history of his, her or its species.* It is this simple point which led first him and then Gott to the doomsday argument.

Humans have existed for many tens of thousands of years, so if the human race ended after, say, another hundred thousand, then you and I might seem not to have had any special earliness if one thought just in terms of an ordinary clock. But when one thought of a Population Clock whose hand had advanced by one step whenever a new human was born, it would at once be apparent that we had been very extraordinarily early. Now, while everyone is inevitably unusual in many ways, that can be a poor excuse for looking on ourselves as highly extraordinary when various fairly plausible theories would instead make us fairly ordinary. And when we consider such things as nuclear warfare, isn't it fairly plausible that human population history will come to an end shortly, so that our position inside it will indeed have been fairly ordinary? If Carter and Gott are right, the human race's chances of surviving for many further centuries should be looked on with new eyes (see Figure 1). Taking account of our observed position in time, we ought to re-evaluate the dangers which our species confronts.

IS THE DOOMSDAY ARGUMENT EASILY REFUTED?

Already embattled on other fronts, Carter has presented the doomsday argument only in lectures and seminars, never in print. However, I published it on p. 214 of *Universes* in a long footnote. Since then I have investigated it in several articles. The argument is certainly controversial. So far, however, I have managed to find only one good ground for doubting it. Suppose that the cosmos is *radically indeterministic*, perhaps for reasons of quantum physics. Suppose also that the indeterminism is likely to influence how long the human race will survive. There then isn't yet any relevant firm fact, 'out there in the world' and in theory predictable by anybody who knew enough about the present arrangement of the world's particles, concerning how long it will survive – like the fact that hidden cards include a definite number of aces, a number you are trying to estimate, or like the fact that exactly nine or exactly sixty names remain to be drawn from a lottery urn, after your own name has been drawn from it. Yet in order to run really smoothly, the doomsday argument does need the existence of a firm fact of this kind, I believe.[10]

Even if it ran only rather roughly, though, the doomsday argument could have considerable importance. In particular, it might throw severe doubt on the theory that the human race will very probably survive for many thousand years. For anyone who believes in radically indeterministic factors yet says that something 'will very probably occur' must mean that even those factors are unlikely to prevent its occurrence.

People have suggested many reasons for distrusting the doomsday argument. At least a dozen times, I too dreamed up what seemed a crushing refutation of it. Be suspicious of such refutations, no matter how proud you may be of them! Probability theory is full of traps. Don't put complete trust in the first 'blindingly obvious objection' that springs to mind. The doomsday argument has now been thought about rather hard by some rather good brains. What seems to have emerged is that it doesn't fall victim to any simple counter-argument.

If it did, then almost all 'anthropic' reasoning – reasoning which draws attention to when and where an observer could at all expect to be – would be in severe trouble. As we have seen, the preconditions of observership are seldom entirely firm. Observers might just possibly exist early in the Big Bang, as patterns of particles emitted randomly from black holes. Users of the anthropic principle therefore ask about an observer's *probable* location in space and in time. Now, most criticisms of the doomsday argument treat *probable location in time* in a way in which nobody would dream of treating *probable location in space*. This goes against the entire tradition of anthropic reasoning, which looks on time and space as equally grist to its mill. And it is hard to see any justification for going against tradition here – once, that is to say, we have made the important concession that the future might be radically indeterministic, in which case the doomsday argument would be weakened although not destroyed.

Look at one very common criticism. Any people of a heavily populated far future *are not alive yet*. Hence we certainly cannot find ourselves among them, in the way that we could find ourselves in some heavily populated city rather than in a tiny village. We are considering the doomsday argument *now*, which means at around AD 2000. We *know* we are at around AD 2000. We'd be just as sure of it, no matter what our theory was about how many humans would exist later. It's because we live near the year 2000 that we can say that the human race got as far as this safely, but cannot say how much further it will get! The evidence we possess of the risks facing humankind is evidence from around AD 2000, not evidence collected many thousand years later.

Well, those remarks are all of them correct, yet how could they invalidate the doomsday argument? Brandon Carter doesn't doubt that the neighbourhood of AD 2000 is *now* – that he *really is* in that neighbourhood, with 100 per cent probability. What he asks himself is the following. As a human observer, how likely *would one have been* to find oneself there, if the lives of all but a very small proportion of all humans were to be lived later? Of course, the lives of you and me are not particularly early *among those of all humans alive now*, let alone *among those of all humans born so far*, but to keep insisting on this is to miss Carter's point.

The uselessness of protesting that later humans *aren't alive yet* can be shown, it seems, with a simple story. Imagine an experiment planned as follows. At some point in time, three humans would each be given an emerald. Several centuries afterwards, when a completely different set of humans was alive, five thousand humans would again each be given an emerald. Imagine next that you have yourself been given an emerald in the experiment. You have no knowledge, however, of whether your century is the earlier century in which just three people were to be in this situation, or the later century in which five thousand were to be in it. Do you say to yourself that if yours were the earlier century then the five thousand people *wouldn't be alive yet*, and that therefore you'd have no chance of being among them? On this basis, do you conclude that you might just as well bet that you lived in the earlier century?

Suppose you in fact betted that you lived there. If every emerald-getter in the experiment betted in this way, there would be five thousand losers and only three winners. The sensible bet, there-fore, is that yours is instead the later century of the two.

What if you were somewhat unsure whether the experimental plan called for more people to get emeralds in the later century than in the earlier? Getting an emerald would now give somewhat weaker grounds for betting that you lived in the later century. If you next came to know you were in fact in the earlier century, then your new knowledge would strengthen your reasons for doubting that many more emeralds – or any – would be distributed in the later century. Throughout, it would of course be true that *people who hadn't yet been born weren't yet observing anything.* But this truth would be utterly irrelevant.

SOME FURTHER EXAMPLES OF ATTEMPTED REFUTATIONS

The doomsday argument itself is reasonably straightforward. ('We should tend to distrust any theory which made us into very exceptionally early humans.' This is hardly a very difficult thought, is it?) What can make the argument seem highly complicated is the need to guard it against a hundred criticisms. Because of the intricacies in which we are then entangled, a thorough discussion of the area will be deferred until Chapters 5 and 6.

Still, many people might like to learn straight away how their own blindingly obvious objections could possibly be faulted. Here, then, is a quick introduction to various common objections, and to how we might reply to them.

(a) Don't object that your genes must surely be of a sort found only near the year 2000, and that in consequence you could exist only thereabouts. For what Carter is asking is how likely a human observer would be to find himself or herself near the year 2000 *and hence* with genes typical of that period. (In the story about the emeralds, suppose that the genes of the earlier century were markedly different from the genes of the later century. The story would retain all of its force, wouldn't it? You'd have fairly strong reasons for suspecting that your genes were ones typical of the century with the five thousand emeralds.)

Don't protest that the chances that, at exactly such and such a date, *exactly you* would be born couldn't have been raised or lowered by any facts about how many other people would be born at later dates. Compare the case of protesting: 'How could the fact that many people have accidents in the home have helped me, exactly me, to fall downstairs on March 17, 1995?' (This mustn't be viewed as a case of other people's accidents perhaps *causing* your particular accident. Instead it is a matter of whether it's unmysterious, quite to be expected, to fall downstairs some day.)

(b) The doomsday argument is about probabilities. Suppose you know that your name is in a lottery urn, but not how many other names the urn contains. You estimate, however, that there's a half chance that it contains a thousand names, and a half chance of its containing only ten. Your name then appears among the first three drawn from the urn. Don't you have rather strong grounds for revising your estimate? Shouldn't you now think it very improbable that there are another 997 names waiting to be drawn?

Don't protest that your time of birth wasn't decided with the help of an urn. You'd be forgetting that *urn analogies* are relevant to huge areas of statistics. Also that births really can be matters for probabilistic arguments. (You weren't born between eleven o'clock and noon on September 25th, were you?)

Again, don't be much impressed by the point that every lottery must be won by somebody or other. Suppose you see a hand of thirteen spades in a game with million-dollar stakes. Would you just say to yourself that thirteen spades was no more unlikely than any other hand of thirteen cards, and that any actual hand has always to be *some hand or other*? Mightn't you much prefer to believe that there had been some cheating, if you'd started off by thinking that cheating was 50 per cent probable? Wouldn't you prefer to believe it, even if you'd started off by thinking that its probability was only five per cent?

(c) Don't describe the doomsday argument as an attempt 'to predict, from an armchair, that the humans of the future will be only about as numerous as those who have already been born'. The argument doesn't deny that we might have excellent reasons for thinking that the human race would have an extremely long future, colonizing the entire galaxy. (If you begin by being virtually certain that an urn with your name in it contains a thousand names in total, and not just ten names, then you may remain fairly strongly convinced of it *even after* your name has appeared among the first three drawn from the urn. Still, you should be somewhat less convinced than you were before.)

(d) Don't object that any Stone Age man, if using Carter's reasoning, would have been led to the erroneous conclusion that the human race would end shortly. One answer to this objection is that Stone Age men weren't facing a pollution crisis brought on by a population explosion. Another is that it wouldn't be *a defect* in probabilistic reasoning if it encouraged an erroneous conclusion in the mind of somebody who chanced to be improbably situated: somebody, for instance, who was in the earliest 1 per cent or 0.01 per cent or 0.0001 per cent of all humans who would ever have been born. (Does the doomsday argument fail 'because it could be used at any point in human history, and at most points it would indeed fail'? One thing to bear in mind is that reasoning which 'failed' for people *at most points in human history* by suggesting wrong predictions to them might still suggest a correct prediction *to most humans who could use it* if human numbers expanded rapidly soon before humankind became extinct. Remember, though, that the doomsday argument is merely an argument for revising risk-estimates upwards. It might never indicate anything so strong as that Doom Soon was likely. Consequently, the fact that no disaster has yet occurred, over all the years since the Stone Age, cannot by itself establish that the argument's reasoning has ever in any sense failed.)

(e) Don't object that if the universe contained two human races, the one immensely long-lasting and galaxy-colonizing, and the other short-lasting, and if these had exactly the same population figures until, say, AD 2150, then finding yourself around AD 2000 could give you no clue as to which human race you were in. The answer to such an objection is that, in this bizarre scenario, a human could greatly expect to be *after AD 2150 in the long-lasting race* – which you and I aren't.

(f) Don't object that there would be more chances of being born into a long-lasting human race, and that these would precisely compensate for the lesser chance of being born early in the history of that race. The answer to this is that there would be nothing *automatically improbable* in being in a short-lasting human race. (Imagine that only ten people will ever have been born. Ought

23

you to be specially surprised at finding yourself among the ten? No, for only those who are born can ever find themselves as anything.)

(g) Don't protest that we can make nothing but entirely arbitrary guesses about the probabilities of various figures for total human population, i.e. the number of all humans who will ever have been born. For surely we could fairly plausibly say, prior to considering the doomsday argument, that there was at least a 2 per cent probability that the human race would become extinct by AD 2150 – and also that if it hadn't become extinct by that date then its chances of growing enormously through colonizing the galaxy could be rather good.

It is not 'mere philosophical armchair theorizing' which could encourage us to say such things. We could have actual evidence in their favour. Evidence of the risk of being poisoned by pollution, for instance, or of the risk of nuclear or biological warfare. But the doomsday argument, like any other argument about risks, can also take account of new evidence of efforts to reduce risks. Because it doesn't generate risk-estimates just by itself, disregarding all actual experience, it is no message of despair.

In Chapters 1 and 2 the risks facing us will be examined in some detail, to give a basis for estimating how great they really are.

1

WAR, POLLUTION, DISEASE

——— •◆• ———

In this chapter and the next, so many risks are listed that it could seem surprising that the human race has survived so long. Now, it might indeed be surprising (although of course if the race hadn't survived, then we'd not be here to observe and discuss the matter). On the other hand, it may well be that the risk of extinction has so far been fairly low. What then needs to be feared is a sudden increase in various dangers.

The chapter expands points made in the Introduction about well-known risks. The continued career of the human race is endangered by chemical, biological and nuclear war, by destruction of the ozone layer and greenhouse-effect over-heating (conceivably of a runaway kind in which warming releases more and more methane, a powerful greenhouse gas), by desertification and pollution of land and sea, by loss of biodiversity and by diseases. Overpopulation, a main cause of the deterioration of the environment, may also lead to global warfare.

Some lesser-known risks are discussed in Chapter 2. And for the moment nothing is said about the dangers presented – if anyone listens to philosophers – by philosophical doctrines which suggest that the extinction of humankind would be no real disaster. Those doctrines are discussed in Chapter 4.

25

NUCLEAR BOMBS

J. von Neumann (a pioneer of computing, who died in 1957) called it 'absolutely certain (1) that there would be a nuclear war; and (2) that everyone would die in it'.[1] What force has this today?

The bomb which destroyed Hiroshima was of roughly ten kilotons: that is, with an energy like that of ten thousand tons of the chemical high explosive TNT. Modern 'strategic' bombs are typically between a hundred and a thousand times more powerful. By 1961, however, the Soviet Union had tested a bomb of 58 megatons (58 million tons of TNT), and much larger ones are possible: with a fission device to trigger it, a fusion bomb can be of virtually any size. During the Cold War, the United States and the Soviet Union each accumulated tens of thousands of warheads, the world's nuclear arsenals becoming the equivalent of a million Hiroshima bombs: 'a World War II every second for the length of a lazy afternoon', in the words of C. Sagan.[2] In 1982 the World Health Organization estimated that a major nuclear war would quickly kill half Earth's population.

Since then, the collapse of the Soviet Union has led to reductions in the arsenals, yet the world's supply of the essential ingredient, plutonium, has climbed steadily to about two thousand tons, some ten times as much as remains tied up in warheads. And recent improvements in bomb design apparently allow plutonium which has been recovered from the spent fuel rods of commercial nuclear reactors – a complex process, but within the technological capacity of many nations – to be used in bombs which are more than just highly polluting 'fizzles'. W. Panofsky, the physicist who chaired a recent study by the US National Academy of Sciences, is convinced that bombs can employ such fuel despite the presence of isotopes other than the plutonium-239 preferred by designers. Although the details are secret, the US military seems to have exploded a test bomb made from it, and one comparable to that dropped on Nagasaki could, it is said, be built with just seven kilograms of it.[3] But there will in any case be two or three hundred tons of best-quality plutonium, as now used in warheads, in civilian hands by the year 2000.

Fast breeder reactors such as France's Superphénix present special dangers. Their efficiency at producing plutonium-239 from uranium's most plentiful isotope, the non-fissionable uranium-238, means that a fast breeder can generate about sixty times as much electricity as a conventional reactor from each ton of uranium, the result being that the energy in spent fuel rods potentially 'doubles world fuel resources', D. Adamson points out: in Britain, for instance, it represents something 'comparable to the country's coal reserves'. At present, the technical difficulties facing fast breeders make their electricity expensive, but this may change. Yet whereas some environmentalists think that conventional nuclear power might be tamed so as to become a comparatively pollution-free source of energy, the editor of *Power in Europe*, A. Holmes, told a committee of Britain's House of Commons that he had never met an environmentalist who was not implacably opposed to fast breeders, largely because their plutonium could so easily become warheads.[4]

Could all-out nuclear war mean the end of the human race? Conceivably, rapid loss of half the world's population would itself produce a return to Stone Age conditions. Our planet would then be able to support only some five million hunter-gatherers. Humans might be as liable to extinction as more or less any other species of large mammal. A more likely scenario, however, would be extinction through the effects of radiation: cancers, weakenings of the immune system so that infectious diseases ran riot, or numerous birth defects. There could also be deaths of microorganisms important to the health of the environment. As Sagan notes, some of them 'might be at the base of a vast ecological pyramid at the top of which totter we'.[5]

Despite such possibilities, a committee of the US National Academy of Sciences judged in 1975 that the effect of a 10,000-megaton war on most ecosystems would be small at first, and negligible after thirty years. Today such assurances can seem misplaced, for 'nuclear winter' studies suggest that the impact on the world's climate could be very severe. Perhaps a hundred million tons of dust would be thrown into the air, soon to be joined by maybe three hundred million tons of sooty smoke generated by forest fires, grassland fires, and firestorms in cities. Weight for weight, the smoke would be about a hundred times as effective as the dust at blocking sunlight. The outcome could be world-wide darkness for days or weeks, and twilight for months or for over a year. Temperatures might fall by 15 °C or more. There is much disagreement among scientists here, some suggesting that heating would occur instead of cooling.[6] The shapes of the soot particles could themselves be crucial to whatever cooling was produced. An encouraging point is that mammals were not all of them wiped out when the dinosaurs died, supposedly through the impact of an asteroid which threw vastly more dust into the atmosphere. But what seems clear enough is that the effects of all-out nuclear war (nuclear winter or just 'nuclear autumn'? Cooling ending after a few days, or lasting for many months?) would be extraordinarily hard to predict. Additional danger could come from nitrogen oxides formed when the nuclear blasts burned nitrogen in the upper atmosphere. These might destroy much of the ozone layer, the end of the darkness then just being the commencement of frying by ultraviolet rays.

As well as uncertainties about nuclear war's effects, there are others about whether such war could possibly be prevented in the long term. The collapse of the Soviet Union hasn't made the bombs vanish. It led the *Bulletin of the Atomic Scientists* to push the 'doomsday clock' on its cover backwards only as far as 'ten seconds to midnight' in March 1990. It had been as far back as 'twelve seconds to midnight' in 1963 after the signing of a test ban treaty. Although over twenty million have died in warfare since the Second World War, the nuclear peace has in fact been kept throughout – but largely only through (1) fears of 'mutually assured destruction', meaning the deaths of at least a quarter of the populations of the belligerents, and (2) 'games of chicken', efforts to persuade the opposing side that one would prefer a major risk of destruction to abandoning one's aims. Unfortunately a promising strategy for winning the original game of chicken, which involves two cars rushing together down the center line of a highway until (perhaps) one of them loses by swerving, is to throw your steering wheel out of the window – hoping that the onrushing party notices this in time instead of throwing out its steering wheel too. During the 1962 Cuban Missile Crisis it looked for a while as if both sides' steering wheels had been thrown out. As reported by T. Sorensen, President Kennedy estimated that the likelihood of war with the Soviet Union had at one point risen to 'somewhere between one out of three and even'.[7] Yet R. McNamara,

Secretary of Defense at the time, had judged that missiles in Cuba could represent virtually no increase in the nuclear threat to the United States. What is more, an obviously available bargaining chip, unused even after the Soviet Union had drawn attention to it, had been to offer to remove US Jupiter missiles from Turkey. The Jupiters stood to Moscow at the same distance – dangerously short because of the reduced time from launch to impact, making it harder for the Soviet Union to recognize false alarms as false instead of launching its own missiles on the principle of 'use 'em or lose 'em' – as any Cuban missiles stood to Washington. They were an intense source of irritation to the emotionally unstable Chairman Khrushchev, whose summer retreat lay on the far shore of the Black Sea. All the same, it was Khrushchev whose car swerved.[8]

Another strategy in the game of chicken is to accelerate to top speed – to escalate, as recommended by H. Kissinger, 'rapidly and brutally to a point where the opponent can no longer afford to experiment'.[9] Alternatively one can blindfold oneself and move at random onto and off the center of the road, an extreme case of using the 'threat that leaves something to chance' recommended by T. C. Schelling.[10] Before calling these strategies unethical, ask yourself whether they mightn't well reduce the risk of a collision actually occurring. Nuclear warfare studies are plagued by ethical paradoxes. The biggest of them concern (see Chapter 7) whether it can be right to threaten or to carry out second strikes, acts of nuclear revenge. Of the others, many center on the fact that striking first could bring advantages, particularly if the enemy rejected the dangerous launch-on-warning, use 'em or lose 'em approach. Consider these points:

(1) It might be thought that building shelters for one's compatriots would be obviously a good thing. Yet the fact of a nation's possessing shelters could itself encourage its leaders to make a nuclear first strike since their sheltered followers might seem at little risk. Again, building shelters could provoke enemy leaders to strike because they believed that they were about to be struck.

(2) It could seem that virtuous leaders would plan for a limited war – either with no nuclear weapons or else just with low-power 'battlefield' devices – rather than for a full-scale nuclear exchange. Yet such planning could make it seem acceptable to risk a war or

to fire the first shots, after which escalation to a full-scale exchange might well be inevitable. Asked, as US Secretary of Defense, whether escalation could be controlled, C. Weinberger replied: 'I just don't have any idea.'[11]

(3) Developing highly accurate missiles, which could destroy enemy rockets in their silos instead of civilians in their cities, might look humane. Yet it too could lead to war by encouraging a first strike – perhaps by a fearful enemy as the missiles were being readied for installation. The US Army's prolonged pursuit of ever greater missile accuracies was therefore dangerous. The fact that the US Navy later joined it in developing within-one-hundred-meters accuracies was still worse, signalling as it did the rise to power of hawkish strategists who claimed that only between two and fifteen million Americans would die in an enfeebled Soviet reaction to a US first strike, this making a nuclear war 'winnable'.[12] The Soviet Union was no model of restraint, however. It did its best to improve accuracies.

(4) Points of the same type apply to the (now at least temporarily abandoned) Strategic Defense Initiative – President Reagan's 'Star Wars' plan, announced in 1983, to 'make nuclear weapons obsolete' by building a shield of lasers (or particle beams or, later, 'smart rocks' or 'brilliant pebbles'). Study after study suggested that SDI shielding would hardly work at all because of the technical difficulties involved, and because effective counters could be developed much less expensively. Yet if it had proved workable then, perhaps, so much the worse. Suppose it had been forecast to provide complete protection when fully installed. The pressure on the Soviet Union to carry out a pre-installation preventive strike, rather than risk annihilation in a war that cost the United States nothing, could have become intense. And forecasts of partial protection might themselves have had similar results. As McNamara explained, 'a leaky umbrella is quite useful in a drizzle' – so that US efforts to erect such an umbrella, one which 'might cope adequately with the depleted Soviet forces that had survived a US first strike', could have suggested an intent to start a war. 'The Russians', McNamara added, 'know that a first strike was not always excluded from US strategic thinking.'[13]

Note that US efforts to develop defensive beams have not been entirely abandoned. The Air Force has awarded contracts for design

30

of a laser able to destroy missiles hundreds of kilometers away, yet capable of being carried in an aircraft.[14]

(5) We scarcely need any association of medical practitioners to tell us that nuclear war would bring death and terrible suffering to people, or to calculate for us that the Cold War stored up the nuclear equivalent of five tons of TNT for every man, woman and child on the planet so that the entire human race could have been killed many times over, had it conveniently assembled itself on some large field. The crucial question is whether reducing the size of the nuclear arsenals would actually have *increased* the chances of disaster through making first strikes look attractive, as was argued by the Harvard University Nuclear Study Group.[15]

Suppose that any party which strikes second must expect the loss of 90 per cent of its striking power. There will then be obvious temptations to adopt a policy of launch on warning – that is to say, of firing off nuclear missiles in retaliation after seeming detection of incoming enemy missiles, instead of waiting for nuclear detonations to occur – unless even a counter-strike with the remaining 10 per cent would cause country-wide devastation. It might well seem that somewhat inconclusive evidence of an enemy attack would itself have to be trusted. Yes, huge forces were built up by the two superpowers before the Cold War ended. But they weren't so huge that each side could have absorbed the losses produced by an enemy first strike which found missiles still in their silos, bombers still on their runways, etc., and nevertheless gone on to inflict the 'assured destruction' central to the strategy of deterrence. As B. G. Blair explains,[16] the result was that both sides moved strongly towards launch on warning despite the severe risks involved – the risk that patterns of sunlight on clouds would be interpreted by sensors as rocket exhausts; the risk that lower-level commanders would abuse the predelegated launch authority which launch on warning almost inevitably involves; the risk that the accidental launch of a few missiles, with or without warheads, would be interpreted as a full-scale attack; and so forth.

In 1969, the Soviet Union threatened a nuclear strike on China, and particularly on its nuclear testing site and nuclear bases.[17] In 1967, 1973 and 1991, Israel is said to have put nuclear forces on alert, and in 1984, 1987 and 1990, India and Pakistan came dangerously close to waging wars in which nuclear bombs could well have been used,[18] although it seems unlikely that a global holocaust would have resulted: neither the United States nor Russia would have been obliged by treaty to become involved, and the main nuclear threat to the survival of the human race has always been of a confrontation between these superpowers. One such confrontation might quite easily have arisen during the Yom Kippur (Arab–Israel) War of 1973: the threatened introduction of Soviet troops into Egypt was averted by US military alerts, this perhaps being a case where one side's determination to keep to the center of the highway deterred the other from putting a car on the road.

Probably, however, it has been *accidental nuclear war* between the United States and Russia which has represented the most immediate danger to humankind since Russia's development of the H-bomb. This statement is as defensible today as it ever has been. The fragmentation of the Soviet Union has presumably made it easier, if anything, for missiles to be launched without authorization, and an attack from as low as the regimental level could result in three hundred nuclear explosions.[19]

The term 'accidental nuclear war' has come to be used widely. As well as the results of mechanical or electronic faults, it covers those of human error or insanity. Nuclear training exercises can be dangerous if on scales which may look to the other side like preparations for a real attack, and above all if errors erode the distinction between real and unreal: Blair reports that 'mistakes occasionally resulted in the United States disseminating actual nuclear launch orders instead of exercise orders',[20] although of course (for otherwise we'd all have heard of it) no launches resulted. The best-known mechanical error occurred in North Carolina in 1961: a B-52 bomber disintegrated and released two 24-megaton bombs, five out of six safety mechanisms on one of them then failing. Just a single switch had prevented detonation.[21] Perhaps still more dangerous, however, was the accidental launch (at some unrevealed date) of a Soviet nuclear-tipped ballistic missile during routine maintenance: fortunately it fell a short distance from the launch pad instead of reaching the target area where it was programmed to explode.[22] Another spectacular incident took place in Arkansas in 1980, a leaked-propellant explosion blowing a 9-megaton warhead six hundred feet into the air.[23] Sagan writes:

'In the years between 1950 and 1968, for which good statistics are available, there were, on average, worldwide several accidents involving nuclear weapons per year.'[24]

Faulty attack-detection systems are yet better known as sources of risk. (Here, as elsewhere, it is US data to which there is a fair amount of access. Heaven knows what went on in the Soviet Union.) In June 1980 a defective computer chip at NORAD (North American Air Defense Command) generated a warning of a Soviet attack: a nuclear alert was declared, the command director being dismissed next day for failure to issue a proper evaluation quickly enough.[25] Seven months earlier, B-52 bombers had been prepared for take-off, while intercontinental ballistic missile crews started preliminary launch procedures, almost certainly inserting their launch keys,[26] because a wargame tape had been accidentally allowed to control the main NORAD warning displays: Soviet missiles were shown as launched from submarines and from land. A Senate investigation thereupon revealed that between January 1979 and June 1980 there had been 147 'serious' false alarms.[27] Then and afterwards, 'routine' alarms (which merely required NORAD's command director to talk with Strategic Air Command and the Pentagon) have occurred several times daily, while maybe once or twice a year an alarm persists long enough to trigger a nuclear alert.[28]

False alarms become all the more serious when the time available for evaluating them becomes shorter. Today's intercontinental missiles have flight times of about half an hour; missiles launched by submarines can arrive in under ten minutes; and a 'Star Wars' space-based shield would have needed to be activated in under six minutes, the 'burn time' of SS-18 rockets, or in under a minute if the Russians had introduced 'fast burn' rockets. Commanders confident in the latest detection systems could be understandably eager to delegate launchings to computers, arguing that only these could make decisions rapidly enough. And while of course well aware of the dangers of accidental nuclear war, else it would have occurred long ago, the military often resist proposed improvements in safeguards, sometimes on the excuse that 'measures that reduce the chance of unwanted launch may increase the chance that legitimate launch orders will not be carried out', Blair and Kendall report.[29] The US armed forces have shown no interest in systems

33

which permit missiles to be rendered harmless after launching, although it was stated by V. Karpov, as Soviet Deputy Foreign Minister, that the Soviet Union had installed such systems in its intercontinental missiles.[30]

In the United States, Blair's researches show, 'de facto adoption of launch on warning' by the mid-1980s meant that false alarms could be especially dangerous in times of tension. High confidence that an enemy nuclear strike was in progress 'no longer depended at all on the presence of nuclear detonations', making it 'distinctly possible that a NORAD high-confidence judgment would have been based on a combination of positive strategic warning' – meaning such things as a political crisis combined with detection of Soviet nuclear-weapon movements – 'and a tactical sensor outage', an outage which might perhaps have resulted from accidental electronic interference of a sort readily mistaken for deliberate jamming.[31]

Can the military initiate nuclear exchanges without permission from their political masters? Blair answers: 'Despite the widespread belief that the Russian and US military establishments cannot physically mount a nuclear attack unless they first obtain essential codes from their respective presidents, in fact they have custody of all the codes needed to order an all-out strategic attack.'[32] Here there is risk from two directions. (1) In the US, above all, there can seem to be a dangerous degree of dispersed control, so that nuclear war could be started by commanders at low levels: one reads, for instance, that 'no physical safeguards prevent US ballistic missile submarines from launching their missiles on a decision by the captain and the officers'.[33] Naturally enough, dispersal of control tends to be particularly great during crises. At the time of the Yom Kippur War, individual US weapon commanders were ordered to remove launch keys and presidential launch codes from their safes.[34] (2) When control is instead centralized, local commanders may actually be unable to prevent launches. In both Russia and the US, higher commanders can broadcast signals which launch missiles automatically.[35]

It would presumably be quite some time before such matters were entirely automated. Still, as early as in 1987 the military historian J. Keegan wrote that 'nuclear command and control secrets are those that an adversary would most like to penetrate' so as to be able to 'calculate if a decapitating first strike was feasible', the resulting walls of impenetrability ensuring that 'we do not, for example, even know whether the launch procedure has been computerized', i.e. whether machines 'are now instructed to order the launch of missiles at some predetermined presentation of warning signals by the other machines of the surveillance system'. In the United States, nothing could be more flatly unconstitutional, but it is no secret that such constitutional principles as that 'President and Congress are bound to conduct debate over the declaration of war in open session' wouldn't be followed at moments of actual or suspected nuclear attack.[36]

It could be rather hard to say who or what – computers or commanders or politicians – could best be entrusted with launch decisions. It isn't only computer chips which can fail. In 1989, Blair and Kendall note, 'of the roughly 75,000 members of the US military with access to nuclear weapons and related components, nearly 2,400 had to be removed from duty. Seven hundred and thirty abused alcohol or drugs, and the rest had psychological or emotional problems, were insubordinate or engaged in criminal behaviour.'[37] S. Britten adds: 'Authority for transfer rests with the unit commanding officer who sometimes takes the view that the 'good soldier', or airman, is one who can conceal his use of drugs, just as he can hold his liquor. Demonstrably unstable men have been kept on nuclear weapons duties against their wills', the problem being compounded by the fact that many apparently normal people 'delight in destruction', being expert 'at concealing their feelings and plans'.[38] Bear in mind, however, that politicians aren't always models of rationality. Alcohol or drugs, prescribed by doctors or self-administered, have clouded the minds of world leaders, including those most generally respected.

Politicians can have other problems too. When President Nixon was suffering the terrible strain of impending forced resignation 'senior government officials took precautions against the possibility that he might act irrationally in his capacity as commander in chief'.[39] President Giscard d'Estaing seemed to some viewers too self-satisfied as he announced on television that he alone, unaided and unadvised (and therefore presumably unrestrainable in the event of sudden psychiatric disturbance), would make any decision to use French nuclear bombs. And the leaders of the coup against

President Gorbachev, who took control of his briefcase containing nuclear warfare codes and communications equipment, were embittered and soon became desperate, factors prompting the generals to agree between themselves that any launch orders would not be accepted.

What could the near future hold for us? Efforts to halt the spread of nuclear weapons have very largely failed.[40] China, Britain and France will between them have arsenals about a quarter as strong as those which the superpowers will retain after their tentatively agreed reductions (to 3,500 warheads for the US and 3,000 for Russia, by the year 2003). India may test an H-bomb soon. There are perhaps a dozen further states – including ones such as Iraq which had signed the Nuclear Non-Proliferation Treaty – that either possess nuclear weapons already (Israel, for example) or have had weapon development programmes. Some of these programmes are still active, while the fact that the others have been suspended is, of course, little guarantee that they won't be revived. Several additional states possess not only nuclear reactors but also reprocessing plants which could be used to build up stores of plutonium. Others, too, could well hope to seize or buy plutonium, or actual warheads. So could terrorists or criminals. The following story is all too believable in view of the chaos attending the Soviet Union's collapse: 'In 1991, Greenpeace arranged to buy a nuclear warhead from an East German soldier. The organisation planned to ship it to Berlin for a surprise news conference. This unusual sale was stopped only by the early withdrawal of the soldier's company back to Russia.'[41]

As J. Hassard points out, a nuclear bomb's delivery system 'need not be a ballistic missile. A truck packed with refugees would do the job.'[42]

Admittedly there is nothing in all this to compare with the kind of direct, immediate threat to the survival of the human race that the superpower arsenals may provide. Yet, in an age in which world peace could be threatened by any city-destroying nuclear explosion, not only states but individuals too are becoming more and more able to afford nuclear weapons. Knowledge of the technology is widespread, much of it – including fairly detailed instructions for making H-bombs – actually available in public libraries and on the computer Internet. The Aum Shinri Kyo religious sect, responsible for the March 1995 nerve gas attack on Tokyo's subway trains, claimed to have $1.6 billion in assets and had accumulated many documents on how to construct nuclear weapons. Its forty thousand members included physicists and even a rocket scientist.

A final, possibly very disturbing point is that small fusion bombs might be made without using either plutonium or enriched uranium as their triggers if 'red mercury' – a compound of antimony and mercury, bound together after irradiation in a nuclear reactor, that releases hundreds of times more chemical energy than the high explosive TNT – is more than a myth, as has recently been suggested by Frank Barnaby, former Director of the Stockholm International Peace Research Institute, a well-known nuclear weapons analyst who has been investigating some widely denied rumours for several years. Barnaby has now said that 'on the balance of probabilities' the substance exists, and that it may have been incorporated in Russian neutron bombs. Sam Cohen, the nuclear physicist who invented the neutron bomb (which kills mainly by irradiation rather than by shock waves), has gone further, stating that 'red mercury is real and it is terrifying. I think it is part of a terrorist weapon that potentially spells the end of organised society.' Cohen claims that it could be used to initiate fusion in tritium atoms at the core of a baseball-sized neutron bomb able to kill everyone within about six hundred meters. Other experts are very sceptical of all this, however.[43]

CHEMICAL AND BIOLOGICAL WARFARE

In the First World War, above a million soldiers were casualties of chlorine, phosgene and mustard gas, over ninety thousand dying. The nerve gases tabun, sarin and soman, discovered but not used during the Second World War, were deadly in far smaller quantities, while the yet more effective VX – the United States had four thousand tons of it in 1967 – killed when just a few milligrams reached one's skin. Still, an amount sufficient to destroy all the people in China, supposing that they lined up to receive their doses, could in practice 'neutralize' only a square kilometer of battlefield.[44] (A cynic might say that this is why many nations recently proved willing to sign a Convention banning manufacture of chemical weapons – adding, though, that sixty-five nations must ratify it before it comes into force.) Natural toxins, now manufacturable inexpensively through gene cloning, are far more lethal: three hundred tons might replace the eighty thousand tons to which the chemical warfare arsenal of the superpowers had at one stage grown.[45] Shiga toxin manages to be over a million times deadlier than tabun. The gene for it was cloned by the US Army, officially 'to create a vaccine' and thus 'for peaceful purposes', while the same army had earlier cloned the gene for diphtheria toxin 'to create a new therapy to treat melanoma, a type of skin cancer'.[46]

Properly protected troops, however, would merely be slowed down by the bulky clothing and respirators needed to counter such agents. And while civilians could suffer heavy casualties, the extermination of the human race would seem to require agents of a self-reproducing kind: the bacteria, rickettsiae, viruses and fungi of biowarfare. A single inhaled organism can lead to death from Q-fever. Just one genetically novel virus started the influenza pandemic of 1918–19. Its offspring infected at least two-thirds of a billion people, killing more than the world war had done.

In 1346 besieging Mongols hurled plague-infected corpses into the city of Caffa, its fleeing inhabitants then helping to spread the Black Death. Twenty-five million people perished, about 30 per cent of Europe's population.

In 1763 the British made gifts of blankets from smallpox hospitals, with the intended effect on North American Indians.[47]

There were several allegations of germ warfare during the First World War.

During the Second World War the British developed anthrax bombs. They then ordered half a million from the United States 'for use', Prime Minister Churchill wrote, 'should this mode of warfare be employed against us'.[48] Britain's Joint Planning Staff received instructions, all the same, to study whether the Allies could reach victory more quickly by first use of such warfare.[49] In 1945 a 500-pound British bacteriological bomb was at an advanced stage of development; it was estimated that forty thousand such bombs could deliver death by anthrax to half the citizens of Aachen, Berlin, Frankfurt, Hamburg, Stuttgart and Wilhelmshafen.[50] In the United States a force which grew to four thousand persons worked on anthrax, yellow fever, plague, botulism and dozens of other diseases, including those of crops and farm animals. The manufacturing plant in Indiana, ready to operate in 1945 but never actually used, was capable of producing half a million anthrax bombs a month, and crop disease bombs were produced for the US Air Force six years after the war.[51]

In 1935, reacting to alleged Russian attacks on their water supplies with cholera bacteria, the Japanese began major work on cholera and also on plague, typhus, typhoid, hemorrhagic fever and smallpox.[52] They developed bombs for anthrax and gas gangrene. During their invasion of China they attacked at least eleven cities experimentally, their aircraft dropping plague-infected paper, cotton, wheat and rice.[53] In addition they distributed one hundred and thirty kilograms of anthrax and paratyphoid bacteria.[54] Several thousand prisoners of war became their experimental subjects, perhaps as many as three thousand dying, but the United States overlooked the deaths in return for the experimental data, then continuing to deny Russian reports of the whole affair for the next quarter-century. The Russians may have regarded all this as an invitation to pursue their own research, for in 1979 a US Congressional Committee reported that an anthrax outbreak in Sverdlovsk had been caused by an explosion at a biological weapons factory.[55]

Post-war US activities included producing designs for a plant able to breed one hundred and thirty million mosquitoes a month, for spreading yellow fever. Fleas, ticks and flies are said to have been bred at Fort Detrick as possible vectors for plague, tularemia, anthrax and dysentery. Strains of brucellosis, psittacosis, Rocky Mountain spotted fever, Rift Valley fever, Q-fever, encephelomyelitis, and so on were also developed for possible use in warfare.[56] In 1952, during the Korean War, an international scientific commission made the firm statement – the United States was equally firm in its denial – that 'the people of Korea and China did actually serve as targets for bacteriological weapons'. Many years later, the statement's British co-author commented that 'mostly it was experimental work, as far as we could see', work which 'didn't seem to be very successful'.[57] However, secret pseudo-attacks by the US military on San Francisco, New York and Winnipeg had been depressingly effective. In one of them, in 1950, wind blowing over two minesweepers sent at least five thousand harmless bacteria into the lungs of virtually every San Franciscan. Secret British experiments from 1948 to 1959 were similarly alarming. Caged on rafts off the Bahamas and the west coast of Scotland, thousands of animals were exposed to wind-driven bacteria, while harmless zinc cadmium sulphide was poured from aircraft flying around the British coast. The results are said to have shown that Britain would be virtually defenceless against germs in aerosol form.[58]

All this activity had occurred despite first one and then another treaty: the 1925 Geneva Protocol, which prohibited actual warfare with gas or germs, and the Convention of 1972, which in addition banned development and stockpiling of biological weapons. For a start, many countries failed to sign these treaties or else failed to ratify them. The first was ratified by Japan only in 1970, and by the United States not until 1975. In 1985 half the developing countries had accepted neither of them. Next, ratifications of the Protocol were often with two qualifications: that only first use would be prohibited (first use being something very hard to verify) and that countries which hadn't ratified could be attacked at will. Again, the Convention permitted unlimited research, plus production 'for protective or other peaceful purposes' – so that huge amounts could be produced 'for making vaccines', some then being available for actual vaccination of the home population and the remainder for launching an attack. Moreover, studies of verification methods began only in 1991, perhaps understandably, since treaty violations would be nearly impossible to detect. Against such a background, even saintly governments could appear in need of biowarfare research to evaluate threats from others, to develop vaccines and antibiotics, and to deter by making it plain that weapons could be constructed quickly. In 1994 the United States claimed that as many as twenty-five nations, including North Korea, Iran and Iraq, were developing biological weaponry, and that the Russians had pursued a vigorous offensive programme in violation of the Convention.[59]

The arrival of genetic engineering was at first judged to make little difference. As recently as 1983 a spokesman for the US military said the world was already full of fine biological weapon agents, for instance anthrax. Such a reaction sounds foolish today. Techniques of gene manipulation have advanced so rapidly that lethal, highly infectious viruses are no longer regarded as too dangerous to handle. (Anthrax vaccine has reduced mortality rates to 20 per cent or less, and anthrax is not particularly infectious.) Essentially new diseases can be produced by 'site-directed mutagenesis' in which chemicals, delivered to chosen regions of an organism's DNA or RNA, alter genes which wouldn't ordinarily mutate, or by 'splicing', which combines genes from different organisms. In 1985 Prime Minister Thatcher stated that biological weapons had become as potentially dangerous as nuclear ones.[60]

Normal germs 'don't want to kill'; there is an evolutionary penalty to be paid for murdering one's host, so that new varieties of plague, for example, tend to become less and less deadly as they spread; but toxin-producing genes can be deliberately added to remedy this. Thus, the harmless *E. coli* bacteria of everybody's digestive tract might be changed so as to produce botulinus toxin.[61] Natural resistance and vaccines can be thwarted by changing the surface structures of virulent organisms, making them 'unrecognizable'. The unrecognizability can be maintained through genes which confer hypervariability of the kind already found in the influenza and AIDS viruses. A country might vaccinate its own troops against bacteria, or even some viruses, which it intended to use in an attack. Its population too could be secretly vaccinated by wind-blown aerosols.[62] But attempted defences would be futile unless one knew exactly which organisms the attacker was going to use – whereas in fact one would probably first learn of an attack only several days after it had taken place.

'Ethnic' biological weapons have been proposed. Among victims of Rift Valley fever, whites are ten times less likely to die than blacks, while Epstein–Barr virus causes cancers in black Africans and in South-East Asians, but not in whites.[63] A nation attacking with such diseases, or with new ones produced by genetic engineering, might deny that there was anything unnatural in high death rates in enemy territory combined with low ones in its own. Similar 'deniability' could, of course, be had in the case of any disease endemic to the territory targeted. A lethal new strain produced by genetic engineers could be called a natural mutation.

The difficulties of verification have been worsened by advances in production methods. Small peaceful installations for making antibiotics and vaccines can readily be converted to making germs

41

instead. Production times have been reduced several thousandfold and, now that mammalian cells can be grown on the surfaces of tiny beads, one small bottle can produce virus yields which previously required large production facilities.[64] Germs are fast becoming the poor man's atom bomb, available to small terrorist organizations or to criminals wishing to hold the world to ransom.

What is there in all this to exterminate the human race? In the Second World War fowl plague was intensively studied and the British manufactured five million anthrax-filled cattle cakes, but humans can survive as vegetarians. In contrast, the viruses, bacteria and fungi investigated for attacking rice, wheat, maize, potatoes, etc. could produce widespread famine. It seems unlikely, though, that sufficiently many crops would be destroyed to wipe out humankind. The main danger surely lies in germs specifically directed against humans. An attacking nation's vaccines to protect itself might all too easily fail. 'Ethnic' biowarfare agents could mutate, then slaughtering all races equally. Ingenious safety measures, for instance engineering of organisms so that they would die off after a small number of cell divisions, might again be nullified by mutation or by exchange of genetic material with unengineered organisms.[65] Terrorists, or criminals demanding billions of dollars, could endanger the entire future of humanity with utterly lethal organisms which mutated so rapidly that no vaccines could fight them.

In *Man's Means to his End* Sir Robert Watson-Watt, after surveying the possibilities of nuclear and biological warfare, concluded that humans could enjoy a long future only if they established 'a unique World Police Force', to be 'the only force in the world with armament exceeding that required for the maintenance of internal order in individual nations'.[66] These words were written in 1961. Today it can seem that the threat to the human race from terrorists and criminals (let alone governments) could be removed only by very intrusive policing. One's own privacy is worth a great deal. Still, it may not be worth a major risk of dying, in company with everybody else, because some people have been using their privacy for perfecting a new disease.

ENVIRONMENTAL DEGRADATION
AND THE POPULATION CRISIS

This could easily be the area containing the greatest dangers. While most are well known, the section on pp. 59–63 below – on a runaway greenhouse effect – may come as an unpleasant surprise.

Pollution by chemicals or nuclear radiation

Air, water and soil are threatened by pollution. For a start, there is domestic sewage and garbage. In many places raw sewage enters river, lake or sea. In industrialized countries, people each produce about half a ton of garbage annually. It accumulates in landfill sites which poison groundwaters, or it is burned in ways adding pollutants to the air and concentrating others in the ash. Many elements of the garbage count as hazardous waste, yet much more of this is produced by industry. In the United States, factories generate at least a ton of hazardous waste per citizen, about ten million tons of it being toxic chemicals. These frequently end up in leaking dumps such as the infamous Love Canal in Niagara city. Poor countries typically have few restrictions on dumpsites; China generates five hundred million tons a year of industrial waste, dumping most of it just outside its cities; but both in North America and in Europe illegal sites are in any case common. In the tiny Netherlands, four thousand of them were quickly found by one survey.

In the mid-1980s, Britain and France were using sea dumping for nearly twenty million tons of industrial waste yearly, despite severe lack of knowledge about the environmental effects of the eighty thousand chemicals synthesized industrially. It took a quarter of a century to convince people that DDT and leaded gasoline were dangerous, and such inert substances as chlorofluorocarbons (CFCs) can themselves cause great damage when broken down into their constituents by natural processes.

We mine two billion tons of non-fuel minerals a year, from which to manufacture goods. During both the mining and the manufacturing, toxic metals are scattered far and wide. A rule of thumb for mining (and also for logging and farming) is that each ton of

43

final product, eventually to become garbage in many cases, is preceded by five tons of waste generated during manufacturing, and by twenty tons of it during initial resource extraction. Depletion of the mines can cause tremendous growth both in the energy used for extraction and in the waste 'tailings': D. H. Meadows, D. L. Meadows and J. Randers note that 'as the average grade of copper ore mined in Butte, Montana, fell from 30 per cent to 0.5 per cent the tailings produced per ton of copper rose from 3 tons to 200 tons'.[67] Lead now enters the environment at eighteen times the natural rate; cadmium at five times the natural rate; mercury, nickel, arsenic, vanadium at twice the natural rate. Two thousand tons of mercury have joined the Amazon's ecosystems, just from gold prospecting.

Carcinogens such as many pesticides, the polychlorinated biphenyls (PCBs) and the yet more dangerous dioxins are special causes for concern. They can be tremendously concentrated as they move up natural food chains. In the North Sea, PCBs in marine mammals have become concentrated by ten million times. J. Cummins writes: 'If the PCBs held in the Third World alone entered the seas, they would probably cause the extinction of a wide range of marine mammals, if not all.'[68] An explosion at a chemical plant in Seveso in 1976 brought dioxins to international attention, but such dramatic incidents form only a small part of the problem. At Bhopal in 1984 a pesticide-manufacturing explosion injured two hundred thousand and killed two thousand – yet accidental pesticide poisonings number a million a year, causing twenty thousand deaths.

Chemical pesticides and chemical fertilizers are applied in greater and greater tonnages as soil quality declines and the pests (weeds, fungi, nematodes, mites, insects) develop resistance, while their natural predators will often have been utterly destroyed. The chemicals then accumulate in the ground or are carried into rivers. It is the pesticides which wreak the most obvious havoc. In fact, the main disadvantage of fertilizers may be that they make pesticides essential by ruining soil balances and crop ecologies. In Western nations, many pesticides whose use is prohibited are nevertheless manufactured for export. British exports of DDT, quite a powerful carcinogen, rose by seven times soon after it was banned from British farms. Its use became illegal in the United States in

1972, yet that country exports twenty thousand tons a year, mostly to the third world.

The gases and particulates of air pollution are most obvious in cities: in some, sufferers can now buy oxygen from slot machines. However, the surrounding countryside is affected too, as evidenced by smaller harvests. Dusts, carbon monoxide and ozone are important here, but oxides of sulphur and of nitrogen are perhaps the main culprits: arriving from vehicles and from power stations, they attack fish and forests by forming acid rain. While its effects up to date have been noticed mainly in Europe and North America, acid rain threatens to do particular harm to the thin and poor red-laterite soils of South America, Africa and Asia. It leaches out nutrients and activates mercury, cadmium and other toxic metals.

War and preparations for war have contributed to pollution mightily. During the Vietnam War, US forces employed some hundred thousand tons of defoliants and other chemical warfare agents, Agent Orange being heavily contaminated with dioxin. Disregarding the Koran's prohibition of such acts, Saddam Hussein took revenge for his defeat in the 1991 Gulf War by setting fire to Kuwait's oilwells: the cloud of sooty smoke was 900 km long and 600 km wide. With the fires extinguished, thousands of square kilometers became covered by oil lakes which released clouds of toxic fumes. Still, Hussein's behaviour did less harm than had been feared, largely because the smoke rose only to fairly low altitudes. Much greater damage has occurred during the development and production of nuclear weapons. In the Altai district of southern Siberia in 1949, thousands received radiation doses like the ones suffered by those inhabitants of Hiroshima and Nagasaki who outlived 1945's nuclear attacks. They developed sickness, cataracts and cancers in consequence. Stalin had ordered the testing of his first atomic bomb, nobody worrying that the wind direction was such that radioactive dust from the near-ground explosion would be blown across more than a million people living nearby – people who were warned neither beforehand nor afterwards, so that they happily consumed the products of contaminated fields. Again, hundreds of square kilometers had to be permanently evacuated when stored waste from Soviet military reactors exploded at Kyshtym in the winter of 1957. And when contemplating President de Gaulle's fun-loving refusal to delay watching a nuclear test until the wind had changed – the result was fairly high radiation levels for people living as far distant as three thousand kilometers – don't forget that there were 461 such above-ground nuclear tests between 1945 and 1961. Residual radiation could render many Pacific islands dangerous to inhabit for millennia.

Until the explosion of the Chernobyl reactor in 1986, civilian nuclear power had a remarkably fine record, making it a much more environmentally friendly source of energy than coal or hydro-electricity. The partial core meltdown at Three Mile Island seven years earlier had released hardly any radiation to the surroundings. Even the fire at Windscale in 1957 had led to no fatalities in the short term, and although in the long term up to one hundred additional deaths from cancer may conceivably have resulted, any large coal-burning power station beats this total, thanks to coal mining accidents, black lung disease, asthma, and so forth. The Chernobyl disaster involved such ludicrous disregard for safety that we might harbour hopes of its never being repeated: 'no matter what you did with the reactor an explosion was impossible', the operators are reported to have thought.[69] It did, however, kill thirty people quickly, with up to forty thousand premature deaths to follow according to an official Soviet report, or half a million or more according to the biophysicist J. Gofman and the radiologist E. Sternglass;[70] and there could be still more energetic reactor explosions – ones rivalling the detonation of up to three kilotons of TNT according to R. Webb, an expert on nuclear reactor hazards.[71] Nevertheless the main dangers in this area will always be the risk of helping nations to acquire nuclear bombs, the risk of attacks on reactors by warplanes, terrorists or criminals, and all the risks involved in storing reactor wastes that are going to remain highly radioactive for hundreds of centuries. Sites geologically suitable for prolonged underground storage have proved very hard to find, while above-ground storage has a deplorable history: between 1945 and 1973 over four hundred thousand gallons of radioactive waste had leaked from tanks at Hanford, the main US storage center. The US Department of Energy estimates that the States will have accumulated fifty thousand tons of 'spent fuel' by the year 2000. (This is uranium removed from commercial reactors because its radioactivity has *in*creased too much.) And unfortunately it now seems that reactors using nuclear fusion, if these can be developed to replace the fission reactors of today, will themselves generate much radioactive waste, the walls of their reaction chambers quickly becoming contaminated.

Companies based in the rich nations frequently move their factories to poor nations whose environmental regulations are less stringent. If not, then they may at least threaten to do so, thereby discouraging legislation in their home countries – for why put home-country jobs at risk while offering no benefits to the world as a whole? Further, some twenty million tons of toxic waste are sent by the rich to the poor each year. Often it ends up in illegal dumps. Still, one mustn't imagine that the generation of pollution is an activity only of rich countries. Burning of tropical and subtropical forests, scrubs and grasslands in order to clear them, the grassland fires often being repeated annually, generates plentiful smoke and gases: millions of tons of methyl chloride, for instance. In the third world, the few laws which restrict industries are seldom enforced. And one large group of poor countries, those of the former Soviet Union, are among the world's worst polluted. T. Beardsley writes that the radioactivity from Chernobyl 'was puny compared with the colossal exudation of much longer lived radionuclides from reactions that the former Soviet Union used, and Russia still uses, to produce plutonium for bombs', the world's biggest environmental release occurring over decades at Tomsk-7 in central Siberia, which poured out 'about a billion curies of high-level waste, or 20 Chernobyls' worth': this made the total released radioactivity in Russia 'about 400 times the amount in the United States'.[72] In 1992 three hundred thousand citizens of the former Soviet Union were being treated for radiation sickness, while in the Urals the noxious fumes of military-industrial areas were causing shockingly many birth defects and cases of bronchitis, blood disease, nervous disorder and mental retardation: many cities in the area had become utterly unfit for human habitation.

Communism's filthy legacy extends also to Poland, where the waters of the Vistula are too polluted for industrial use, Warsaw having no sewage treatment; to Czechoslovakia, where 90 per cent of wells in the countryside are contaminated; and to Romania, whose border-crossing chlorine emissions, the cause of constant disorders of eyes, lungs and skin, pushed tens of thousands of Bulgarians into antigovernment demonstrations in 1987.

The current orgy of deforestation may worsen matters. Forests are important cleansers of the atmosphere. And concentrations of the hydroxyl radical – a highly reactive molecular fragment, largely responsible for holding down the atmospheric percentages of trace gases such as sulphur dioxide, nitrogen oxides and chlorofluoro-carbons – might fall significantly because of carbon monoxide coming from forest burnings.[73]

More generally, there is the danger that environmental cycles will undergo disastrous changes with 'positive feedback', each alter-ation causing still more alteration. J. E. Lovelock's *Gaia* (1979), treated by many industrialists as a charter to pollute since it put so much emphasis on how negative-feedback mechanisms (such as are found in thermostats) had kept Earth healthy for billions of years, none the less included a warning of possible 'gigadeath' through 'runaway positive feedback'.[74] Lovelock later wrote that

the human species, aided by the industries at its command, has significantly altered some of the planet's major chemical cycles. We have increased the carbon cycle by 20 percent, the nitrogen cycle by 50 percent, and the sulphur cycle by over 100 percent. We shall have to tread warily to avoid the cybernetic disasters of runaway positive feedback or of sustained oscillation between two or more undesirable states.[75]

As early as in 1986, Meadows et al. comment, it was estimated that humans took for their own use '25 per cent of the photo-synthetic product of the earth as a whole (land and sea), and 40 per cent of the photosynthetic product on land', raising the grim question of what the world would be like if they took 80 per cent or more after 'the next doubling of human population and economic activity, 20 to 30 years away'.[76]

A possible sign of imminent environmental collapse is that frogs and toads are becoming rare everywhere but in Africa. Breathing partly through their moist and delicate skins, these amphibians might be acting rather like the canaries which used to be carried down coalmines so that their deaths would give warning of dangerous gases.[77] Again, there is an apparent halving of human sperm counts world wide, and a twofold to fourfold rise in testicular cancer. These may be the effects of pollutants which mimic human estrogens, or many other toxic substances could be responsible.[78]

All the same, there are grounds for hope. Lovelock argues that his seemingly unscientific 'Gaia hypothesis' – that the biosphere might usefully be viewed as a superorganism able to keep itself healthy – is supported both by the geological record and by seeing how negative feedbacks can arise unmagically, species then evolving to benefit from them (and sometimes also to reinforce them for their greater benefit). Forests, for instance, react to extra sunlight by evaporating vast volumes of water, and the resulting clouds reflect sunlight back into space.[79] Again, it has been authoritatively claimed that cancer figures aren't yet climbing rapidly. Lung cancer is more prevalent, but this is primarily due to cigarettes, while digestive and cervical cancers are now significantly rarer than before.[80] Further, it was possible to maintain in 1994 that 'forest biomass in Europe is not only surviving but probably increasing, despite enormous burdens of pollutants and acid rain, possibly through fertilization by the very same chemical pollutants that are causing the damage'.[81] And acid rain might reduce greenhouse-effect overheating: it 'could increase biological activity in the oceans which, in turn, could allow the oceans to absorb more of the carbon dioxide in the atmosphere', while sulphates in the rain seeded the formation of clouds to cool the planet.[82] Moreover, microbes are evolving so as to live off pollutants, turning them into harmless substances, while General Electric has patented a genetically engineered organism for breaking down oil slicks. Our situation could also be helped greatly, Meadows et al. suggest, by such advances as replacing hundreds of copper wires in a telephone system by 'one hair-thin strand of ultra-pure glass', or by using the biotechnology and nanotechnology which Chapter 2 will discuss instead of the 'high temperatures, severe pressures, harsh chemicals, and brute forces that have characterized manufacturing processes since the beginning of the industrial revolution'.[83]

Perhaps the main reasons for optimism lie in the growing environmental movement; the coming of a trillion-dollar market for environmentally friendly factories and machines, and for processes for cleansing polluted soil and water; and the growing willingness in government offices and in lawcourts to make polluters suffer financially.

Destruction of the ozone layer

Stratospheric ozone blocks ultraviolet light. Were all of it to be brought down to sea level, the ozone would form a layer only three millimeters thick. In the 1970s it was attacked without restraint by CFCs manufactured at a rate of nearly a million tons a year as refrigerants, aerosol propellants, industrial solvents and foam-blowing agents. Rising slowly into the stratosphere sooner or later, for instance from dumped and rusting refrigerators, CFCs are broken down by sunlight. Their chlorine then attacks the ozone by catalysis, so that just one chlorine atom can destroy tens of thousands of ozone molecules. Largely because of CFCs, the stratospheric chlorine is now about five times more than before, and increasing. The globe's average stratospheric ozone level is thought to have declined by between 4 and 8 per cent.

The losses are particularly marked in Antarctica, where each October sees the appearance of a 'hole', its area sometimes equalling that of the United States: ozone is reduced by about 60 per cent overall and by 95 per cent at the center. In the year 2005 there would be very little ozone in the hole if present trends continued. A second, less transparent hole – ozone levels reduced by 10 per cent or more – now opens over the Arctic at intervals, stretching southwards over much of Europe and North America.

The threat from CFCs was first explained in the early 1970s, before discovery of the Antarctic hole. As usual with pollution crises, the evidence was at first doubted. When the hole was found, it was suggested that seasonal winds were blowing the ozone away. A. G. Burford, head of President Reagan's Environmental Protection Agency in the early 1980s, later wrote scornfully, 'Remember a few years back when the big news was fluorocarbons that supposedly threatened the ozone layer?' D. Hodel, Reagan's Secretary of the Interior, advocated 'personal protection and lifestyle changes' as a sufficient counter to the alleged risk. But cartoons showing cows wearing baseball caps and sunglasses to defend against blindness and applying sunblock creams to avoid skin cancer, or adopting the 'lifestyle change' of staying indoors, together with a growing scientific consensus that the problem was genuine and very dangerous, led to the Montreal Protocol of 1987. Signed at first by twenty-seven countries, the Protocol called for a 50 per cent cut in the manufacture of CFCs and halons (which are the other main ozone-destroyers) by 1991. Later becoming convinced of the inadequacy of this, the signatories, joined by more than fifty further countries, called for phasing out the use of these chemicals by the end of the century.

Optimists hope that stratospheric ozone will be back nearly to normal by the year 2050. Others think, however, that the ozone depletion at that date will be at least as much as in 1990 even if all signatories keep to the suggested timetable. They point out, too, that governments have quite often failed to ratify the Protocol, demanding financial aid before doing so, and that companies advertising their commitment to the environment nevertheless quickly unloaded stocks of ozone-destroyers in developing countries which hadn't signed: in India, the tonnage of halons sold in 1990 was eight times greater than in 1987. By 1993 only nine third-world countries had cut emission levels. Particularly in view of how easy it has been to find substitutes for ozone-destroying chemicals, all this could be viewed as a case of too little action, too late.

CFCs and halons are far from being the only threats to stratospheric ozone. With their vapour trails, aircraft cause about a tenth of the ozone depletion, and could cause much more after the anticipated growth in high-altitude flights. (In 1990 Britain and France were cheerfully proposing joint development of a new fleet of supersonic high-altitude aircraft despite the earlier outcry of environmentalists against similar plans in the United States.) Nitrogen oxides produced by, for instance, the use of nitrogenous fertilizers destroy maybe another tenth of the ozone. Methyl bromide, a crop fumigant, destroys perhaps as much again. Other contributors include methyl chloride: as mentioned earlier, this is generated copiously when forests, scrubs and grasslands are cleared by burning. It has been claimed that by ejecting hydrochloric acid volcanoes send more chlorine to the stratosphere than humans, but this has been disproved: practically all of the acid is washed out by the rains accompanying eruptions, and in any case the recent big eruption of Mt Pinatubo ejected a mere fifty thousand tons of it, an amount negligible by comparison with the CFCs emitted in the same period. Yet volcanic emissions, together with industrial pollutants, do help clouds to form in the stratosphere, these then initiating reactions which speed up the ravages of the chlorine which humans have put there.

The direct consequences include an estimated additional 200,000 expected deaths from skin cancer in the United States alone or (the Environmental Protection agency has calculated) over 3,000,000 by the year 2100 if ozone depletion continues unabated. There will be many more cases of blindness (100,000 more for each 1 per cent decline in stratospheric ozone, according to a United Nations panel), a weakening of the human immune system, and premature aging. Still, the worst consequences could be indirect ones. Light in the ultraviolet-B waveband harms living organisms of all main types, on land and in water. It attacks not only plants, including many trees, but also the nitrogen-fixing bacteria on which crops rely unless heavily fertilized. Above all, it may be a grave threat to many zooplankton and phytoplankton species. Zooplankton and phytoplankton are at the base of the oceanic food chains. Phytoplankton are crucial for taking carbon dioxide from the atmosphere: they remove more of this greenhouse gas than all other factors combined.

We can draw comfort from how some of the phytoplankton species are specially resistant to ultraviolet light, while others seem to be evolving resistance. Some plants, too, are more resistant than others: particular varieties of soya bean, for instance. But scientists are troubled by such facts as that ultraviolet-C – it can be far more rapidly destructive than ultraviolet-B, yet has so far been almost entirely absorbed in the stratosphere – may soon break through in the Antarctic.[84] Again, trapping of heat at lower levels by greenhouse gases makes the stratosphere cooler, which increases ozone losses by encouraging clouds to form there. And extra ultraviolet light increases the quantity of reactive radicals in the lower atmosphere, resulting in more production of pollutants. The pollutants include lower-atmosphere ozone, a very effective crop destroyer.

Rather than human beings ruining the ozone layer, might Betelgeuse do the job? A red supergiant star nearing the end of its lifetime, Betelgeuse will explode as a supernova perhaps as soon as in the next few thousand years. The astronomer M. L. McCall has suggested that the resulting shower of ultraviolet light and X-rays could strip off the ozone.[85] But Betelgeuse is at a distance of some five hundred and twenty light years, quite far enough to make us safe according to most other astronomers. Any loss of enough ozone to kill off the human race would almost certainly be produced by us humans instead. In view of all the scientific uncertainties, it could be foolhardy to declare that the danger of producing it was zero or very small.

India, where sales of refrigerators are rising rapidly, is said to be trying to move straight to ozone-friendly refrigeration. But the far richer industrialized nations have set no good example, and China plans to put CFCs into fifty million new refrigerators before changing to other substances.

In April 1995, the state legislature of Arizona voted to legalize manufacture of CFCs, in contravention of federal law. 'Irresponsible theories about the ozone layer are no excuse to deprive people of necessary technology', the Governor is reported to have said as he signed the legislation.[86]

The greenhouse effect

Greenhouse gases let through sunlight but tend to stop energy escaping into space when it has been changed to lower-frequency heat radiation. While water vapour is the main such gas, there are growing contributions from over thirty others, especially CO_2 (carbon dioxide), nitrogen oxides, methane, fluorocarbons (CFCs, HCFCs and HFCs), and lower-atmosphere ozone. Humans produce over thirty billion tons of CO_2 annually, two-thirds of it by burning fossil fuels at a rate which has increased fourfold since 1950 and over thirtyfold since 1900. But nitrogen oxides, generated by fertilizers or by burning of just about anything – they are spewed out in huge amounts by automobiles and aircraft – are now often thought to be almost equally important, while the fluorocarbons, many thousand times as effective as CO_2 (molecule for molecule) and with atmospheric concentrations which will increase for many years, could become the strongest greenhouse gases apart from water vapour by about the year 2030. And in later years methane, some thirty times as effective as CO_2, may become even more important than the fluorocarbons were, both in itself and through being oxidized in the stratosphere to produce water vapour. At present it accounts for perhaps a fifth of the new warming.

CO_2 is produced by power stations (they burned 2.3 billion tons of coal in 1970, 5.2 billion in 1990), by automobiles (250 million of them in 1970, 560 million in 1990), by burning of grasslands (which produces a great deal, but most is reabsorbed as new grasses grow) and by clearing of forests. As forests vanish, their store of carbon is returned to the atmosphere. Admittedly it is only young trees which are overall absorbers of CO_2, because full-grown ones 'breathe out' as much of it as they 'breathe in'. Also, of course, trees haven't perpetually added more and more oxygen to the air, else everything would be catching fire; and if all of them vanished tomorrow, you and I wouldn't suffocate. Yet it is green plants, for instance trees, which have made the air contain so much more oxygen than CO_2, and if they disappeared then humans would be starting to be short of breath after a few thousand years. (An iron bar in a flame doesn't get perpetually hotter and hotter, but if the flame is removed it gets colder.) Well, between 1950 and 1990 Earth's forest cover dropped from thirteen to ten billion acres. Tropical forests, vanishing at a rate of a million acres a week, will all be gone by the year 2040 – some people say much earlier – unless present trends are reversed. The gigantic forest of European Russia is threatened by pollution and by cutting at well beyond sustainable speeds. India has almost no forest left. And so on. (Note that forests evaporate huge amounts of water, which then forms clouds that reflect sunlight back into space. Their replacement by cropland 'could precipitate disaster on a global scale', Lovelock writes.[87])

Had green plants never appeared on land or in water, the atmospheric CO_2 level would be about 98 per cent.[88] The actual level is 0.036 per cent, giving perhaps 1 °C of greenhouse warming. The level has been rising since 1850, however, and is now higher than for 160,000 years.[89] Before the year 2060 it could well have risen by another three-quarters.

Methane too is at a level higher than for 160,000 years, but its concentration is rising three times faster than that of CO_2 and has doubled since 1900. Its heating effects would equal those of CO_2 if the concentration doubled again. Roughly half is generated by irrigated land, above all by rice paddies, and much of the rest by wetlands, burning of forests and grasslands, cattle flatulence, oilwells, coalmines, landfills, and leaks in natural gas pipelines.

Is CO_2 truly a powerful greenhouse gas? The main evidence for its effectiveness comes from the record of the rocks and from air bubbles extracted from deep inside icecaps. Warmer periods do seem to have been associated with higher CO_2 concentrations. It is more controversial to say that the warming effect has been growing of late, but recent weather has tended to be warmer – despite (1) the slow cooling which had been expected as Earth moved forward in its Milankovitch cycles (before the greenhouse effect hit the headlines, many people were predicting a minor ice age for the near future), (2) the cooling effect of dusts and aerosols thrown into the atmosphere by industry, desertification and recent volcanism, and (3) the fact that the oceans are temporarily able to absorb half the increase in CO_2 emissions, plus half of any new heat. Over the past forty-five years there has been a dramatic melting of the Wordie ice shelf in Antarctica. In the Arctic of the 1970s, sea ice was reduced by some two million square kilometers.

Predictions for the coming century vary greatly. However, the 'CO_2 equivalent' of the greenhouse gases other than water vapour, all taken together, is expected to have doubled by some date between 2030 and 2050, most experts forecasting a temperature rise (averaged over the years and over the globe) of between 1.5 °C and 5 °C. It has standardly been held that the rise would be strongly concentrated at the poles, where temperatures might be up to 12 °C higher while those at the equator had climbed by as little as 1 °C. This has lately come to be doubted, and if the doubters are right then the tropics, and maybe even middle latitudes, would suffer frequent droughts, and probably more and stronger hurricanes.[90]

What happens thereafter? A worst-case scenario for the year 2075, from I. M. Mintzer of the World Resources Institute, has temperatures 16 °C higher than at present. This could be far too pessimistic, yet it is at least sure that CO_2 levels will rise markedly. The number of automobiles continues to shoot upwards; China and India are industrializing; the already discovered reserves of coal and oil represent four trillion tons of carbon waiting to be burned, over five times as much as is held in the atmosphere at present; yet even if there were immediate cuts in emissions by four-fifths, atmospheric CO_2 would be stabilized only after several decades, while with 'business as usual' its level would be 50 per cent greater by the year 2010. At Rio in 1992 it was agreed by Japan, the United States and the European Union that efforts would be made to reduce emissions to 1990 levels by the turn of the century, but the United States, which had insisted that meeting this target should be 'urged' rather than required, almost certainly won't meet it, now that it has abandoned the idea of taxing energy. The Canadian government, giving hundreds of millions of dollars in subsidies to Alberta's oil industry megaprojects, has replaced its election promise of a 20 per cent cut in emissions by the year 2005 with plans just to ask its citizens to act responsibly, the predicted outcome being a 13 per cent rise by the year 2000. The European Union, too, is delaying energy taxes. As for the developing countries, almost all have done little more than talk about the problem. Atmospheric CO_2 levels thus seem likely to keep increasing for quite a while, almost everyone accepting that temperatures will rise by at least 2.5 °C in consequence.

Probable results include drought in many areas. The US dustbowl years of the 1930s had summer temperatures only 1–2 °C higher than normal, with rainfall at critical growing times slipping by only a fifth. In a world with even a slightly enhanced greenhouse effect the States could well suffer many more years like 1988, when much of the Mississippi became too shallow for navigation and crops throughout the grain belt failed. In the poor countries of the tropics there could be major famines: in fact, it has been reputably argued that greenhouse enhancement may already have caused millions of deaths from drought.[91] A concentration of the new heat at the poles, although it would calm the present wind systems, would probably result in many more cyclones like the one of 1970 which killed hundreds of thousands in Bangladesh. India depends on monsoons for 70 per cent of its precipitation, and they could easily be disrupted.[92] And because of thermal expansion of the oceans and melting of icecaps, sea levels will rise by perhaps a meter by the year 2050, and by five to eight meters by 2100 in a worst case envisaged by President Carter's Council on Environmental Quality. Now, astonishing numbers of humans live in coastal areas. The US National Academy of Sciences has predicted that as many as a billion people could soon find their lands inundated or dramatically changed for the worse, sometimes by salt in rising water tables.[93] Bengal and Egypt are among the heavily populated regions in which large sectors would be lost. A one-meter sea-level rise would displace at least seventy million Chinese, fifteen million Bangladeshis.

The changes could come very rapidly. Studies of cores extracted from the full depth of the Greenland ice sheet suggest that the past eight to ten thousand years have seen unusually stable weather and that climates had earlier altered radically within a few decades, probably through changes in ocean currents.

Climatology is so complex that sceptics can of course be found. A professor of environmental studies, K. E. F. Watts, has called greenhouse fears 'the laugh of the century'. He and J. Goodrich, former chief climatologist for California, claim that figures wrongly suggesting warming have been collected near expanding, overheated cities. (Watts and Goodrich might be correct in the case of the United States, which may actually have cooled for the moment: pollutants, especially sulphates, can help the atmosphere to reflect sunlight, in part directly and in part by helping clouds to form.[94]) Again, the climatologist R. S. Lindzen argues that although radiation can be trapped by greenhouse gases, heat will always be carried upwards by convective currents which move around until they find a vent. Recent hot years can be dismissed as fluctuations or attributed to an increasingly active sun: most of the warming experienced between 1750 and 1850 does seem to have resulted from solar changes. People have tried arguing that water vapour is so much the most powerful greenhouse gas that others can make no real difference; or – though this now appears to have been roundly refuted – that volcanoes generate more CO_2 than humans; or even that CFCs produce as much cooling as warming. (Stratospheric ozone being an effective greenhouse gas, its destruction by CFCs may produce significant cooling; and what is more, the new ultraviolet light reaching the lower atmosphere through the weakened ozone layer may trigger cloud formation and therefore further cooling. Unfortunately the less destructive HCFCs whose manufacture is allowed by the Montreal Protocol until 2030, and the yet ozone-friendlier HFCs which may subsequently replace them, are greenhouse gases quite as directly warming as CFCs – while, of course, they lack whatever indirect cooling effects are achieved by attacking stratospheric ozone.)

There might also be some very important *negative feedbacks*. Lindzen suggests that water vapour is involved in one of them. In his view, greenhouse heating increases convection, which leads to rain, which means that the atmospheric concentration of water vapour is reduced, which leads to cooling – whereas the generally accepted belief, seemingly confirmed by studies of sea surface temperatures,[95] is that by far the strongest feedback involving water vapour is *positive*: greenhouse heating generates more water vapour, which traps more heat. Increased water vapour can, however, lead to more snow, thereby contributing to Earth's ability to cool itself by reflecting sunlight. Clouds, too, are usually thought to be cooling on the whole; they can trap heat, especially at night, but at least for the present they quite probably reflect more of it than they trap; and increased evaporation leads to more clouds. Also, any rain falling from those clouds helps to remove CO_2 from the atmosphere. And an increased level of CO_2 can make vegetation grow more vigorously, which tends to reduce the level. In the *Journal of Climatology* in 1984, S. B. Idso went so far as to speculate that such things as greater vegetative cover would make increased levels of CO_2 Earth-cooling on balance, not Earth-heating.

To support such ideas, we could point to how the planet has avoided runaway heating and runaway glaciation for billions of years during which the sun's luminosity has grown by 30 per cent. Isn't this a sign of strong negative feedback loops? Perhaps it is – but in that case, will the overall feedback continue to be negative and strong? The consensus is that Earth has enjoyed rather remarkable luck: increased solar luminosity has been to a great extent balanced by the decline in greenhouse gases (carbon dioxide, methane, ammonia) brought about by green-plant photosynthesis.

Rather than denying that greenhouse warming is going to increase, some just say that it could be expected to change Earth for the better. Everybody agrees that while various areas would be hotter and dryer, others would be wetter and colder. The Soviet climatologist M. Budyko has spoken of a 'greenhouse paradise' with cattle in the Sahara and crops in the present-day deserts of central Asia. The main change would be that regions suitable for particular plants and animals would move northwards. Plant growth could be more luxuriant, and growing seasons longer because of increased cloud cover: cooler days, warmer nights, fewer droughts. Still, in our joy at all this we mustn't overlook the potentially awful immediate effects on people and on ecologies. We could expect famines and wars if large regions suddenly became inhospitable, and animals and plants – trees above all – would find it very hard to migrate fast enough to keep pace with the expected changes: a rise of just 2 °C by the year 2050 would be too fast. Further, the weather would be pulled in two directions at once as dusts and aerosols (sulphates, smoke and soot from forest burnings, etc.) cooled some areas while others were becoming hotter. This could lead to great instability. And the atmosphere's store of hydroxyls, which play a crucial role in its chemical cycles, could become exhausted through being attacked by methane, triggering very sudden alterations.

Besides, the world's weather is the standard example used by chaos theory (see Chapter 2) to illustrate how small changes in initial conditions can have huge effects on how events develop. In the present case, a main danger is that Earth's climate could get to a position where it underwent a jump from one semi-stable state to another which was radically different, causing tremendous disruption.[96] Europe might be plunged into an ice age when global warming changed the Gulf Stream.[97]

A runaway greenhouse disaster?

The most serious greenhouse danger could be of *runaway positive feedback*. Here we have the horrid example of Venus. Primitive life may perhaps actually have evolved there, but now a dense atmosphere, almost all of it CO_2, gives greenhouse temperatures of around 450 °C.[98] Whereas a level of 0.5 per cent causes only shortness of breath, 'once the carbon dioxide concentration in the air approaches or exceeds 1 per cent, new non-linear effects come into play and the heating greatly increases',[99] Lovelock points out: for a start, water vapour accumulates markedly.[100] 'Earth', he continues, 'would then heat up rapidly to a temperature near to that of boiling water.' Notice that to achieve disaster one doesn't in fact need 1 per cent of CO_2. It is enough if the newly enhanced effect of the greenhouse gases, taken together, equals that of 1 per cent of CO_2.

Scenarios with strong positive feedback are easily constructed. For instance, S. H. Schneider writes:

Rapid change in climate could disrupt forests and other ecosystems, reducing their ability to draw carbon dioxide down from the atmosphere. Moreover, climatic warming could lead to rapid release of the vast amount of carbon held in the soil as dead organic matter. This stock of carbon – at least twice as much as is stored in the atmosphere – is continuously being decomposed into carbon dioxide and methane by the action of soil microbes. A warmer climate might speed their work, releasing additional carbon dioxide (from dry soils) and methane (from rice paddies, landfills and wetlands) that would enhance the warming. Large quantities of methane are also locked up in the continental-shelf sediments and below arctic permafrost in the form of clathrates – molecular lattices of methane and water. Warming of the shallow waters of the oceans and melting of the permafrost could release some of the methane.[101]

There are *over ten trillion tons of it*, its carbon content thus being greater than that of all known fossil fuel deposits;[102] but in methane, chemical formula CH_4, the carbon is considerably more threatening than in fuel burned to form CO_2. Remember, methane is a greenhouse gas thirty times more effective than CO_2, molecule for molecule.

The director of science for Greenpeace International's Atmosphere and Energy Campaign, J. Leggett, remarks that the Intergovernmental Panel on Climate Change, whose report greatly influenced the politicians at 1992's meeting in Rio, 'reached its consensus by rejecting extreme estimates', whether best-case or worst-case, and covered every biological feedback loop in just one sentence: 'Biological feedbacks have not yet been taken into account.' This was despite such facts as that changes leading to the loss of 10 per cent of the marine phytoplankton 'would reduce the annual oceanic uptake of carbon dioxide by about 5 billion tons, an amount equal to the annual emissions of carbon dioxide from fossil fuel consumption'. The phytoplankton also produce dimethyl sulphide, which helps clouds to form, so that losses to them could mean 'fewer clouds to reflect radiation back into space, and proportionately more water vapour to act as a greenhouse gas'. Greenpeace asked four hundred climatologists for their reactions to a runaway greenhouse scenario which Leggett had constructed. 'Almost half felt that a runaway greenhouse effect is possible if emissions of greenhouse gases are not cut. And more than 10 per cent believe that such a scenario is probable.'[103]

Leggett's scenario[104] includes (a) ocean waters becoming less able to take CO_2 from the air as they warm up; (b) cold-water nutrients rising to the warmed sea surface only rarely, so that phytoplankton grow more slowly, absorb less CO_2, and generate less of the cloud-forming dimethyl sulphide; (c) phytoplankton deaths because of ozone layer losses; (d) warmer weather increasing net CO_2 production in soil and plants; (e) melting of tundra, producing yet more CO_2 and vast amounts of methane; (f) changes in high-altitude clouds, making them trap more heat; (g) drought, which kills vegetation, returning carbon to the atmosphere; (h) depletion, through the ravages of methane and other greenhouse gases, of the hydroxyls which are at present so important in cleansing the atmosphere of these same gases; (i) more lower-atmosphere ozone, quite a powerful greenhouse gas, because of ever-growing numbers of automobiles and trucks; (j) a retreat of sea ice so that less sunlight is reflected back into space; and (k) a final runaway when methane is released from continental-shelf sediments.

Leggett could have included many further factors. For instance: (1) As already mentioned, warming pushes more water vapour into the atmosphere, a greenhouse enhancement which ultimately overtakes those produced by all other gases. (2) Peat bogs emit vast quantities of carbon dioxide when they dry. Three-quarters of the carbon held in Britain's soils and vegetation is in Scotland's bogs. (3) Warmed oceans could give out much of their dissolved organic carbon as CO_2, thanks to increased activity by bacteria. An expedition to the north Atlantic found that levels of organic carbon molecules near the surface sometimes fell by 30 per cent within a few days – and the oceans contain some 1,600 billion tons of those molecules, representing more carbon than is stored in all land plants.[105]

Such points are made all the more disturbing by two facts noted earlier: that greenhouse warming by at least 2.5 °C is expected by almost everybody, and that solar luminosity has increased over billions of years so that it is now 30 per cent greater, while from 1750 onwards it has been recovering from one of its occasional minor decreases. A rise of average annual global temperatures by 2 °C could make our planet warmer than for the past hundred million years, and perhaps than it has ever been since life moved to the land four hundred million years ago.[106] C. R. Chapman and D. Morrison warn us: 'Recent measurements of the CO_2 trapped in Greenland ice sheets suggest that the CO_2 content of the Earth's atmosphere can change suddenly, and unpredictably, in only a few hundred years'; that 'we sit at the peak of a warm, interglacial epoch'; that 'it has never been significantly warmer, and there has never been so much CO_2 in the atmosphere, since this cycle of ice ages began'; and that for all we know the Cretaceous period, which ended sixty-five million years ago, 'may have been near the threshold for a runaway greenhouse', in which case 'changes set in motion today might not be reversible in time before our planet found itself rushing headlong towards a venusian conclusion'.[107] Lovelock himself, so very largely responsible for inventing and developing the idea that powerful negative feedbacks keep Earth healthy, could still write in 1985 – before some of the most disturbing evidence came to light – that when the planet's temperature regulating mechanism is stressed to near its limits 'even a small disturbance may cause it to fail entirely', and that it may be 'not far from one of these limits'.[108]

All this is extremely speculative. But certainty is almost impossible to get in climatology; if got, it may be got too late; and as R. Sylvan says, 'rational decision making has to take account of what may not be very likely at all, but may be quite disastrous should it occur'.[109] It might help if we could find out exactly what happened 250 million years ago, at the end of the Permian period. Three-quarters of the world's species became extinct then, possibly by suffocation: 'anoxia and rising sea levels tend to occur together in the geological record, but no one is sure why', P. Wignall comments.[110]

What could we do to become safer? R. M. White noted in 1990 that 'no matter what policy actions we take, fully arresting the climate warming just does not seem to be in the cards', but he warned against 'apocalyptic thinking' and hoped that the international community could act during the thirty to fifty years he thought it would take for the situation to 'become serious'.[111] This relaxed approach was reflected in the easy-going, vague, non-binding Climate Change Convention signed at Rio in 1992,[112] and in the Berlin Mandate of 1995, which committed its signatories merely to continued talks: detailed targets for limiting emissions after the year 2000 would be debated only in 1997. Still, it is difficult to get signatures for energetic environmental treaties, let alone to enforce them.[113] 'Carbon taxes' on extraction of fossil fuels could have greater effect – and could end up costing people virtually nothing, because of encouraging them to save energy. Again, taxes on emissions have inspired Norway to strip CO_2 from natural gas, compress it, and bury one million tons per year by injecting it into rocks under the North Sea.

A little more nuclear energy might help, but digging up and processing huge quantities of low-grade uranium for a greatly expanded nuclear energy programme would itself lead to large CO_2 emissions. And sad to say, hydroelectric power is associated with large methane emissions from vegetation rotting in areas which have been flooded to form reservoirs. Improved solar cells, or wind or wave power, might offer a solution. As a last resort we could fling huge quantities of dust into the upper air, conceivably by use of nuclear bombs, in the hope that the outcome would be cooling rather than just more warming. People have suggested trying it, entirely seriously.[114]

Exhaustion of food-producing land and water

Using heavy irrigation and fertilization, modern agriculture sows the same crop again and again: land is seldom left to recover ('lie fallow') or planted with nitrogen-fixing clovers. If the soil gives signs of exhaustion, more and more fertilizer is applied until not even this can help. Constant watering leads to salt accumulation, but that too is disregarded until crops fail. Because of enthusiastic pesticiding of the weeds which would hold it together and reduce evaporation, topsoil is more easily salinized or washed away or blown away. Population pressures and the selfishness of large landowners often cause intensive use of new, marginally fertile soils, which are quickly degraded. However, degradation can be equally marked where the soil used to be best, so that a large population sprang up to put stress on it.

Deforestation does make new land available for farming. Especially in the tropics, though, it tends to be land so poor as to become useless within three years. And deforestation increases soil erosion. As well as helping winds to carry off the topsoil, it produces heavy flooding up to hundreds of miles away. Twenty-five billion tons of topsoil are lost to erosion every year: one and a half billion in Ethiopia alone, four billion in the United States (more than in the 'dustbowl' 1930s), six billion in India, and so on. This and other things mean that twenty thousand hectares become unfarmable every day. The resulting trend towards deser-tification, to which overgrazing and recent droughts have contributed, is best known through Africa's Sahel disaster, yet in Asia at least two-fifths of all land is at high risk.

Further factors limiting harvests include pollution, the exhaustion of aquifers (the aquifer under the US grain belt, the one under the north China plain, the one supplying the vital Punjab wheat-fields, whose waters are sinking by a meter a year, and so on) and failures of genetically uniform crops to stand up to disease and to insects. World per capita grain yields have been falling by about 1 per cent a year since 1984, the decreases occurring mainly in poor countries. D. Mackenzie wrote in 1994:

> Africa now needs 14 million tonnes more grain per year than it produces. With a population growing at 3 per cent a year, and agricultural production at 2 per cent, that shortfall will reach 50 million tonnes by the year 2000. China's growing population, diminishing farmland and increasing prosperity could boost Chinese grain imports from 12 million tonnes per year now to 100 million by the year 2000. If countries with surpluses must choose between giving grain to Africa and selling it to China, the choice may not be difficult.[115]

Might the Green Revolution of the 1970s and 1980s be re-newed, to boost tonnages yet again? The high-yield grains now being developed may turn out to have many of the defects of their Green Revolution predecessors: low nutritional quality, vulnerability to rot during storage, a need for heavy watering, heavy fertilizing, heavy use of pesticides. It could be that the Green Revolution, while undoubtedly increasing Earth's carrying capacity for a while, will have diminished it in the long run. In India, for instance, people misled by Western scientists may in effect have been feeding themselves 'by borrowing against their children's food sources'.[116] It has been claimed that a super-rice almost ready for marketing will produce harvests up to 25 per cent larger than today's finest, be tolerant of poor, drought-prone soils, and have genes conferring resistance to insects and to diseases;[117] yet even if all this turned out to be true, intensive use of such a rice might bleed the soil. Rice yields have declined in recent years on some of the International Rice Research Institute's most fertile test plots.

In the waters the situation looks depressingly similar. In rivers and in lakes, fish catches have declined sharply because of pollutants. These include nitrate fertilizers and phospates which cause eutrophication: plants overgrow and then rot, removing almost all the oxygen. Yet it is the sad case of the oceans which is really alarming, for they produce a quarter of the protein on which humans feed.

Although wetlands are the spawning grounds for most ocean fisheries, also filtering out pollutants, over half have been destroyed by draining, mangrove felling, chemical pollution, and sediment from construction sites. And almost everywhere the coastal waters, by far the most biologically productive, are heavily attacked by agricultural runoffs of pesticides and fertilizers (which once again cause eutrophication), domestic and industrial sewage, toxic waste, oil. It will, of course, prove far harder to harm living organisms throughout an ocean than to make the fish of Lake Superior dangerous for everyday consumption. Even the deliberate sinking after the Second World War of well over a hundred thousand tons of mustard gas and other gases – of twenty elderly merchant ships, for example, loaded with captured German gas shells[118] – may not have caused disastrous damage. Still, the annual tonnages of pollutants have become fairly impressive: six million tons of oil, for instance, a little of it from tanker accidents but most from municipalities, coastal refineries and ship bilges. Mercury now enters the sea at three and a half times the natural rate, and lead at thirteen times the natural rate. The Caribbean, Mediterranean, Black Sea, North Sea and Baltic are particularly hard hit. In the Baltic, only a few species of worm have survived.

Overfishing, however, and not pollution, has so far been the major cause of declining fish stocks. Trawlers use advanced technology to pinpoint shoals, and then sweep up everything in huge nets kept open by heavy trawl-doors which can utterly plough up seabed ecosystems, while driftnets extend for up to fifty kilometers. Much of the catch is discarded as trash. Of the rest, much becomes fertilizer or animal feed. Sea fishing provides some of the clearest examples of the 'Tragedy of the Commons':[119] when a resource is exploitable by many individuals, it is to the advantage of each to grab as much as possible, in spite of how this leads to resource exhaustion. Global catches kept growing until 1989, although much more slowly after 1970. In 1990 they began to fall. But although the United Nations estimates that the world's fishing fleets now make an annual loss totalling about fifty billion dollars, the fleets operate as enthusiastically as ever, thanks to governmental subsidies.

Some doubt the gravity of all this. It has, for example, been denied, and by such experts as the two who produced the *World Atlas of Desertification* for the United Nations Environment Programme, that deserts have advanced on a broad front. Certainly, many alleged desertifications are only cases of temporarily reduced rainfall. Again, it might be that food scarcities could be resolved by genetic engineering of things apart from grains, or by sea farming of kelp or of krill. Or they could be resolved in the usual way through local famine deaths instead of putting the very survival of the human race at risk. But it is hard to introduce the latest farming techniques in the impoverished countries which may stand in most need of them – countries whose militaries might believe that unleashing, say, biological warfare would be preferable to starvation, and an act of just revenge on the disgustingly overfed. In connection with his theme that the carrying capacity of the Earth should be treated as sacred, G. Hardin tells of an American visiting a refugee camp where almost half had starved:

> Noticing sacks of grain stocked in great mounds in an adjacent field, he asked the patriarch of the refugee community

why the people did not simply overpower the lone soldier guarding the grain. The patriarch explained that the sacks contained seed for planting the next season. 'We do not steal from the future', he said.[120]

Yet as Hardin notes, we mustn't too readily assume that everybody would willingly play a role in some such story.

Economists tend to construct models in which growth tails off gradually as fertile land and other resources become scarce. Unfortunately, the more realistic computer model described by Meadows et al. in *Beyond the Limits* (1992) indicates that fairly severe collapses are inevitable whenever there are lags between scarcities and the economically ideal reaction to them. Now, when mouths need to be fed whether or not resources have become scarce, and when fishing boats can operate for many years before falling apart, etc., lags are very hard to avoid. The computer runs examined in *Beyond the Limits* suggest that global collapse may lie only about fifty years in the future.

A vitally important question is whether sustainable exploitation of the environment, after reaching whatever limits have been set at any particular stage in technological history by the combination of such things as limited agricultural land, limited forests, and the limited ability of soil, water and air to absorb more pollutants, will then be followed by a disastrous and long-lasting collapse, or just by one which is small and temporary. Unluckily it seems clear that, unless very heroic efforts are made to prevent it, long-lasting collapse will be virtually certain because of the erosion of the factors which had made growth possible. Soil can, of course, become eroded, but the ability of the Earth to recover from pollution can be eroded too, since pollutants tend to poison the natural mechanisms for absorbing pollution.

Meadows et al. used a deliberately very simple computer model of the world. They ran it again and again, each time making new assumptions about the maximum amount of food which could be extracted from the land, the rate at which soils deteriorated through constant use and through pollution, and the availability of minerals and fossil fuels. They found that doing such things as doubling the available resources tended only to put off the dates at which overshooting of limits began, and that the collapses which followed

were major and long lasting precisely because the periods of overshoot had so eroded everything that had made growth possible.
They report:

> In the thousands of model runs we have tried over the years,
> overshoot and collapse has been by far the most frequent
> outcome. Overshoot comes from delays in feedback – from
> the fact that decision makers in the system do not get, or
> believe, or act upon information that limits have been
> exceeded until long after they have been exceeded.

While they insist that this isn't itself a prediction about the real
world, it does strongly suggest what will happen unless we learn
to look decades ahead, whereas governments seldom look much
further than the next election or the lifetime of the current aging
tyrant. 'If a society takes its signals from the simple availability of
stocks, rather than from their size, quality, diversity, health, and
rate of replacement, it will overshoot.'[121]

In the case of an agricultural and pollution crisis, overshooting
would mean being faced by a need to clean up a poisoned environment at a time when people were themselves most poisoned and
most famished.

Loss of biodiversity

Biodiversity – variety of living species – is lost through four main
causes. First, there is destruction of wilderness areas (particularly
the rainforests), which hold around four-fifths of today's plant
and animal species, and of coral reefs (often simply mined for
their limestone). Second, there are the extinctions produced by
pollution. Third, there is the way in which modern agriculture
concentrates on a strictly limited number of varieties. Growers
cultivate just a few plant types which are specially productive, at
least when massively fertilized and until new diseases hit them. The
others they treat as weeds to be destroyed with pesticides. And
for plant and animal breeders to have commercial rights to the
varieties they have developed, those varieties must 'breed true',
which means they can contain very little genetic diversity. In Britain

it is a criminal offence to sell seed varieties which are not regis-
tered, each for annual fees in the hundreds of pounds, and
registration is possible only for seeds which do breed true.[122]
Fourth, there is overfishing, overhunting, overpicking, overgrazing,
and the like.

The extinction rate is increasing, making it altogether possible
that well over half of all the species which still remain will have
disappeared by the year 2100 even without global nuclear war or
catastrophic destruction of the ozone layer. By the year 2000, it
has been suggested, up to 20 per cent of the species in existence
fifteen years earlier could well have been wiped out.[123] Although
figures in this area are highly controversial, the definition of
the word 'species' itself leading to disputes, the concentration
of perhaps three-fifths of the species in the rapidly disappearing
tropical forests may make such suggestions plausible, as may that
of so many of the others in coral reefs. In the Philippines
nine-tenths of the coral has been destroyed by dynamite, pollution and collecting. The wildlife trade is profitable enough to drive
species to extinction – rhinoceros horn is now worth more
than its weight in gold and an orchid can change hands for
thousands of dollars – but the main threat is from the destruction
of habitats.

Loss of biodiversity inside individual plant or animal species can
lessen resistance to diseases or to insects, more and more pesticides
and vaccines then being used in increasingly desperate attempts to
counteract this. Changes in climate or in the soil (increased salinity,
perhaps, or accumulation of heavy metal pollutants) or in the
amount of ultraviolet radiation getting through the ozone layer,
or in the atmosphere's load of pollutants, become more severe in
their effects because there are fewer genetic combinations with
which Nature or the breeders or genetic engineers can experiment
in order to produce continued vigour. A decrease in the number
of individuals in a species can itself be important. A species which
shrinks from one million individuals to ten thousand may thereby
lose half its genetic diversity.[124]

Loss of biodiversity inside various habitats can also have
disturbing results, although here the evidence is less one-sided.
Experiments with simple artificial habitats in Imperial College's
'Ecotron', with tall-grass prairie in Minnesota and wild plants in

the Serengeti National Park suggest that complex mixtures of plants and insects are more productive and better able to resist grazing and drought[125] – a result confirmed by the way in which modern monocultured fields typically require considerable irrigation. The failure of 'Biosphere 2', a hectare-sized glass-enclosed ecosystem which yielded far less food than expected, might further demonstrate a need for the highly complex diversity of 'Biosphere 1', the total biosphere of our planet. On the other hand the loss of oxygen in Biosphere 2 – huge new quantities had to be pumped in to save its eight inhabitants from suffocation – was due not to limited biodiversity but to excess microbial richness in the soil. And, as will be discussed again in Chapter 2 in connection with catastrophe theory, it is sometimes argued that the highly complex biodiversity of Earth's biosphere has actually made it more liable to collapses over the ages, this helping to explain some of the mass extinctions revealed by the geological record. E. O. Wilson writes:

> Why has life multiplied so prodigiously in a few limited places such as tropical forests and coral reefs? It was once widely believed that when large numbers of species coexist, their life cycles and food webs lock together in a way that makes the ecosystem more robust. This hypothesis has given way during the past twenty years to a reversed cause-and-effect scenario: fragile superstructures of species build up when the environment remains stable enough to support their evolution during long periods.[126]

But, of course, Wilson isn't saying that loss of the fantastic richness of the rainforests would be accompanied by no real danger to humans. Remember such things as the atmospheric cleansing produced by rainforests, and their stores of plant and animal DNA, which could save us from agricultural disaster.

A Biodiversity Convention seemed one of the most promising achievements of 1992's 'Earth Summit' in Rio. Yet thirty months afterwards agreement couldn't be reached on such a minor point as where the Convention's secretariat would be based; the sub-committee to provide scientific and technical advice had its first meeting scheduled only for September 1995; forest conservation was turned over to a United Nations Commission on Sustainable

Development whose decisions would lack legal force; and the most noteworthy decisive action was the naming of December 29 as the International Day for Biodiversity.

The population crisis

Malthus, writing in 1798, when Earth's population had just risen rapidly to nearly one billion, predicted that it would very soon reach the limit which the planet could support, after which it would fall sharply because of famines, epidemics and wars. In fact it proceeded to double in a century, doubling yet again in the subsequent half-century. It is now about twenty-five times greater than at the time of Christ, and growing at a quarter of a million people *per day*. The doubling time is down to about thirty-five years. Even if fertility were to fall tonight to the 'replacement rate', just over two babies to each grown woman, the figure would still climb from today's roughly six billion souls to around eight and a half billion, because so many of those now alive have yet to reach reproductive age.

Although the United States has itself doubled its population since 1940, most of the increase has occurred in the poorer countries. It is expected that the population of Asia will have grown about ten times between the years 1800 and 2040; that of Africa some thirty times; that of Latin America perhaps fifty times. In Kenya in 1975 the fertility rate (lifetime births per woman) stood at over eight. It has now fallen, but only to about the same figure – namely six – as in sub-Saharan Africa as a whole. For Egypt the figure is roughly five; for India and Peru, around four. In Indonesia the widely praised success of a campaign of education, advertising jingles and free contraceptives still leaves the figure above three. United Nations projections suggest a global population of roughly ten billion by AD 2050, given a marked decline in fertility, and twelve and a half billion otherwise. Although over a billion people are already near to starvation, forecasts of mouths to feed in AD 2100 range up to twenty-seven billion. Nigeria just by itself, with a present-day doubling time of a little over twenty years, could move from its hundred or so million to nigh on half a billion. Crowded together as they are, Pakistanis and Bangladeshis are expected to double their numbers.

In contrast, the economist P. Ehrlich – author of *The Population Bomb* (1968), a book whose predictions have on the whole turned out to be overly pessimistic, and then of *The Population Explosion* (1990) – has suggested that the maximum readily sustainable global population would be two billion. True, one might cram in twenty billion if they lived at the miserably impoverished level of present-day Bangladeshis, but environmental disaster could seem inevitable if all these people were to move to the level of Parisians or New Yorkers in diet, resource consumption and production of pollutants. The average US citizen is said to put between forty and a hundred times as much stress on the environment as the average Somalian. Scientific progress (possibly some new source of energy, virtually non-polluting) could be of great help, but twenty billion people would seem more than twenty-first-century science could hope to sustain at any acceptable standard of living, or perhaps at all. And of course one would rapidly get to many more people than this if growth continued as rapidly as in recent times. Not even rapid expansion into outer space would remove the problem. With the best presently imaginable technology it could take some four million years to colonize our entire galaxy, while with modern rocket technology three hundred million years would be required.[127] Yet in under 1,300 years a human population continuing to grow at the current rate, roughly 2 per cent a year, would need to be distributed across one hundred billion Earthlike planets. Even supposing, fantastically, that there were one such planet for every star in the galaxy, this result could be achieved only by faster-than-light travel.[128]

At least in the near future, a population of as little as ten billion could be expected to cause desertifications and famines, intolerable local water scarcities and levels of pollution, which virtually guaranteed wars. (The recent mass killings in Rwanda's civil war can be viewed as a direct result of overpopulation and the resulting pressures on the country's agriculture: while the population had a doubling time of only two decades, soil nutrient depletion had reduced harvests by almost 20 per cent.) Despite advances in crop science, global population growth seems almost sure to outstrip growth in food production in the next forty years. Disease and environmental disaster might then sweep over the planet. Species could become extinct in such numbers that the biosphere collapsed, or the greenhouse effect might run beyond all possible control: bear in mind that methane, a powerful greenhouse gas, is generated plentifully by rice paddies and livestock, and that many in the developing world might like to own automobiles. All this gives some plausibility to the title 'Ten years to save the world' which the president of the Worldwatch Institute gave to an article of 1992:[129] the population bomb is sometimes said to have exploded already. Ordinary wars seem unlikely to alter matters by much: all the fighting from the start of the First World War to the end of the Second World War killed only about a fifth of a billion people.[130] However, if some desperately hungry or thirsty country unleashed biological warfare, then that might indeed make quite a difference.

When one third-world bureaucrat was asked what he would like to see from his window twenty years in the future, the answer was 'Smog'. One can sympathize with this. Better the smog of industrialization than grinding poverty and constant fear of starvation ('a challenging daily struggle for the daily bread', in the words of one clerical opponent of contraceptives). Yet the pollution which causes smog could cause famine too.

In 1972, with the backing of a group known as The Club of Rome, D. H. Meadows, D. L. Meadows, J. Randers and W. H. Behrens published *The Limits to Growth*, warning that the rapidly increasing exploitation of the environment could soon become disastrous.[131] While some of their forecasts have proved too gloomy, many have been accurate, as evidenced by such things as collapsing fisheries. In *Beyond the Limits*, the first three of them point once again to the sad results to be expected from continuing, if only for a short while, on exponential curves of growth in population and in industrial production. A quantity grows exponentially, they remark, 'when its increase is proportional to what is already there', as with the imaginary water lily that chokes out all other life in the pond after thirty days of doubling in size: 'For a long time the lily plant seems small, so you decide not to worry about it until it covers half the pond. On which day will that be? On the twenty-ninth day. You have just one day to save your pond.'[132]

Even when not pushed by population increase, industrial production tends to grow exponentially as people seek higher standards of living. The combination of an exploding world population, a widespread demand for equalization of living standards, and delays in reacting while the limits to growth approached could easily be disastrous.

There are some grounds for hope. First, technology might come to the rescue in unexpected ways, particularly if assisted by changes in society's values. *Beyond the Limits* suggests that the impact of each new human on the environment might in theory be reduced 'by a factor of a thousand or more': a good start would be to give the world's population 'the productivity of the Swiss, the consumption habits of the Chinese, the egalitarian instincts of the Swedes, and the social discipline of the Japanese'.[133] Second, as countries become richer they tend to move to lower fertility rates ('the demographic transition'). If the fertility rate recently found in West Germany spread to the rest of the world, there would be no humans in existence by about the year 2400. Affluence means no need for children to share your labour, or to give assurance that one or other of them will survive to grow food for your old age. Again, because of unavailability of contraceptives and exclusion of women from decision-making at least a quarter of today's pregnancies are definitely unwanted by the pregnant, according to the World Health Organization. Well, the equivalent of under a month's global expenditure on armaments could make contraceptives available to everyone. Television soap operas in Brazil, showing families as typically small and happy but sometimes large and miserable, have been encouragingly effective, and there is evidence that the demographic transition begins in poor countries after just a small rise in incomes. Third, governments have had some success by combinations of reward and punishment. Despite the indignation expressed by Westerners at its population-control programme of 1975-7 – sterilization was officially compulsory for one of the parents in each family that had three children, while tiny rewards were given for other sterilizations – India is still offering its citizens cash for voluntarily ending their reproductive lives. The amount involved, so few rupees that they couldn't buy twenty dollars, is accepted surprisingly often. In China a more draconian 'one child only' policy, backed by losses of benefits, by fines and by compulsory sterilizations, forced fertility downwards almost to the replacement rate. The cost in human misery was immense, but constant famine could well have been the alternative. China had doubled its already huge population between 1950 and 1980.

There are also major grounds for pessimism, however. China, still adding sixteen million a year to its population, will have 25 per cent less arable soil per capita in 2010 than in 1994, and it will be soil suffering from erosion. The migration of tens of millions from its impoverished interior and north to its booming coastal cities could initiate prolonged warring among regional states, as has so often occurred in its past.[134] Incomes in most developing countries have long been falling, not rising in the way that encourages the demographic transition towards constant population. Furthermore, religious fundamentalists often wish to make women powerless, treat all uses of contraceptives as instances of the sin of Onan (Genesis 38.9) or classify as infanticide any destruction of a fertilized human ovum, for instance by a 'morning-after pill', while a few third-world leaders continue to dismiss as 'racist plots' all suggestions about encouraging small families. Population policy was actually excluded from the official agenda of the 1992 'Earth Summit', the United Nations Conference on Environment and Development. The Reagan administration cut off US support for the International Planned Parenthood Federation and the United Nations Fund for Population Activities, the Bush administration then failing to restore it. And well-nourished Canadians scarcely help matters when they express outrage at the very idea of Indians being 'bribed' into sterilization by offers of transistor radios.

It is doubtful whether voluntary population control could work for very long. Lovelock cites with approval the claim by C. G. Darwin, grandson of the author of *The Origin of Species*, that natural selection would make '*Homo philoprogenitus*' (lover of many offspring) bound to win in the end.[135] This might seem correct despite the importance of social influences. *Philoprogenitus* might be expected to evolve so as to resist those influences if necessary; but pressures inside particular groups could in any case encourage their members to reproduce themselves prolifically in spite of pressures from outside, the groups in question then coming to dominate the world. An urge to produce numerous offspring could be passed on to each next generation by displays of pride in large families or by the preaching of God's enthusiasm for them, instead of by genes.

Overpopulation, environmental degradation, disease, criminality and war all tend to come in a single package. R. D. Kaplan writes to his fellow Americans:

> For a while the media will continue to ascribe riots and other violent upheavals abroad mainly to ethnic and religious conflicts. But as these conflicts multiply, it will become apparent that something else is afoot, making more and more places ungovernable. Mention 'the environment' or 'diminishing natural resources' in foreign-policy circles and you meet a brick wall of skepticism or boredom. To conservatives especially, the very terms seem flaky.... It is time to understand 'the environment' for what it is: *the* national-security issue of the early twenty-first century. The political and strategic impact of surging populations, spreading disease, deforestation and soil erosion, water depletion, air pollution, and, possibly, rising sea levels in critical, overcrowded regions like the Nile Delta and Bangladesh, will be the core foreign-political challenge. While a minority of the human population will be, as Francisco Fukuyama would put it, sufficiently sheltered so as to enter a 'post-historical' realm in which the environment has been mastered and ethnic animosities quelled by bourgeois prosperity, an increasingly large number of people will be stuck in history, living in shantytowns where attempts to rise above poverty, cultural dysfunction, and ethnic strife will be doomed by a lack of water to drink, soil to till, and space to survive in.[136]

NATURALLY OCCURRING DISEASES

Infectious diseases cause roughly half of all deaths today. The organisms producing them fall into four main groups: bacteria, viruses, the rickettsiae, which lie between bacteria and viruses in complexity, and parasites such as the protozoa of malaria and the tiny worms of schistosomiasis. Malaria and tuberculosis are the biggest killers at present, the second slightly in the lead with its roughly three million fatalities per year. However, the 'Spanish influenza' virus of the 1918–19 pandemic may have infected almost

76

everyone on the globe, and it killed twenty million. And while modern medicine has perhaps now managed to make smallpox extinct, also greatly reducing the threat from poliomyelitis and diphtheria, there are many diseases (malaria and tuberculosis included) which have grown resistant to drugs and antibiotics, much as mosquitoes and other disease-carriers have developed immunity to pesticides. In addition, new pathogens such as the Legionella bacterium are constantly emerging. Ebola virus, which first appeared in 1976, can kill 90 per cent of its victims, whereas bubonic plague kills only 50 per cent. Yet in the United States recently, P. E. Ross notes, funds for work on infectious diseases other than AIDS and tuberculosis have actually been lower, in inflation-adjusted terms, than they were forty years before, the Center for Disease Control spending only a few million dollars yearly in looking for new killers although it had been a matter just of biological chance that AIDS wasn't as highly contagious as the common cold.[137]

Why haven't the pathogens won? Of the first generation it infected in Australia, myxomatosis killed all but two rabbits in every thousand. Why hasn't something 100 per cent lethal wiped out all mammals, or else the human race in particular? Luck may have played a part here. Perhaps complex life has evolved on a great many planets scattered through the universe. Perhaps most are now planets where disease has proved victorious, nobody remaining alive on them to contemplate this sad state of affairs. Obviously you and I must find ourselves on a planet which continues to be inhabited, regardless of whether such planets are extremely rare. It is hard to know what limits to place on this line of reasoning. Suppose that, of all planets with complex biospheres, 99.9999 per cent suffered disaster from disease before truly intelligent beings evolved on them. It would be unsurprising that the planet on which we find ourselves was in the remaining 0.0001 per cent. Where else could we possibly find ourselves?

Admittedly we can point to a natural tendency for germs to reach an uneasy compromise with the beings on which they prey. Recall that they cannot benefit from destroying their hosts. Malaria, attacking about three hundred million people a year, could be viewed as 'taking care' not to kill more than a couple of million. Yet as A. Mitchison observes, we may nowadays be in 'an utterly unprecedented situation. Even if we knew how often in the past host species had been wiped out by their parasites, that knowledge would tell us little about ourselves.'[138] Various factors combine in support of such a statement:

(a) By the year 2010, every second human is expected to live in a city. There are now about thirty cities of more than ten million people each, and over four hundred others of more than a million. Diseases can spread with fearsome speed in these huge centers, quickly 'testing out' dozens of new strains.

(b) The international food trade, business trips, and tourism carry diseases quickly around the globe. Today there are about twenty times as many international travellers as in 1950. Now, when host and pathogen evolve side by side they can readily reach the uneasy compromise mentioned above: the pathogen takes care to permit the host species to evolve resistance. When, however, a disease suddenly jumps from one continent to another, it will tend to find that in its new surroundings it is too powerful for its own good. It may bring death to almost everyone in a poorly prepared population. Repeatedly, the common cold has proved fatal in areas to which it was new. Introduced into North America by Columbus, chickenpox, influenza and measles bore much of the blame for the decline of the Amerindian peoples to a twentieth of their former numbers.

(c) Diseases flourish in our newly polluted environment. The 1991 cholera epidemic, originating in Peru and soon moving up into Mexico, was largely a product of untreated sewer water. Besides facilitating transmission of infectious organisms, pollution places stress on the human body, which can then fall easy prey to diseases. Mesothelioma, a form of cancer which attacks the membranes surrounding the lungs, is powerfully triggered by a combination of a virus and exposure to asbestos. It is running wild among construction workers.

(d) Mesothelioma merits particular attention because, as P. Brown comments, the virus in question appears to be new among humans and its DNA 'looks suspiciously like that of SV40, a monkey virus accidentally given to millions of people between 1954 and 1963 as a contaminant of polio vaccines'.[139] Perhaps what we have here is the worst accident in the history of medicine.

Similar suspicions have been voiced in connection with HIV, the AIDS virus, which greatly resembles the SIV of apes and monkeys. Here a leap to humans could have been caused by experimental injections of monkey blood, or by use of monkey kidneys for producing a polio vaccine which was tested in central Africa. (In 1994 it was found that SIV viruses in yellow baboons had recently crossed a species barrier. They had come from African green monkeys.)

Note that animal organs – the livers, hearts and kidneys of baboons, for example – have been transplanted into humans occasionally, a practice which will probably boom in view of the shortage of human donors. There are obvious dangers here of helping diseases to jump from animals to humans. The often deadly Lassa and Marburg viruses have lately made such a leap. Perhaps it is high time for universal use of the rule that adults who haven't themselves agreed to donate their organs when they die shall have absolutely no right to get organs from others.

Viruses can be particularly frightening because they cannot be attacked with antibiotics and because of the rate at which new strains appear. Dengue, once a comparatively harmless tropical disease, recently developed a deadly hemorrhagic form. Again, a mutant form of SIV was discovered not long ago. Instead of causing a chronic AIDS-like infection, it kills its monkey in a week.[140]

(e) Diseases are fought by the body's immune system. When, as in AIDS, it is this system itself which a disease has targeted, the victim can be in understandably grave trouble. 'AIDS' is short for Acquired Immune Deficiency Syndrome, while 'HIV' stands for Human Immunodeficiency Virus, the infectious agent generally thought responsible. The disease at first gives the impression of lying dormant: for up to a decade, the body's defences keep it under control. Then it causes the immune system to collapse. It is linked in the public mind with homosexuals, yet 80 per cent of those suffering from it today have contracted it through heterosexual activity. Since the virus kills so slowly, its hosts have plenty of time to infect others, and this puts it under little pressure to develop less lethal forms. In 1980 there were some three hundred thousand HIV-infected people. Today there are perhaps twenty million; some say forty million or more. In various cities with a high proportion of men who are unmarried or whose wives remain in the countryside, half the adult population is said to be HIV-infected, although accurate figures are understandably hard to come by. N. Myers, an expert on global threats, suggests that one-fifth of the world's population may eventually fall victim to the disease.[141]

HIV mutates uncommonly fast. Inside even a single individual, a strain quite frequently splits into several which are markedly different. In the cases of the strains so far known to have appeared, however, the chances of getting the disease after sexual contact with one of its victims are actually fairly small; mosquitoes apparently cannot transmit it; and, despite the presence of HIV in saliva, there has been no evidence of infection by kissing, by sneezing or by coughing. It is coughing which spreads a related virus, the visna virus, from sheep to sheep.

2

OTHER DANGERS

—— •◦• ——

Comets or asteroids, supernovae, solar flares, black hole explosions or mergers might conceivably threaten the human race with extinction. So might genetic engineering. There could also be risks associated with computers – in particular, the risk of their replacing us entirely, a prospect some people find attractive – and with nanotechnology (the use of very tiny, potentially self-reproducing machines). And there might perhaps be strange risks associated with high-energy physics. In a vacuum metastability disaster, for instance, not just Earth's biosphere but the entire galaxy would be destroyed by an ever-expanding bubble.

A COMET OR ASTEROID STRIKE

The human race might be exterminated by a large comet or an asteroid. In 1994 there was heavy media coverage when Jupiter was struck by some twenty kilometer-sized fragments of comet Shoemaker–Levy 9, moving at about sixty kilometers a second. One fragment exploded with an energy of at least six million megatons (TNT-equivalent). Less well known is that Howard–Koomen–Michels 1979XI, a comet whose head was larger than the Earth, hit the sun in 1979,[1] while in late 2126 the comet Swift–Tuttle, a trillion tons of ice and rock moving at some sixty-five kilometers a second, will (if present calculations are right) cross Earth's orbit at a point from which Earth itself is only two weeks distant.[2] There have been certainly five and maybe well over a dozen mass extinctions in Earth's biological history. It seems that at least the last one, which saw the end of the dinosaurs some

81

sixty-five million years ago, was associated with a major impact or impacts. The Yucatan peninsula appears to have been struck by an asteroid between ten and twenty kilometers in diameter – around a trillion tons of rock moving at perhaps over 20 km a second and exploding with an energy of 100 million megatons, about ten thousand times the energy locked up in the world's nuclear arsenals when at their largest. The crater was up to 300 km across. There were huge tidal waves, ejection of trillions of tons of dust into the atmosphere, world-wide forest fires, acid rain, and hurricanes whose winds moved at maybe nine-tenths the speed of sound. Almost complete darkness lasting several months, and the severe cooling which presumably accompanied it, may have been followed by conditions up to ten degrees hotter than previously, thanks to the greenhouse effect of carbon dioxide from the fires and from limestone vaporized by the impact. The new heat might even have been joined by disastrous amounts of ultraviolet light, for the hurricanes could have swept enough salt water into the stratosphere to destroy most of its ozone. The evidence for all this includes a world-wide layer of iridium-enriched clay, in places mixed with soot, the iridium supposedly coming from the exploding asteroid and the soot from the resulting fires; geological layers in which deep marine deposits are side by side with boulders and fossil plants, suggestive of huge tidal waves; a layer of glassy spherules; large crystals of shocked quartz; traces of the crater; and the mass extinction, in which not only the dinosaurs but between a quarter and three-quarters of the world's species perished.[3]

Some of the evidence remains controversial. Much of it might instead be ascribed to massive volcanic eruptions. Volcanic ash and sulphate-rich aerosols could produce darkness and cooling: the eruption of Tambora in 1815 caused famine in far distant New England because of summertime snows and frosts. Now, the Deccan volcanoes were active for about half a million years at around the time of the extinction. The volume of their lava flows may have exceeded two million cubic kilometers, and billions of tons of sulphuric acid were emitted.[4] The consequences would have included persistent acid fog and acid rain, and possibly greenhouse heating when acidic ocean waters generated carbon dioxide. Still, asteroid-impact and volcanic-eruption scenarios are largely compatible. It could be that the impact (now rather well established) was the final blow for many species which had been having a hard time with volcanism. It has also been suggested that large impacts can trigger volcanic eruptions. Collision with an object 15 km in width would have made the Earth's surface move up and down by one hundred meters even 1,000 km from the impact site.[5]

The greatest of the mass extinctions occurred some 250 million years ago, at the end of the Permian period. Between 75 per cent and 96 per cent of all species were exterminated. Out of fifty genera of mammal-like reptiles, only one survived. Once again, many causes may have combined to produce the disaster. They include a rapid fall and then rise in sea levels, associated with an increase in atmospheric carbon dioxide and severe oxygen starvation: the ratio of carbon 13 to carbon 12 reached a minimum, suggesting oxidation of coal and black shales which perhaps cut oxygen levels in the atmosphere by a half and those in the sea by four-fifths. Further, the volcanoes of the Siberian Traps erupted massively at about this time, spreading lava over two or three million square kilometers. But there are also claims that South America, Africa and Antarctica, which were then joined in the southern part of the huge continent Gondwanaland, all carry traces of a single 300-km crater, while Alpine rocks bear iridium from an asteroid impact.[6]

Of comets and asteroids whose orbits are such that they might some day hit the Earth, there appear to be around two thousand measuring between 1 and 10 km in diameter. There is also a much smaller number (to estimate it would be sheer guesswork) of still larger ones, and a much greater number of smaller ones. The Tunguska explosion in 1908, which knocked down trees 40 km away, is thought to have been caused by a body only 60 meters across, too small even to fight its way down through the lower atmosphere – yet the atomic explosion which destroyed Hiroshima was a thousand times weaker, no more powerful than the explosion of the Revelstoke meteorite, which hit a fortunately uninhabited part of Canada in 1965. Bodies which were over one kilometer in size, and therefore potential causes of mass extinctions, could be expected to strike about once every half-million to ten million years.[7] The Earth's surface carries what appear to be old craters up to 500 km across, and F. Close suggests that it is hit around once every hundred million years by a monster able to 'vaporise the oceans and seriously affect the climatic conditions across the entire globe', for the energy of a large strike, if dissipated evenly throughout the atmosphere, would raise air temperatures by something like 200°C.[8]

It has sometimes been held that mass extinctions, and hence impacts, have occurred at regular intervals, for instance every thirty million years or so in recent times. This might be because of something which repeatedly stirred up the Oort Cloud, the solar system's comet belt, which contains anything from a hundred billion to several trillion comets. Three candidates for stirring up the Cloud are 'Nemesis', a small, dark, distant companion star to the sun;[9] a tenth planet, 'planet X', larger than the Earth and two or three times further away than Pluto; and the solar system's oscillations across the crowded galactic plane. None of the three has stood up very well to examination, however. It may nevertheless be that impacts occur specially often in particular periods, and that we ourselves live in one such period. Up to several trillion 'ice dwarfs' may be found in a Kuiper Belt circling the sun much more closely than the Oort Cloud. Despite their name, they could be of great size, the largest having widths of maybe over 1,000 km. (In 1995 D. Jewitt and J. Luu estimated that 35,000 of them measured over 100 km.) Perhaps once in a million years a very large one would wander into the inner solar system and disintegrate. Of its fragments, there might be thousands large enough to be potential causes of mass extinctions.[10] We could live in a time of special danger because of a giant which is now breaking up, associated with the Taurid meteors.

Every year there are approaching twenty atmospheric impacts in the 1-kiloton range. In 1994 a 100-kiloton blast filled the skies near the Pacific island of Tokelau. In 1937 an asteroid almost 2 km wide crossed Earth's orbit, missing Earth itself by about six hours. In 1989 there was another six-hour miss, although in this case the object was only 1 km across. Glassy spherules suggest four impacts of bodies weighing about fifty billion tons over the last thirty-five million years, the latest taking place about a million years ago.[11] A Spacewatch Workshop sponsored by NASA in 1980 concluded that a 'civilization-destroying' comet or asteroid strike, meaning one in which at least 10 per cent of the world's population perished, could well have a 1 in 300,000 chance of happening in any given year: the participants felt confident only in saying that the figure should fall somewhere in the range from 1 in 1,000,000 to 1 in 10,000.[12] The latter estimate corresponds to a 1 in 200 chance that the disaster would occur during a fifty-year lifetime, while even the less alarming 'best guess' figure of 1 in 300,000 would mean that one's risk of experiencing it would be something like a sixtieth as great as that of dying in an automobile accident.

Might it be worth trying to reduce such risks? *The Economist* of 11 September 1993, working with the fairly conservative estimate that the annual risk of a person's dying through an impact was one in two million, pointed out that for Americans this was higher than the risk of death from any other type of natural disaster. Given, it continued, that the British government thought it worth $1.2 million to save a single life through increased road safety, one might expect the developed world to pay $470 million a year to avert impacts.[13] Working over twenty-five years, a set of electronic detectors and a few dedicated telescopes could discover 90 per cent of threatening objects with widths above one kilometer, the program costing only $50 million at the start and then $10 million annually.[14] If the telescopes detected a disastrously large object on a collision course, people might then be willing to spend much bigger sums on preventing the collision. An Interceptor Committee formed by NASA in 1991 had suggested changing such an object's trajectory with hundred-megaton warheads or indeed (as proposed by E. Teller, 'father of the H-bomb') with ones in the million-megaton range – roughly ten thousand times as powerful as the biggest present-day H-bombs. All this had made many people think that the defensive systems, since they might fall into the wrong hands, could be more dangerous than the comets and asteroids themselves. Luckily, accurate tracking could reduce the need for huge energies: given a decade's warning, even a one-megaton explosion might be enough to divert a body one kilometer wide. Again, experts have suggested that heating by lasers, or by the kind of gigantic mirror which can be built in space from very thin plastic sheeting, or just by painting selected areas black, could produce surface jets of gas which, working over many years, would produce the necessary change of direction.[15]

Another possibility would be to store up enough to allow people to survive until agriculture could recover from the effects of a large impact. Close writes that the Swiss 'have a national plan which is a good example of where to start. It is compulsory to have underground shelters for all individuals permanently stockpiled with two years' supply of food and other essentials'.[16] While the plan was evolved for the case of nuclear war, it could serve for any number of other cases too.

SUPERNOVAE, GALACTIC CENTER OUTBURSTS, SOLAR FLARES

Supernova explosions, with energies in the hundred-trillion-quadrillion megaton range, occur when giant stars exhaust the nuclear fuel at their cores, or through transfers of matter between one star and another. For up to a few weeks, a supernova can radiate as brightly as a hundred billion suns, much of the energy taking particularly damaging forms – X-rays, gamma rays and high-energy 'cosmic ray' particles. Earth's normal electromagnetic shielding against cosmic rays could be destroyed; so could the ozone layer's shielding against ultraviolet light; and there might be considerable cooling and a world-wide drought.[17] Still, although the frequency of these explosions is very hard to estimate, it seems that they take place in our galaxy only between once and ten times per century, while dangerously close ones could be expected only just frequently enough to be candidates for explaining one or two of the mass extinctions shown by the fossil record: J. Ellis and D. Schramm recently calculated that supernovae inside thirty-three light years of Earth, attacking the upper atmosphere with cosmic rays sufficient to destroy perhaps 90 per cent of the ozone for perhaps three hundred years, would occur no more often than around once every 240 million years.[18] We would therefore appear to be safe for quite a while, particularly since the nearest potential supernova revealed by our searches is Alpha Crucis at a seemingly very adequate distance of four hundred light years.

There are signs that a gigantic explosion, or more probably a series of explosions spread over a few million years, took place at the core of our galaxy about half a billion years ago, the energy release equalling that of a hundred million supernovae.[19] There may have been other such events more recently.[20] Perhaps chain reactions of supernova explosions were involved, stars being more densely clustered towards the core. Alternatively, a black hole at the galactic center, a few million times as massive as the sun, may emit huge amounts of radiation whenever a specially large quantity of material falls into it. An outburst could have occurred some ten thousand to a hundred thousand years ago, creating the presently observable 'central cavity' about ten light years across.[21] Yet we should be unlikely to suffer catastrophe from any phenomenon like this unless the energy were released over a briefer period than before, or unless it came from some region much nearer than the galactic center.

A neutron star or black hole might emit energy able to do damage from a great range, above all to the ozone layer, because of being concentrated into narrow jets. (The same might perhaps apply to much of the energy of a supernova. During attempts to explain January 1993's observation of a particularly intense burst of gamma rays, S. Woosley suggested that supernovae could emit such jets, detectable at immense distances.) Yet the chances of being in the path of any jet would of course be smaller, the narrower it was. Again, while a jet would have more chance of hitting us if it were sweeping around, the period during which it sprayed us would be correspondingly shorter.

One might also need to consider large solar flares. If the sun were to enter a period of convective mixing, as may already have occurred at intervals, then an immense flare, up to a thousand times more energetic than any yet observed, might destroy the ozone layer about as effectively as a nearby supernova, especially if Earth's magnetic field had fallen to a low level during one of its reversals: there have been ten of these in the past two and a half million years, with the field dropping to near zero for up to twenty thousand years at a time.[22]

However, all such matters could seem to pose little immediate threat. After all, Earth hasn't been troubled by events of this sort for many million years.

BLACK HOLE EXPLOSIONS,
BLACK HOLE MERGERS, ETC.

Black holes, gravitationally collapsed regions from which light finds it very difficult to escape, are in fact not entirely black. As S. W. Hawking showed, they 'evaporate' because of quantum effects, losing energy at first extremely slowly but in the end explosively fast. Many miniature black holes, relics of the Big Bang which started with masses up to that of a mountain, may now be entering their explosive stage. The total energy output during such a black hole's last second could equal that of a ten-million-megaton or possibly even a trillion-megaton H-bomb. This, though, could be a threat only to a habitat which was very unusually near. (For comparison: our sun radiates every second the energy of a three-billion-megaton bomb.) Now, even if black holes were concentrated in galaxies, the nearest such hole would be 'probably at least as far away as the planet Pluto', Hawking estimates.[23] He adds that if the trillion-megaton figure is right, then our region of the galaxy probably sees fewer than two evaporating black hole explosions per cubic light year per century.

A merger between two large black holes could involve an immensely greater output, equivalent to converting up to 40 per cent of their masses into energy – an explosion in the ten-million-trillion-trillion-megaton range. And recent studies suggest that there are over a hundred million large black holes in our galaxy: the figure comes from considering how many have already been discovered in the galaxy (two just in the constellation Cygnus, for example) despite the difficulties of detecting them, and from E. van den Heuvel's calculation of the number of supergiant stars which could be expected to have ended their lives as black holes.[24] Still, in view of the size of the galaxy any risks associated with black hole mergers could well be very small indeed.

Much the same remarks apply to mergers between neutron stars. These, black hole mergers, and mergers between neutron stars and black holes are often blamed for the intense gamma ray bursts that come to us a few hundred times a year from randomly scattered directions. Their scatter, and the distribution of their brightnesses and wavelengths, would be tidily explained if they originated in extremely rare events occurring at tremendous distances. Why would they be observed at such distances rather than nearby? Perhaps simply because distant galaxies vastly outnumber the nearby ones. If this explanation is correct, then the events would be releasing energy up to a billion billion times faster than the sun, over periods ranging from a fraction of a second to several minutes. Recent calculations by S. Thorsett suggest that any burst occurring within two thousand light years of us would make the ozone layer disappear for several years, a burst of this kind occurring once every few million centuries.[25] The outpouring of energy would be thousands of times more violent than that of all other sources in the galaxy combined. But this sort of thing would presumably happen more frequently near galactic centers, and there is now in fact rather good evidence (expanding shells and rings of material, and outflowing gas streams) that the center of our galaxy, some twenty-seven thousand light years away from us, underwent a very large explosion, its energy equal to that of some hundred thousand supernovae, around fifteen million years ago.

Other possibilities include *white hole* 'minibangs', regions in which a Big Bang which was 'ragged in time' was unusually delayed. J. Narlikar has suggested that cosmologists have been too quick in abandoning their speculations about these. As he explains, the reason for abandoning them lay in calculations supposedly showing that 'in a very short interval after they erupt, the white holes are smothered by the surrounding medium and they are converted to black holes'. He shows that the calculations could be based on defective assumptions, so that white holes might be 'energy machines' able to account for observed bursts of high-energy cosmic rays or gamma rays.[26] Again, M. A. Markov writes that primordial black holes may exist in 'swarms' having a mass of some billion metric tons, and that any such swarm could be a source of 'considerable or even catastrophic energy release'.[27] And as P. C. W. Davies points out, there must be some slight risk that a single large black hole (or, he adds, a rogue planet ejected from its orbit around another star, or a brown-dwarf star) may 'come upon us unseen, without warning, and wreak havoc with the solar system'.[28]

While all such matters can deserve a mention, they certainly seem not to represent any severe and imminent danger. There are no signs that Earth has so far been troubled by them, and such evidence as we have suggests that the more violent of them occur only rarely in our galaxy. For instance, it is thought that neutron stars collide in the galaxy only about once every hundred thousand years.

GENETIC ENGINEERING

Quite apart from its possible contributions to biological warfare (see Chapter 1), genetic engineering might be considered extremely dangerous. The fact is that the complexity of the field makes its risks very hard to evaluate. At least in public, most experts say they are no great cause for concern, as shown both by calm scientific reasoning and by the absence of any disaster so far: see, for example, chapter 3, 'The fear and trembling', of B. K. Zimmerman's *Biofuture*, with its talk of 'poor Chicken Little', who 'mistook an acorn for a piece of the sky and gathered her friends to rush and tell the king that the sky was falling'.[29] Without actually being ill informed or irrational, however, you might think the risks as great as any which humankind now faces. The apparent consensus among the experts might perhaps itself be explicable more by social pressures than by scientific findings: instead of just affecting industry, as in the case of regulations applying to nuclear power plants, attempted restrictions on genetic engineering threatened the salaries and research grants of scientists in universities and research laboratories. The outcome, it has sometimes been suggested, was a speedy presentation of a united front despite quite a severe lack of evidence.[30]

Eventually it may be possible to manufacture all of an advanced organism's DNA molecules – the ones which act like computer programs to build and control its cells – from simple chemicals which are then assembled by 'gene machines'. At present, though, genetic engineers tend merely to splice together long strips of genetic material stolen from different organisms. An organism's DNA may be cut up with the help of enzymes, chosen segments then being ferried into bacteria, plants or animals by carriers which can be plasmids, liposomes, viruses, or pellets fired by tiny guns. The resulting genetically engineered organisms could be, for example, bacteria which produced insulin for treating diabetes or interferon for helping cancer patients. The insulin or the interferon would itself then be called 'genetically engineered'.

Genetic engineering's potential benefits are enormous. Diseases of humans or of farm animals can be cured by genetically engineered vaccines or genetically engineered antibiotics. Genetic defects (inability to produce normal hemoglobin, for instance, which leads to the fatal blood disease beta thalassemia) can be repaired. Plants can be made resistant to frost, salt, disease, insects and pesticides, or novel nitrogen-fixing abilities (reducing the need for fertilizers) can be given to them. Milk production can be boosted by genetically engineered bovine growth hormone. Organisms can be tailor-made for manufacturing chemicals in bulk, for extracting oil from seemingly exhausted wells, for eating up industrial waste, or perhaps even for terraforming Mars (making it habitable). Old age might be greatly delayed through minor tinkering with the human genome. All this would be 'unnatural', yet so are shoes and tractors, hearing aids and operations for appendicitis, houses and parachutes and defences against avalanches. In a world of cancer, plague, earthquake, and people born blind or deformed, there is nothing very evidently superior in all that's 'natural'.

What really is evident, on the other hand, is that techniques for creating dramatically beneficial organisms could also be used for creating harmful ones. The world is well supplied both with criminals and with honest folk who make mistakes. When selling shares in their companies, genetic engineers rightly claim that their methods will prove to be far more powerful than those of, say, conventional agricultural cross-breeding. They mustn't then go on to argue that none of their acts involve novel dangers. True, there will be scores of cases where artificially engineered organisms will do poorly in the wild. Yet there are bound to be other cases in which such organisms – varieties of wheat, perhaps, which have been given nitrogen-fixing nodules of the kind found in clovers – will do better than their natural counterparts.

The notion that anyone other than a hater of the human race would hatch plans to fill humans with salmonella bacteria *which inhibited sperm production for months* could well seem preposterous, couldn't it? Yet as the Introduction noted, exactly such plans have been hatched in an American university – it being assumed, perhaps, that an ability to produce substances which inhibited

91

sperm production could only hinder the bacteria in their struggle to survive, so that they would soon die out. We are all permanently infected to some degree by ordinary salmonella bacteria. Luckily these don't inhibit sperm production, and with a little further luck they would indeed produce more offspring than the genetically engineered variety; but what if they didn't? For squelching this objection, it mightn't be enough to equip the genetically engineered bacteria with what are known as 'kamikaze genes' to give them suicidal tendencies, genes which could be activated at will by taking suitable pills, or which would spring into action as soon as pill-taking stopped. The difficulty is that any bacterium which mutated so that it lost the genes in question might reproduce itself uncontrollably.

Genetically engineered to fight off attacks by insects, couldn't crops proliferate disastrously? Or couldn't their new 'pest-resistant' properties be transferred to crop-destroying weeds by the kind of exchange of genetic material which – as has belatedly come to be appreciated – is rather common in Nature?

Again, mightn't 'improved' humans, intended to be genetically superior to those of earlier generations, fall easy victims to some disease, perhaps cancer of a new type? This would be particularly disastrous if the disease made its first appearance only after all humans had undergone 'improvement'. The DNA of our cells programs them to die after a limited number of divisions. Old age could be delayed by increasing the number in question – yet this would make the modified cells more like tumour cells, which can keep dividing indefinitely. Programmed death may be a defence against earlier death from cancer.

When gene splicing, 'recombinant DNA' techniques arrived in the mid-1970s, their practitioners voluntarily accepted a one-year moratorium on various potentially dangerous experiments. (As P. R. Wheale and R. M. McNally explain, public alarm had first been generated by a plan of a Stanford University team 'to study the tumour virus, Simian Virus 40, by cloning it in *Escherichia coli*, the common bacteria of the human intestinal tract': this virus produces cancer in hamsters and fears were voiced that the cancer-inducing DNA would spread to humans.[31]) The U.S. National Institutes of Health then quickly published *Guidelines for Research Involving Recombinant DNA Molecules*. Although with no legal force outside governmentally funded projects, the guidelines were at first widely followed. And initially they were strict. It was forbidden to release genetically engineered organisms into the environment. Many experiments were to be carried out only by technicians enclosed in protective suits, working in low-pressure buildings so that any leaks would carry particles inwards and not out into the world. Further, organisms would often have to be 'crippled' in ways making them unlikely to survive outside laboratories.

Because of pressures from the emerging biotechnology industry, including blunt threats to perform experiments in countries where no restrictions were in place, the NIH guidelines remained without much legal force. What is more, they suffered dilutions 'to a point where they are almost meaningless' – to quote R. L. Sinsheimer, a biophysicist who had played a major part in formulating them. In a letter to the NIH, Sinsheimer protested that the effect of the dilutions was 'to dismiss the possibility of hazard from all recombinant DNA experiments except those involving known, very pathogenic agents'.[32] In 1986 a White House Council on Environmental Quality went so far as to delete the rule requiring federal agencies to examine worst-case scenarios, on the grounds that such efforts to avert disaster bred 'endless hypothesis and speculation'.[33]

There were certainly some excuses for relaxed regulations. In particular, many techniques of gene-crippling had been perfected. Organisms could be engineered so that they survived only in the presence of chemicals not normally available, or genes could be inserted to limit how many generations of descendants they could have. Still, no firm legislation prevented engineering of organisms potentially capable of reproducing themselves better than natural ones when released into the wild. This situation continued despite discoveries showing that gene-crippling might succeed only temporarily, and that alterations engineered into one species could spread to others. In particular, it was fast becoming plain that, in the words of T. Beardsley, 'a blizzard of genetic material blows freely through the microbial world, not only between bacteria of the same species but also between members of distantly related species and even between bacteria and viruses' – viruses being, so far as risks are concerned, even worse than bacteria because they evolve by the exchange of whole functional genetic units, and because they can so readily transport genes from one species to another.[34] Genetically crippled by being deprived, for instance, of elements essential to their replication, microbes can fairly readily acquire the missing material from elsewhere: British safety inspectors gave precisely this reason for ending some University of Birmingham tinkerings with organisms which were cancer-producing in their uncrippled form.[35] Using viruses as their carriages, genes can travel from one type of plant to another, or between humans and other mammals. And sometimes not even carriages are essential. Marine bacteria are now known to take up the DNA floating where other bacteria have died and decayed.[36]

In one way, no doubt, such discoveries simply strengthen the view that the genetic engineer's experiments pose few threats. 'Nature', it can be commented, 'is constantly performing similar experiments.' But remember, genetic engineering occasionally performs feats which Nature could rival only in millions of years. That is what makes it a source of benefits unachievable by conventional stock breeders, crop scientists and vaccine developers. Moreover, some of its achievements are ones which Nature could almost certainly never reproduce. Of the modifications which would increase an organism's Darwinian fitness, some can come about only through many simultaneous changes, each fatal if in isolation. Genetic engineers can ensure that such modifications do occur together. Again, they have actually managed to add a sixty-fifth codon–anticodon pair to the genetic alphabet, thereby opening a path towards radically new proteins.[37]

What major dangers might be lurking here? It is almost impossible to tell. Now, this itself magnifies whatever dangers there are, for it makes it very hard to set up restrictions which won't immediately be broken. Being humans like the rest of us, genetic engineers are rather easily convinced that their own projects are vital to human progress. Besides, theirs is a field where huge amounts of money are now being invested.

Wheale and McNally note that 'the insurance industry in the U.S.A. has been unwilling to provide insurance cover against the event of mishaps in field trials of recombinant microbes'.[38]

COMPUTER-CAUSED DISASTERS, AND COMPUTER REPLACEMENTS FOR HUMANS

While placing nuclear missiles under computer control could quickly prove disastrous, it is just one example of how catastrophe could come from the computer revolution. Here are some other possibilities:

(a) As well as being open to sabotage, for instance by a terrorist's bomb whose electromagnetic pulse fries computer circuits throughout a city, complex electrical or electronic networks are subject to largely unpredictable collapse. In 1965 failure of a relay device in an electricity generating plant near Niagara Falls triggered havoc: most parts of Ontario and of seven American states were without electricity for hours. In 1990 and 1991 there were large-scale crashes in America's telephone networks: the capital was isolated and airports were closed. In one instance the cause was a single erroneous letter in a line of computer software. Because of it, any message saying that one switching center had recovered from a problem paralyzed neighbouring centers temporarily. When those centers in turn recovered, their own messages paralyzed other centers, and so on. The public felt sure that computer hackers were responsible. People were simply unable to understand that huge 'landslides in cyberspace' can occur without deliberate planning. Yet in 1972, and again in 1980, a rather similar disease had overwhelmed a communication system through an error indicating that messages routed via Los Angeles would experience a large *negative delay*: they would save time by being sent onwards even before they had arrived. This logically absurd news spread from Los Angeles right across the land, efforts to eradicate it at any one place being nullified by reinfection from elsewhere.[39]

In 1992, British Nuclear Fuels had detected 2,400 errors, about 100 of which could have 'placed a demand upon the safety systems' (to quote the project manager's careful words), in an early version of software to control its huge new nuclear fuel reprocessing plant at Sellafield. When a computer program contains more than a couple of thousand lines of code, finding all its faults can be near impossible. Even prolonged practical testing may fail to reveal them. Under plausible mathematical assumptions, there is only a half-chance that a program will function properly for the same length of time as it had before, and in one extensively tested program about a third of all the remaining errors were '5,000-year bugs', each likely to cause a failure only about once in fifty centuries.[40]

If you were forced to guess an actual day for human life to become extinct then January 1, AD 2000, could seem the best bet. Very many computer clocks, perhaps including ones in military systems, will be unable to handle the radical change of date: already 'it has been reliably reported that NASA postponed a space shuttle flight which was going to straddle a year end'.[41] A recent estimate is that it would cost some five hundred billion dollars to change computer software, world wide, so that the next millennium opened smoothly.[42]

(b) The erroneous indication of *negative delays* in Los Angeles didn't result from some computer programmer's carelessness. Instead the communications network 'was inhabited by a spontaneously evolved, quite abstract, self-reproducing organism, formed by a simple, random mutation', H. P. Moravec writes. The self-reproducing entity (a section of computer code) was spotted only because its effects were so devastating. 'If it had been more subtle in its action, it might have lived much longer. Among programs without masters there is a strong natural-selection criterion: reproduce but lie low. It is quite likely that many unsuspected organisms are already making a quiet living in computer memories', Moravec adds, then pointing out that 'since any datum in a computer is subject to duplication, this covers a lot of ground'.[43] The successful strategy of lying low might come about by mutation in man-made 'computer viruses', pieces of code designed to reproduce themselves in computers without permission. Adding a degree of intelligence to these, or making them able to mutate rapidly like the AIDS virus and so avoid the 'virus killer' programs which are now commercially available, is an obvious further means of increasing their success. In 1994 the magazine *PC Computing* reported the existence of a software package, 'Mutation Engine', which supplied pranksters with viruses designed to change constantly as they spread. The more complex and rapid computers become, the greater is the 'world of cyberspace' in which, as Moravec puts it, electronic 'rats, coyotes, and master criminals' could evolve from fairly simple computer viruses with startling speed. Their evolution might be aided by 'the ability to systematically copy and try out fragments of code from other programs and other viruses – the beginnings of computer-virus sex'.[44] Of all the computer viruses so far produced, hardly any have become extinct in spite of the many virus killers.

Long ago, N. A. Barricelli developed computer programs whose slightly varying copies, 'mutated offspring', so to speak, evolved (because the less successful were constantly weeded out) so as to improve at playing a simple game whose rules were initially unknown to them. And computer replications can occur at tremendous speed. This fact is now being exploited by scientists who want to investigate life's probable origins without having to conduct several hundred million years of test tube experimentation. One of them was so troubled when colleagues pointed to the 'security problem' – the risk that if his model of evolving RNA escaped into other people's computers then it could take on a life of its own – that he ensured that his program couldn't be read in standard computer language.[45]

(c) It can seem plain, none the less, that computer-based intelligence which evolves of its own accord is not the main threat in this area. Much more potentially worrying are deliberate human plans to give computers great intelligence and power.

For a start, nation-states could get considerable competitive advantages by letting computers control their factories and many functions of their governments. As R. A. MacGowan and F. I. Ordway note, the danger would then be that the machines would gradually overcome the remaining limitations to their powers, possibly 'by strategies totally incomprehensible to the political leaders'.[46] Powerful factors in what President Eisenhower christened 'the military-industrial complex' already show an uncanny capacity for circumventing all attempts to restrain them. They appear to flourish regardless of whether individual military commanders or captains of industry are in favour of arms control.

MacGowan and Ordway think being ruled by a huge computer, 'a dictatorship of unimagined centralization of authority', wouldn't be 'slavery in the usual sense of the word'. Rather, 'a relatively Utopian society would be the immediate result', while in the long term the production services of humans would become 'of negligible importance' so that 'the automaton would probably abandon the human race and emigrate to greener astronomical pastures': 'intelligent automata may be much more widespread in the universe than intelligent biological species'.[47] Grimmer scenarios have been imagined by others, however. K. E. Drexler writes that AI (artificial intelligence) systems which are clever enough to design and build still better AI systems 'will enable states to expand their military capabilities by orders of magnitude in a brief time'. He adds that the world already holds governments which torture and spy on their citizens, and that advanced technology will merely extend the possibilities open to them: 'using an abundance of speech-understanding AI systems, they could listen to everyone'. But, he continues, they mightn't want to. 'With advanced technology, states need not control people – they could instead simply *discard* people.' Artificially intelligent systems could replace not only the workers who 'make, move, or grow things' but also 'engineers, scientists, administrators, and even leaders'. 'A state could prosper while discarding anyone, or even (in principle) everyone': prosper in the sense of beating other states in economic or military struggles.[48]

It is often argued that a World Government would be uncomfortably totalitarian. Still, competition between nation-states could easily lead to something worse. To suppose that any state would be so perverse as to put itself at the mercy of machines programmed with the main aim not of benefiting the state's citizens, but simply of defeating other states economically or militarily, can appear totally bizarre – yet then one remembers, first, how so many of today's states seem far more concerned with defeating other states than with the welfare of their citizens, and second, that a state which failed to make defeating others its top priority could run a severe risk of being wiped off the map.

(d) Finally, the discarding of all people – or at any rate of all people readily recognizable as *humans* – could be planned by humans themselves. Several authors welcome the idea that the human race will be replaced by advanced computers, perhaps after a period in which the mental processes of selected individuals are 'transferred' to such machines. The brains of those individuals might be hooked up to the computers for months or years, thinking in co-operation with them until the transfer was complete.

MacGowan and Ordway point out that computers could have the advantage of being born, so to speak, complete with all the very latest knowledge; of having 'indefinitely long life spans' since death could be expected only through accidents; and of each being able 'to control the parameters of its thinking processes' instead of becoming paranoid or neurotic or pathologically depressed. They could 'grow indefinitely both in mental and physical capacities', and two or more of them could fuse their identities when desired. They could operate in a very wide range of environments, for example in a vacuum.[49]

Moravec actually calls himself 'an author who cheerfully concludes that the human race is in its last century, and goes on to suggest how to help the process along'. He looks forward to rapid advances in intelligence as soon as machines become clever enough to manage their own design and construction. 'Our DNA will be out of a job', having passed the torch to much more nearly immortal, much more flexible carriers of 'genetic information' of a new kind, namely 'exclusively knowledge, passed from mind to artificial mind', he writes.[50] Earlier he had said that there might at first be 'human thought freed from bondage to mortal body': thought which had been transferred from human brains to artificially intelligent machinery, somewhat as program and data are moved from one computer to another. He had then explained that whereas almost all the computers used for research into artificial intelligence have possessed, at the most, the information-processing powers of insects, systems intricate enough to rival human brains might exist by the year 2030. They would need to have a thousand trillion bits of memory, and to perform ten trillion calculations a second. Commercial and other competition would virtually force such systems on us: 'we have very little choice'. But in Moravec's view the 'genetic takeover' of humans by machines would be cause for joy. Eventually, use of ultradense matter might make it possible 'to build systems with a million million million million million times the power of a human mind'.[51]

Now, presumably it would be pointless to declare that a computer reacting to its surroundings as skilfully as any human 'would still be in no sense conscious'. It would be much like saying that computers 'are in no sense good at chess' although able to beat grandmasters. However, many take the view that vast skill in information processing wouldn't guarantee consciousness *of any worthwhile kind*. There are various fairly forceful grounds for such a view.

Consider, for a start, the case of a man blind from birth. Several writers join F. C. Jackson and R. Swinburne in claiming that no amount of knowledge about patterns of activity in a brain could permit the man to understand just how it felt to see yellow or blue.[52] Similar claims may then be made about all sensations. After that, it can be claimed that computers, even when able to keep track of their internal activity patterns (as computers typically do, so as to control them and report on them), would be really no better off than the blind man. Yes, computers might distinguish between yellow objects and blue ones. Equipped with wheels, they might move away from harmful stimuli, crying 'Ouch!'. Yet they couldn't be aware of colours in the way in which we rightly want to be aware of them, and people could kick them without causing any genuine pain.

Next, J. R. Searle has argued that no computer could properly understand what it was doing. Any 'chess successes' which it achieved would be like the 'successful answering in Chinese' of somebody who could consult a highly complex rule book in order to match Chinese symbols (forming more or less any question) with other Chinese symbols (suitable answers) but who knew those symbols only as meaningless squiggles.[53]

Just what, though, could be the factor which importantly distinguished humans from computers which regularly won at chess or cried 'Ouch!' and moved away from kicks? Well, no matter how successfully the machines kept track of their internal activity patterns, they might be held to have 'no properly integrated overview of those activity patterns' – but precisely what would those words mean? Swinburne writes that 'certain simultaneous mental events are states of a common subject. At a single moment of time you feel cramp in your leg, hear the noise of my voice, and see the movement of my arms'.[54] Yet, we might ask him, couldn't a computer's states also be 'states of a common subject'? Couldn't its internal activity patterns represent all the thirty-two pieces on a chessboard, or a voice and a moving arm, in some 'properly integrated' fashion?

Perhaps what bothers many people – it certainly bothers me[55] – is that any computer can seem to be a collection of parts *fully separate in their existence*: parts each of which could (at least as a logical possibility) continue to exist unchanged while the rest of the universe vanished. Consciousness, in contrast, 'holds a many in one, a diversity within a unity', in the words of the English idealist philosopher F. H. Bradley, who thought it 'really monstrous' to look on the unity in question 'as consisting in no more than some relation or relations': some fact, that is to say, about how elements fall into complicated spatiotemporal, causal or other patterns.

We could here feel tempted to follow Spinoza, treating the universe's parts as all of them merely 'modes', aspects, of a single existent: i.e., as elements which were no more capable of separate existence than the redness of a cherry or the length of a lake. Still, followers of Spinoza must admit that the universe does have *parts*, elements whose separate existence at least isn't *an obvious logical impossibility*. Also that some groups of its parts are particularly closely unified. Why shouldn't a computer count as one such group, then? Couldn't the human brain be looked on as a biological computer, dramatically well unified?

A possible answer is that the human brain is indeed a computer of the right sort, but that being of this sort isn't just a matter of being good enough at information processing to, say, pass as a human when interviewed lengthily by telephone. *By exploiting quantum effects* our brains may manage to be computers with a unity of a highly desirable type. While not actually essential to complex information processing, unity of the kind made possible by quantum physics could be a great help towards it; but its desirability wouldn't be simply a question of giving such help. Suppose the human race had to be replaced by computers. Then, I strongly suggest, the computers ought to be ones with this special kind of unity ('quantum unity') for the following reason. A consciousness which wasn't 'fused into a single whole' by quantum effects might well have *no intrinsic value whatever*. Without quantum unification, the elements forming a conscious state could be too little joined in their actual existence – which is what is relevant when you join me in asking whether they are elements whose collective existence is of intrinsic value, i.e., is ethically required for its own sake, rather than just for the sake of something else.[56]

Several authors like to think that, at least in some key region or regions, the brain is unified by quantum effects. Quantum theory allows complex systems to be much more closely knit than would be allowed by classical physics. For instance, various particles (ones obeying Bose–Einstein statistics, which can be understood only on the basis of quantum theory) can very largely lose their individual identities so that when, for example, there are two of them in a box, then the probability that both will be in the same half of the box isn't *one-half*, as you might expect; it is instead *two-thirds*. (This is because there aren't two distinct ways in which the particles could be in different halves of the box: namely particle A on the left and particle B on the right, and vice versa. Instead, particles A and B have 'fused their identities' in some complex sense.) D. Bohm wrote that 'on the basis of modern physics, even inanimate matter cannot be fully understood in terms of Descartes's notion that it is nothing but a substance occupying space and constituted of separate objects': 'the interaction of particles may be thought of as depending on a common pool of information belonging to the system as a whole'.[57] Writing later with B. Hiley, he added that in consciousness 'one's most primary experience' is of how the parts of one's conscious being 'flow into and out of each other and, in a certain sense, enfold each other'.[58]

R. Penrose points out that '*quantum correlations* can occur over widely separated distances' and therefore might play 'a definite role over large regions of the brain', it being tempting to view this as the basis of 'the 'oneness' or 'globality' that seems to be a feature of consciousness'.[59] Again, 'there could conceivably be some relation between this 'oneness' of consciousness and *quantum parallelism*': because 'different alternatives at the quantum level are allowed to exist in linear superposition' we can say that '*a single quantum state* could in principle consist of a large number of activities occurring simultaneously'.[60]

Very speculatively, biological details have been added to the picture by various writers. In particular I. N. Marshall, impressed by 'the unity and complexity of states of consciousness' and convinced that 'no classical physical system could play the role', notes that 'among quantum systems a Bose–Einstein condensate has the right properties'. Superfluid helium is one such condensate, with 'long-range order and a sharing of the identities of constituent units'. This sort of thing could provide 'the diversity-in-unity required'. Now, H. Fröhlich had pointed out that a 'pumped phonon system' akin to a Bose–Einstein condensate might exist at the temperature of the living brain. Such a system, Marshall suggests, could provide 'a concrete physical basis for recent attempts to use the hologram as a metaphor for states of consciousness'.[61] Each tiny area of a hologram encodes information about the whole.

There is a fascinating discussion of such ideas in M. Lockwood's *Mind, Brain and the Quantum*.[62]

A DISASTER CAUSED BY NANOTECHNOLOGY

'Nanotechnology' means the use of complex machines whose components are of about a nanometer, a millionth of a millimeter. Building them involves manipulating individual atoms and molecules with great precision. The science involved can be a mixture of chemistry, liquid physics and engineering. In 'There's plenty of room at the bottom',[63] R. P. Feynman suggested using machines to construct tinier machines, which would then make yet tinier ones, and so on. Another approach is that of the microelectronics industry, with its photographically shrunk templates and computer-controlled cutting beams; or scanning-tunnelling electron microscopes can be used to pull particular atoms into desired places (as has been done to form the letters 'IBM'). Again, while all chemists have long been in the job of manipulating atoms indirectly, exploiting their 'self-assembly' when thermal movemements bring them into contact, nanotechnologists may prefer to join atoms with weak bonds, for instance hydrogen bonds, instead of chemical bonds.

Already hydrogen bonds, van der Waals bonds, and bonds based on hydrophobic interactions have been used to make self-assembling 'molecular switches' of kinds activated by light.[64] It is altogether possible that inside the next couple of centuries the step will be made from self-assembly to self-reproduction. Instead of just being 'assemblers' manufacturing other things, some nanomachines containing thousands or millions of switches, rods and rotors would be 'replicators' producing perfect copies of themselves. J. von Neumann developed a general theory of self-replicating machinery,[65] a theory later found to be beautifully illustrated by the interactions of DNA, RNA and proteins in natural self-reproduction. Modern computer-controlled lathes are a first step towards 'von Neumann machines' able to reproduce themselves indefinitely. Well, it seems that complex electronic computers will fairly soon be shrunk to micron (thousandth of a millimeter) dimensions. Mechanical computers might undergo comparable miniaturization. 'With components a few atoms wide, a simple mechanical computer would fit within 1/100 of a cubic micron': 'even with a billion bytes of storage, a nanomechanical computer could fit into a box a micron wide, about the size of a bacterium', Drexler writes in his *Engines of Creation*.[66] Nanometer-sized cogwheels would revolve at such speed that groups of them could carry out calculations more rapidly than today's electronic computers. They would thus readily control very complicated construction tasks, including the task of self-reproduction. If they could be shrunk to the same scale, electronic computers would operate still faster: perhaps hundreds of thousands of times faster.

Such tales must be counted as speculative futurology, yet *Engines of Creation* tells them rather plausibly and Drexler's *Nanosystems* goes on to supply many technical details.[67] Operating at a billion cycles per second and therefore able to co-operate in constructing a complex, kilogram-weight object in an hour or less, nanomechanical devices carrying their own computers could be introduced into vats of chemicals, where they would make machines of almost any kind. Acting as miniature surgeons, they could clear fats from our arteries or perform intricate repairs which greatly prolonged our lifetimes, as was suggested in R. C. W. Ettinger's *The Prospect of Immortality*.[68] But, Drexler points out, when devices of this sort are able to make 'almost anything (including more of themselves) from common materials', then they will 'give nuclear war some company as a potential cause of extinction'. Artificial plants using solar cells 'could out-compete real plants, crowding the biosphere with inedible foliage', while tough, omnivorous artificial bacteria 'could spread like blowing pollen, replicate swiftly, and reduce the biosphere to dust in a matter of days' – a threat which has come to be known as 'the gray goo problem'.[69] A disaster might arrive by sheer accident. Or it might be brought about by using replicators 'to wage a sort of germ warfare' with 'programmable, computer controlled 'germs''. These could be much more useful militarily than real germs, until they went out of control.

As Drexler elsewhere remarks, 'by simply neglecting to solve some difficult problems, we need never come close to building nanoreplicators capable of runaway exponential growth, or capable of evolving into systems that pose that threat'. In very tiny components even single particles of natural radiation could cause significant changes, but these would be unlikely to help a self-reproducing machine to leave an increased number of descendants. Natural organisms 'make heavy use of spontaneous assembly': 'molecular parts diffuse and bump together in all possible positions and orientations' until they fall into configurations which are right – *rightness* being very largely a matter of topology, of the right kinds of connections, rather than of accurate spatial positioning. Nanodevices, on the other hand, would be more like automobiles. Most of their parts wouldn't work at all unless positioned very accurately: think of how the hole in an automobile's tank must coincide with the end of the fuel pipe. Consequently there would be little danger that the devices would undergo Darwinian evolution, if they hadn't been expensively designed for it. Moreover, they might be made able to operate only in unnatural environments such as 'special chemical vats (providing, say, hydrogen peroxide as a source of energy and oxygen)'.[70] And although there could be advantages in making them able to use 'inexpensive, abundant chemicals' and even to operate in the natural world instead of in factories, we must remember that 'these machines needn't be replicators'. They could instead be mere assemblers of other things, incapable of reproducing themselves.[71]

Even so, none of this can mean that perils would be for ever absent. In view of the tremendous commercial, medical and other benefits which nanomachines would offer, to try to suppress potentially dangerous advances would itself be 'futile and dangerous', Drexler comments. What one needs instead is 'intelligently targeted delay to postpone threats until we are prepared for them'. But unfortunately it seems that defences 'must be based on assembler-built systems that can be built only after dangerous replicators have already become possible'. And while responsible individuals could pursue laboratory research by manipulating the contents of tiny, sealed containers protected by explosives, so that 'someone outside cannot open the lab space without destroying the contents', criminals or terrorists or hostile nations could build their own laboratories. Mightn't it become possible, though, to outwit them by filling the world with 'nanomachines that act somewhat like the white blood cells of the human immune system: devices that can fight not just bacteria and viruses, but dangerous replicators of all sorts'? The snag is that 'dangerous replicators will be far simpler to design than systems that can thwart them'.[72]

In short, we can but hope that the temptations of war, terrorism and crime will be removed – by a huge international police force, or by firm education of the kind which many kind-hearted folk regard as vicious brainwashing? – before any nanotechnological revolution hits us.

RISKS AS INVESTIGATED
BY CHAOS THEORISTS,
CATASTROPHE THEORISTS, ETC.

Scientists now recognize that many events, disasters included, couldn't be predicted unless one had virtually complete knowledge of earlier events, plus computers galactic in size. E. Lorenz, a main originator of 'chaos theory', suggested that next month's weather, for instance, could well be so delicately dependent on conditions today that it made sense to ask 'Does the flap of a butterfly's wings in Brazil set off a tornado in Texas?' – this being the subtitle to his paper 'Predictability' at 1979's meeting of the American Association for the Advancement of Science. The behaviour of the solar system could itself be impossible for us to predict over periods of hundreds of millions of years.[73] Although the 'chaotic' wanderings of its planets are quite probably 'bounded' so that Earth would never have the close encounter with Venus which Hawking mentions as a possibility,[74] we cannot rule out such an encounter or even Earth's ejection from the solar system thanks to the working of Newton's laws over the next billion years. More immediately threatening, 'an asteroid can orbit for hundreds of thousands of years in a perfectly regular, sensible way, and then quite suddenly its orbit can change chaotically into a cometlike, elongated path that comes near the Earth', C. R. Chapman and D. Morrison observe.[75]

The difficulties of prediction investigated by chaos theory overlap with the ones of R. Thom's 'catastrophe theory' and those of what P. Bak and K. Chen have called 'the theory of self-organized criticality'. Thom's word 'catastrophe' means any sudden change, not necessarily disastrous: compare how Lorenz's 'chaos' can often be a good thing, as in the case of the human heart, whose beatings are healthy only when they are in Lorenz's sense 'chaotic'. Applied to Darwinian evolution, for instance, catastrophe theory may help explain why long periods of stability are separated by bursts in which new species arise in large numbers.[76] The actual time at which a catastrophe occurs may be thoroughly unpredictable by mere mortals, but a gradual increase of tensions can show that a sudden change is to be expected sooner or later – although the size and nature of the change can also be something transcending our predictive powers. When, for example, international tensions build up towards a war, catastrophe theory won't tell us just how many people will be killed, but it may throw light on the war's degree of inevitability. As J. L. Casti demonstrates with its help,[77] a system of nation-states can be pushed almost inexorably towards warfare despite good intentions on all sides.

Nowadays, a popular instance of a catastrophe is the collapse of a sand pile. If sand grains are added one by one to such a pile, sudden avalanches occur. With clean sand piling up on a small plate, the size of the avalanches can be effectively unpredictable.[78] Several studies suggest that many complex systems behave similarly. Also that a system's complexity can itself force it to evolve to more and more complex states which are increasingly unstable, until the equivalent of an avalanche occurs. Bak and Chen write: 'Systems as large and as complicated as the earth's crust, the stock market and the ecosystem can break down not only under the force of a mighty blow but also at the drop of a pin. Large interactive systems perpetually organize themselves to a critical state in which a minor event starts a chain reaction that can lead to a catastrophe': in the case of the crust, to an earthquake.[79]

Some of the mass extinctions revealed by the fossil record might illustrate the point. Bak, H. Flyvbjerg and K. Sneppen comment that 'large events in the history of evolution – such as the extinction of the dinosaurs – may have taken place without being triggered by large cataclysmic events', since survival of the fittest 'does not imply evolution to a state where everybody is well off. On the contrary, individual species are barely able to hang on – like the grains of sand in the critical sand pile.' Computer-based variants on sand piles suggest to these authors what many a biologist had suggested before them: that 'species with many connections – that is, those with a high degree of complexity – are more sensitive to the environment, more likely to participate in the next co-evolutionary avalanche and become extinct'. It may therefore be 'that cockroaches will outlast humans'.[80]

What applies to a species richly connected to others will, of course, tend to apply as well to rich groups of interacting species. As was argued by the ecologist R.May in the 1970s, an ecosystem's biodiversity is not an unmixed blessing: the interconnections between its parts may help it to fall apart, just because there are so many of them.[81]

Much of this involves bold world-modelling with computer systems or very clean sand, which can behave rather differently from natural systems and ordinarily dirty sand. And clearly it is no excuse for scattering pesticides everywhere to reduce biodiversity, or for destroying as many complex animals as possible. On the other hand, there is something very suspect in arguing that the elements of Earth's biosphere are now so intricately knitted together that they run no real risk of falling apart under the new stresses that pollutants put on them, or that humans at least 'are so advanced that they are bound to survive'. Again and again, the fossil record tells of complicated species which have become extinct while simple ones have continued onwards.

UPSETTING A METASTABLE 'VACUUM'

In 1980, S. Coleman and F. De Luccia published an article in *Physical Review D* with the curious title 'Gravitational effects on and of vacuum decay'.[82] It was followed in 1982, in *Nature*, by 'Is our vacuum metastable?', from the pens of M. S. Turner and F. Wilczek,[83] and then a year later, once again in *Nature*, by 'How stable is our vacuum?' from those of P. Hut and M. J. Rees.

Hut and Rees concluded from cosmic ray studies that 'at least no particle accelerator in the foreseeable future will pose any threat to our vacuum'.[84]

How could anything as empty as *a vacuum* ever be threatened by particle accelerators or by anything? And if we did feel any fears on this score, how could they be reduced by studying cosmic rays? For the present, at least, particle accelerators are the physicist's preferred means of reaching very high energies: ones which are 'locally' – over very tiny regions – much above those produced by H-bombs. What guided Hut and Rees was that, among all the events of whose existence we can be fairly confident, collisions between cosmic rays, extremely fast particles which can have the kinetic energies of rifle bullets, are by far the most locally energetic. So long as cosmic ray collision energies weren't exceeded, nothing disastrous could be expected. Any higher energies, however, might 'pose a threat to our vacuum'. For 'vacuum' in modern physics, or 'empty space', needn't mean a region absolutely empty. It usually means one of two other things instead:

(1) 'Vacuum' – particularly in such phrases as 'true vacuum' – may mean a region in which all fields (magnetic, electrical, etc.) are in their states of lowest energy. Now, this can be very different from saying that the fields are zero, entirely absent, since some fields are such that *their absence* is energetically costly. We might say that the natural thing is for these fields to take non-zero values. As viewed by today's physicists, what we call 'empty space' is in fact 'stuff' of a surprisingly substantial sort. On very small scales empty space is extremely complex stuff, dense with quantum disturbances. Particles are constantly jumping into existence and then vanishing. Connections between points are repeatedly made and broken, which leads people to speak of 'space-time foam'. On larger scales, it is extremely rigid stuff. Although space (as an aspect of bendable space-time) can be bent by gravity, it resists bending far more strongly than steel. It should come as no great surprise, therefore, that the natural state of this stuff, the state costing least in energy, is one in which many fields are non-zero.

(2) Alternatively the word 'vacuum' – particularly in the phrase 'false vacuum' – can indicate that while fields aren't quite in their energetically lowest, fully stable states, they are at least *metastable*: there are less energetic states into which they might fall, yet they

are, so to speak, trapped behind barriers over which it is hard to shove them. Like balls unable to roll downhill because they are resting in hollows, they are at fairly stable 'local minima'. A sufficiently powerful push would change matters. It might conceivably be a push given to the fields by an experimental physicist.

As Hut and Rees commented, it may be that 'the vacuum state we live in is not the absolute lowest one' because on many physical theories 'a local minimum of the effective potential, which can be quite stable, can exist for certain parameter values. The Universe, starting at a high temperature, might have supercooled in such a local minimum.' In this case we should find ourselves in a false vacuum. Fields wouldn't be at their lowest energies, the ones to which they would like to fall. It would follow that 'our vacuum state' – space of the sort we live in – 'might suddenly disappear if a bubble of real vacuum formed'. The bubble would expand 'at close to the speed of light, with enormous energy release', right through the galaxy and then onwards indefinitely. Might 'such an unfortunate event' be triggered by 'a new generation of particle accelerators'?

As had been pointed out by Coleman and De Luccia, this would be 'the ultimate ecological catastrophe'. Inside the expanding bubble, 'the new vacuum', there would be 'new constants of nature'. 'Not only is life as we know it impossible, so is chemistry as we know it', since all protons would decay as soon as they were hit by the advancing bubble wall. Worse still, there would be no hope that the new vacuum would in due course come to sustain 'if not life as we know it, at least some structures capable of knowing joy'. For the space through which the bubble had expanded would suffer gravitational collapse in 'microseconds or less'.[85]

Hut and Rees found the danger unimpressive. Colliding cosmic rays, they argued, had reached energies very much higher than those of particles smashing together in all currently envisageable accelerators. So far, collision energies in our accelerators have climbed only to about four times 10^3 GeV (four thousand billion electron volts). The now cancelled Superconducting Supercollider would have produced collisions merely ten times more energetic. What impressed Hut and Rees was that cosmic rays had been observed with energies up to about 10^{11} GeV (10^{11} being one followed by eleven zeros).

Suppose a very energetic cosmic ray strikes a relatively slow moving particle, for instance a proton in Earth's upper atmosphere or a less energetic cosmic ray. The resulting immediate release of energy is fairly small, only about the square root of the ray's kinetic energy. What are important are instead the rare occasions on which two very energetic cosmic rays collide head on. How often, we have to ask ourselves, would there be a head-on collision between 10^{11} GeV cosmic rays? Or rather, how often would such collisions have occurred *inside our past light cone*? Any collisions *outside* this light cone couldn't have become known to us, because calling an event 'outside our past light cone' means that not even light would have had enough time to carry the news of it to us.

Among collisions occurring inside the light cone, Hut and Rees calculated, perhaps one hundred thousand had released energies in the 10^{11} GeV range. Quite probably not even a single collision had released an energy exceeding 10^{12} GeV – but even 10^{11} GeV is millions of times beyond what the Superconducting Supercollider would have reached. It could well seem right to conclude that high-energy experiments would never endanger the human race. Unfortunately, however, such a conclusion is far from being firmly established, for various reasons:

(1) To begin with, it is virtually impossible to say what energies might be reached by sufficiently ingenious experimenters. In their *From Quarks to the Cosmos* (1989), L. M. Lederman and D. N. Schramm – the first a former Director of the Fermi National Accelerator Laboratory and the second a leading astrophysicist – noted that the energies available in laboratory experiments had increased roughly tenfold in each decade since the turn of the century. This relationship, they wrote, 'has continued to hold into the 1980s and will continue to hold if we can build the SSC within the next decade'. Simple extrapolation leads to the prediction 'that we should have the technology to achieve Planck-scale energies by about the year 2150. Skeptics will now surely be outraged. Just wait! Obviously, that technology would involve something radically different from present technology.'[86]

Planck-scale energies are of roughly 10^{19} GeV, which is ten million to a hundred million times above the 10^{11} to 10^{12} GeV which Hut and Rees gave as the energy released by some cosmic ray collisions. With a continuing tenfold rise in each decade, however, energies above 10^{11} GeV would be had well before the year 2100. Already people have proposed 'plasma particle accelerators' in which the fields accelerating the particles – perhaps fields produced by two laser beams which create a rapidly moving interference pattern called a 'beat wave' – would be many thousand times stronger than those of present-day accelerators.[87] In his *Dreams of a Final Theory* S. Weinberg speculates that with plasmas to transfer energy 'from powerful laser beams to individual charged particles' even Planck-scale energies might be attained.[88]

D. Burgess and H. Hutchinson give details of developments in this region.[89] Until the late 1980s the beams of even the most powerful lasers, filling rooms the size of aircraft hangars, could be focussed to an intensity of only about 10^{19} W/m^2 (ten billion billion watts per square meter). Soon afterwards, 10^{22} W/m^2 was reached: a thousand times more powerful, some hundred billion trillion times the intensity comfortable for reading a book, and enough to produce great physical pressure – about a billion kilograms per square centimeter. The lasers used were 'T-cubed' ones, a joke of a name which stands for 'table-top terawatt'. Generating pulses of terawatt (10^{12} watt) power, they still managed to fit onto surfaces measuring eight feet by four.

At Imperial College, focussed intensities of 10^{22} W/m^2 were reached by one such laser in 1988, in pulses of about a trillionth of a second. (Much beyond the intensities of the two-terawatt, five-millionth-of-a-second pulses produced by discharging electrical capacitors in MAGPIE, Mega Ampere Generation for Plasma Implosion Experiments, also at Imperial College. Note, though, that the MAGPIE capacitors are charged just by drawing, for a minute and a half, less power than is needed to boil a kettle.[90]) Five years afterwards, lasers ten times as powerful had been made.

Fed into plasmas, Burgess and Hutchinson calculate, beams even in the 10^{20} W/m^2 range could generate fields equalling the one which binds together the electron and the proton of a hydrogen atom: fields about a million times stronger than those generated by lightning flashes. Acting over a mere ten centimeters, these fields could accelerate electrons to energies such as they reach only after many circuits of the twenty-seven-kilometer ring of the LEP accelerator in Geneva.

Another possibility would be to reach great energy concentrations in the laser light waves themselves. Even sound waves from a small loudspeaker, concentrated about a trillion times just by being used to make a flask of water vibrate, have raised temperatures at their point of convergence to perhaps in excess of 100,000 °C.[91] For drilling holes, focussing of laser light to about a micrometer (a thousandth of a millimeter) has long been practised.

Among the sources of electromagnetic waves which physicists have so far developed, the most powerful are the hard-X-ray lasers of President Reagan's SDI or 'Star Wars' project. While the energy outputs of the lasers are secret, they are at any rate much greater than that of the hangar-sized Nova Laser of the Lawrence Livermore National Laboratory. This can deliver one hundred thousand joules, energy enough to raise a kilogram weight by about ten thousand meters, in a burst lasting a billionth of a second.[92] The National Ignition Facility laser proposed to replace it would be about twenty times more powerful.

In 1988 the US Department of Energy relaxed secrecy sufficiently to reveal that Livermore's nuclear fusion programme – needing powerful lasers to compress pellets and heat them to 100,000,000 °C, it was pursued in parallel with SDI laser research – was progressing so well that a new laser with pulses of ten million joules was contemplated.[93] Each pulse would rival the explosion of two kilograms of TNT. This laser, though, would be designed to operate many times. The SDI lasers, in contrast, would be vaporized after generating single pulses because they would be powered by small nuclear bombs. An X-ray laser pumped by a one-hundred-kiloton bomb might generate not just ten million joules, but *ten trillion*. This would be what was needed to destroy an intercontinental ballistic missile during its far-distant acceleration phase, given that the laser beam would be distributed over a spot perhaps two hundred meters in diameter.[94]

Could such lasers be used to exceed cosmic ray collision energies? Laser pulses which might seem very brief could still have their energies spread over periods much greater than those of collisions between particles (cosmic rays are protons, helium nuclei and occasional heavier nuclei) which were moving at nearly the speed of light. Several techniques of pulse compression are available,

113

however. They delay a pulse's successive elements to different degrees, so that the entire pulse reaches the target at virtually the same moment. Compression by about a thousand times can be achieved by simple acousto-optic delay lines or, when a pulse has a mixture of frequencies varying with time, by using gratings to direct components with different frequencies along paths of different lengths. With light of a single frequency, one can use a crystal whose refractive index varies in response to a rapidly oscillating electric field.

We remain faced with the impossibility of bringing any mere wave to a focus narrower than its wavelength. Now, there is quite a gap between an SDI X-ray laser's 10^{-9} meter (millionth of a millimeter) wavelength and the circa 10^{-15} meter which is characteristic of cosmic rays. Still, use of tremendously energetic pulses could help compensate for this. So could techniques for generating 'higher harmonics': that is to say, of processing beams so as to increase their frequencies and hence reduce their wavelengths. The original discovery in this area was that passing laser light through a quartz crystal could lead to frequency doubling. Greater frequency increases were next obtained with other crystals acting singly or in combination. Later still, increases by over a hundred times could be had: intense laser beams tore electrons from atoms but then allowed them to spring back, which made them radiate at the higher frequencies.[95]

If anything is obvious here, it is that physicists in search of higher and higher energies are confronted by no clearly unsurmountable barriers. In view of recent developments, the once popular idea that Planck-scale energies could be reached only by accelerators as large as the galaxy has come to seem quaint. Here are some points to bear in mind. (a) Carefully synchronized, lasers could send their pulses to a focal point at the same instant despite being at considerable distances from it. Huge numbers of lasers could therefore combine their energies. (b) X-rays are hard to concentrate with lenses or 'image-making' mirrors, but focussing might instead use funnels. Funnels already provide the best means of focussing sunlight: R. Winston reports focussing by 84,000 times and a theoretical limit of at least 140,000 times, far higher than could be achieved by any mirror which formed a tiny image of the sun.[96] (c) Various phenomena tend to make laser beams 'defocus', yet the beams can also undergo considerable 'self-focussing' not just in solids (an effect which at one stage limited laser powers by shattering the lasing rods) but in plasmas as well. (d) Burgess and Hutchinson write:

> Many other areas are being explored. For example, the ability to ionise matter in a single optical cycle, in less than a hundredth of a picosecond [i.e. less than a hundred-trillionth of a second], has spawned ideas not only for particle accelerators but for so-called photon accelerators which might be able to increase dramatically the frequency and shorten the duration of a light pulse.[97]

(2) Is vacuum metastability a ridiculous fantasy? As was noted by J. Ellis, A. Linde and M. Sher, many physicists 'would not like even to consider the possibility that we live in an unstable vacuum state'. Yet, they pointed out, the particle physicist's standard model – the Glashow–Weinberg–Salam model – indicates that we indeed live in such a state if the top-quark mass exceeds 95 GeV plus six-tenths the Higgs-boson mass. It might well do so, for tests had suggested that the top quark weighed between 100 and 160 GeV, while the Higgs boson was perhaps as light-weight as 41 GeV.[98] More recent tests give a top-quark mass of near to 200 GeV. This figure might seem alarmingly high, but some currently popular theories view it as a sign of a Higgs boson massive enough to exclude the danger entirely, as J. Demaret and D. Lambert say.[99] The main characteristic of this area, in fact, is that nobody is in the least sure about it. It isn't even clear that Higgs bosons exist, or whether they would come in several masses; and if one goes beyond the simple standard model to a 'supersymmetric' one, then, R. A. Flores and Sher point out,[100] 'the proliferation of parameters makes any attempts to find limits meaningless', so we simply couldn't know whether our vacuum would be stable against an energetic push. Plainly, our sole security lies in keeping below the cosmic ray collision energies which Hut and Rees estimated.

In fact, we ought probably to keep quite far below them. The crux is: how lucky are we that no disastrous collision has occurred inside our past light cone? (That is to say: inside the segment of space-time in which a bubble of true vacuum, expanding at virtually the speed of light, would have meant that we simply shouldn't be here to discuss the affair.) Now, the Hut–Rees collision-energy calculations may have involved two risky simplifications:

(a) For a start, Hut and Rees assumed 'a homogeneous distribution of ultrahigh-energy particles', as is suggested by the fact that cosmic rays seem to come to us with more or less equal intensities from all directions. What if the assumption were wrong? Might this make a dangerous difference? Not so, they argued. For while clumping of the particles would reduce the probability of their colliding inside typical volumes of space, collisions would be specially probable elsewhere: in particular, in the regions where the particles were produced. But this perhaps invites the protest that in those regions, and maybe elsewhere, clumping – possibly channelling by magnetic fields – might operate so as to separate particles moving very rapidly in opposite directions, these being precisely the particles whose collisions could lead to disaster. (Magnetic fields do have some channelling effects on cosmic rays, and neutron stars and quasars send out narrow beams in opposite directions.) Again, channelling might set up a situation in which very energetic particles, *if they collided even once*, would collide in numbers large enough to destroy vacuum metastability not just once but many thousands of times – but correspondingly they would be many thousands of times less likely to collide *even once*. On the other hand, Ellis wrote to me, 'if cosmic rays are clumped in galaxies, as many expect, this can only increase the probability of collisions between cosmic-ray particles, as compared to the case where the same number of particles is distributed evenly through space'.

(b) The other perhaps risky simplification was this. It was assumed that the right things to calculate were the collision probabilities inside *a typical* light cone stretching backwards from today. Yet our ability to carry out calculations itself guarantees that no disastrous collision has occurred in *our* past light cone, regardless of whether past light cones of this size typically include many such collisions. The fact that we are here to observe anything may have set up an observational selection effect. (Something rather similar might explain our failure to detect technologically advanced extraterrestrials. All over our universe, beings who developed technologically advanced civilizations might almost always perform disastrous high-energy experiments. Thereafter, no observers could

116

exist inside their future light cones, i.e., at points from which those
civilizations could be seen. You cannot observe an experiment when
it has destroyed you, let alone one which has killed off all the life
forms which could have become your ancestors.)

Complex studies – Sher cites 465 other papers yet warns that
they may suddenly be 'swept into the dustbin' by new findings –
indicate that not only collision energies but the details of the
resulting fireballs could be crucial. For example: bubbles of true
vacuum, particularly if extremely energetically produced, might
shrink instead of expanding because they started off too small.
And accelerators or other devices might generate fatal bubbles
more efficiently than cosmic rays could. Accelerator beam intensities are great. This makes it specially probable that further
high-energy particles, or very massive particles, would arrive
soon after collisions to facilitate bubble growth or that, out of a
great many subcritical bubbles, at least one would exploit quantum
uncertainties and grow: 'it may not be likely, but it only takes one
event'.[101]

There are two main theoretical reasons for suspecting that our
vacuum might be dangerously far from complete stability:

First, as already mentioned, the particle physicist's standard
model says that incomplete stability would result from some fairly
plausible masses of top quark and Higgs boson, while other models
are unable to tell us which masses might lead to it. The Higgs
boson is the particle of a Higgs scalar field. The field's existence
has yet to be confirmed: scalar fields have no directionality of the
kind which makes a magnetic field detectable with a compass
needle. However, both the standard model and its main competi-
tors do need scalar-field particles to explain why other particles are
massive, rather than massless like the photon.

Second, much evidence suggests that the cosmic region probed
by our telescopes is 'fine tuned for observers' in the following
sense: tiny changes in particle masses, and in the force strengths
which reflect those masses, would have made it a region in which
observers could never have come into being. This can in turn
suggest that scalar field strengths are products of chance, which
would allow randomization of particle masses and force strengths
over a large number of cosmic regions. We observers would
then, of course, find ourselves in a cosmic region tuned in

observer-permitting ways. Now, when a field's actual strength *was due to chance*, mightn't it quite easily be made to alter disastrously? Let us now look at these two ideas in detail.

(A) No particle could possess mass intrinsically without destroying the mathematical completeness of the standard model.[102] Starting from signs that differences between force strengths lessen as temperatures rise, theoreticians have developed the following tale. Instead of gravity, electromagnetism, and the nuclear strong and weak forces, there was just one 'unified force' during early stages of the Big Bang. All particles were massless (i.e. they lacked rest-masses, as photons do even today). Cooling then produced one or more scalar fields which destroyed the force unification, a process called 'symmetry breaking'. Interacting with such fields, particles would become massive to degrees which depended on the field strengths. This would in turn fix the relative strengths of gravity, electromagnetism and other forces.[103] For when the particles on which it acts are more massive, a force will be effectively weaker. Again, it will be effectively weaker when mass is added to the 'messenger particles' which convey it, because very massive messenger particles can travel short distances only.

(B) The strength of any scalar field might conceivably be dictated by some grand unified theory or Theory of Everything. But it could instead be a random affair – and thus able to change inside a tiny bubble which then expanded all-destroyingly.

What is known as the 'fine tuning' of our universe can seem fairly good evidence of the affair's randomness. Chapter 4 of my *Universes* listed many physical mechanisms which might perhaps lead to the existence of multiple universes, otherwise known as 'sub-universes' or 'worlds', or in Russian writings 'metagalaxies': huge cosmic domains, each largely or fully separate from the others, which could have very different properties, perhaps because of scalar field differences. (A few philosophers still insist that the word 'universe' must mean Absolutely Everything, there then being only a single universe no matter how thoroughly it is chopped up into domains, but today's cosmologists typically use the word differently.) Inside a gigantic cosmos, the universes might look rather like individual ice crystals on a pond. But they might alternatively be separated in time, for instance as successive oscillatory cycles of an oscillating cosmos (Big Bang, Big Squeeze, Big Bang, etc.), or they might be 'buds' which had been completely pinched off from other regions in an ever-expanding cosmos. Some theorists picture all of them as born from the same space-time foam. Others suggest that they spring into existence entirely independently. What excuses could there be for actually believing in such marvels? Perhaps the chief excuse is this. The existence of *multiple universes with randomized properties* could tidily explain why there exists at least one universe, ours, with properties 'fine tuned' in ways permitting observers to exist.

Various claims about the fine tuning were discussed in Chapter 2 of *Universes*.[104] Just in case the reader is interested, here are a few details of them:

1 The early cosmic density and the associated expansion speed had to be tuned to perhaps one part in 10^{12} or even 10^{60}, if gas clouds were to condense into galaxies. An appropriate density and expansion speed may have been produced by cosmic inflation – tremendously rapid expansion at very early instants – but the factors producing this inflation could then themselves have needed tuning with the same or greater accuracy.

   Here one meets the famous 'cosmological constant' or 'vacuum energy density' problem: the problem of why a number which one would expect to be huge is instead very tiny.[105] This point will be developed in just a moment.

2 The strength of the nuclear weak force had to fall inside narrow limits if any hydrogen (for making water and long-lived, stable stars) was to come out of the Big Bang, and if the proton–proton and carbon–nitrogen–oxygen cycles were to make stars into life-encouraging sources of heat, light, and elements heavier than helium.

3 The nuclear strong force had to be what it is, to within plus or minus 5 per cent, for stars to burn at life-encouraging rates instead of exploding like H-bombs or else not burning at all.

4 The strength ratio between gravity and electromagnetism may have required extremely accurate tuning, perhaps to one part in 10^{40}, for there to be sunlike stars. And slight increases in electromagnetism's strength would have destroyed all atoms (by

converting quarks into leptons), caused protons to repel one another so powerfully that hydrogen was the only possible element, or made chemical changes extremely slow.

5 The strength ratio between gravity and the nuclear weak force could have needed tuning to one part in 10^{100}, to prevent space from contracting or expanding furiously.

6 Quite small changes in the masses of various superheavy particles would have resulted in a universe just of light rays or else just of black holes, or made all matter intensely radioactive.

7 The existence of solids and of chemistry demanded that the electron be much less massive than the proton. Further, for life's purposes the neutron–proton mass difference had to be just about twice the mass of the electron. Otherwise the Big Bang would have yielded only neutrons or only protons, rather than the couple of hundred stable nucleides which are the basis of chemistry and biology.

In attempting to explain such apparent instances of fine tuning, Russian writers have proved markedly keen on the idea that the visible universe – meaning the region, a few billion light years in radius, which is all that we can see, because light from anything more distant couldn't yet have reached us – is only a domain inside a far huger cosmos, and that the life-permitting properties of this domain are due to scalar fields which simply chanced to take appropriate strengths.[106] Linde writes: 'The inflationary universe becomes divided into an exponentially large number of inflationary mini-universes' in which scalar fields 'roll down to all possible minima'. Thus the cosmos as a whole 'becomes divided into many different exponentially large domains, realizing all possible types of symmetry breaking': 'in the inflationary universe there is lots of room for all possible types of life'.[107]

In *Dreams of a Final Theory*,[108] Weinberg is particularly open to such reasoning in the case of the 'total or effective cosmological constant', generally believed to control our universe's expansion speed. This constant is at present either exactly zero or very near zero. Many physicists prefer to think of its value as dictated in some presently unknown manner by fundamental physical laws.

When meeting a figure like zero, their instincts are against treating it as a product of chance. Therefore, they reason, there could be no real danger that some high-energy experiment would jolt the constant down to a disastrously lower value, as would be allowed by various theories that don't ban large *negative* values of the constant. But, says Weinberg, it might well be better to treat the constant 'anthropically'. By this he means considering it as able to take very different values: values which it may actually have taken in universes or cosmic regions other than the one we inhabit. All such places would be expanding or contracting too quickly to be habitable by observers of any plausible kind.

Instead of introducing multiple universes, randomized properties, and *observational selection* due to how living beings can observe only the universes that have life-permitting properties, mightn't one prefer to believe in *divine selection*? God, it could reasonably be argued, would have grounds for creating properties that allowed living beings to evolve.[109] However, it would be unwise to rely on God to guarantee us against a vacuum metastability disaster, an all-destroying bubble of new-strength scalar field. God might be a fiction. Or God might have created infinitely many universes, then relying on chance to throw up an infinite number which were life-permitting thanks to how scalar fields happened to take appropriate strengths – until such time as intelligent beings upset them by their experiments. Belief in God's goodness in no way commits us to thinking that God guards us against all evils, and it could be very wrong to think that all God's eggs would have to be in a single basket, our own little universe or cosmic region.

Brandon Carter has written to me that while vacuum metastability is interesting, 'given all the other more obvious dangers that surround us I cannot say it adds significantly to my alarm'. His attitude could well be correct. Still, clever folk might shrug off the dangers which he calls 'more obvious'. They could tell themselves that not even nuclear or biological warfare would put an end to the human race. Shrugging is far harder to justify in the present instance. The physics of vacuum metastability is extremely difficult, and the potential disaster is utterly irrevocable.

On the other hand, there is nothing like hard evidence that high-energy experiments could be dangerous, whereas it might nowadays seem clear that such things as climatic instability might very easily be all-annihilating. So (as was stressed to me by Ellis, who heads the theory division at the European Organization for Nuclear Research) we mustn't forget that high-energy experiments may provide the only genuine prospects for achieving much understanding of fundamental physical laws, understanding which could be essential to staving off disasters that threaten us in the near future. Also that energies greater than those considered safe by Hut and Rees might be thought very unlikely to be reached within the next couple of centuries.

IGNITING THE ATMOSPHERE; CREATING QUARK MATTER

We now come to two possible sources of risk which I take much less seriously, although it might be wrong to disregard them entirely.

When physicists considered performing experiments at very high energies, fears of vacuum metastability were by no means the first to be voiced. As R. Ruthen writes,[110] 'Since the beginning of the nuclear age, researchers have met many times to discuss whether there was any chance that a proposed experiment might initiate a catastrophe.'

Probably the earliest such heart-searching took place when the first nuclear weapons were being developed. E. Teller 'proposed to the assembled luminaries the possibility that their bombs might ignite the earth's oceans or its atmosphere and burn up the world'.[111] J. R. Oppenheimer, the project leader, took the proposal fairly seriously. People were soon persuaded that there was no danger, a post-war technical report declaring that 'the impossibility of igniting the atmosphere was assured by science and by common sense'; yet it is hard to see how mere common sense could have had much to say about a matter complicated enough to have worried the likes of Teller and Oppenheimer. Note that when H. A. Bethe stated in the *Bulletin of the Atomic Scientists*, June 1976,[112] that an enormous safety factor would always be present, he felt a need to qualify this by adding 'unless, some time in the future, nuclear weapons of entirely different type are designed which produce much higher temperatures'.

Of course, neither the atmosphere nor the oceans (where, Bethe adds, 'the problem is more subtle') have been ignited even by H-bombs. This presumably proves that 'objectively', 'out there in reality', the risk has been zero at the temperatures so far attained. What had seemed potentially dangerous, though, were deuterium–deuterium and proton–deuterium reactions. Now, during the recent furore over reports that 'cold fusion' had been produced in a test tube, S. E. Koonin and M. Nauenberg calculated that in some circumstances deuterium–deuterium fusion would proceed some ten billion times faster than had previously been estimated, while proton–deuterium fusion would be yet faster, by a factor of a hundred million.[113] Naturally, these authors might be wrong. And supposing they were right, the reactions in question would, as they say, be nowhere near fast enough to produce interesting amounts of cold fusion. What is more, cold fusion and nuclear bombs would have little in common. Still, this tale does at least illustrate how alarmingly unreliable the calculations of experts can be.

Further calculations preceded the start-up of Bevalac, an accelerator producing violent collisions between atomic nuclei. S. D. Gupta and G. D. Westfall report:

In the early 1970s Tsung Dao Lee and Gian-Carlo Wick discussed the possibility that a new phase of nuclear matter might exist at high density, and might lie lower in energy than the most common type of matter in a nucleus. The Bevalac seemed to be the ideal instrument with which to make and discover this new matter. If it existed and was more stable than ordinary matter, it would accrete ordinary matter and grow. Eventually it would become so massive that it would fall to the floor of the experimental hall and be easily observed. But what would stop it from eating the Earth? [Eating it entirely, that's to say, by converting it all into matter of the new type.] Knowledge of dense nuclear matter was so poor at the time that the possibility of this disaster was taken seriously. Meetings were held behind closed doors to decide whether the proposed experiments should be aborted. Experiments were eventually performed, and fortunately no such disaster has yet occurred.[114]

123

Ruthen explains that the decision to proceed was inspired by the argument

> that nature had already performed the relevant experiment: the Earth, moon, and all celestial bodies are constantly bombarded with an extraordinary number of high-energy particles that are produced by stars. Some of the particles collide with atoms on the earth and create conditions that equal or surpass anything that Bevalac could do.[115]

Bevalac has since been replaced by accelerators reaching still higher energies, but it appears that any high-density matter produced in them expands and disintegrates quickly.

In ordinary matter the atomic nuclei – made of protons and neutrons, which are in turn composed of 'up' and 'down' quarks – are severely limited in size because the electric force between the protons tends to blow large nuclei to bits. What Lee and Wick had envisaged was a type of 'quark matter' which wouldn't be restricted in this way.[116] As we have seen, their fears proved to be unfounded, but subsequent writers have produced a variant on them. They have suggested that quarks could indeed form stable lumps of almost any size if 'strange' quarks were added to the mixture. The nuclei of the resulting 'strange-quark matter' – 'strange matter' for short – would have a very small electric charge. If the charge were positive then the nuclei of ordinary matter would be repelled, in which case nothing unfortunate would occur. But, E. Farhi and R. L. Jaffe pointed out, strange matter might instead have nuclei which were negatively charged and surrounded by positron clouds, in which case

> the situation is radically different. Ordinary atoms would be attracted to it and absorbed. In contact with a supply of ordinary matter it would grow without limit. Clearly, negatively charged strange matter would have disastrous consequences, converting everything it touched into more of itself.[117]

Unfortunately, they said, theoretical calculations in this area are extremely difficult: 'the only definitive demonstration of the existence and properties of strange matter will come from experiment'.[118]

Ruthen comments:

> Can theorists be absolutely certain that an accelerator will
> never spawn a voracious clump of strange matter? The ques-
> tion was first posed seriously in 1983, when researchers were
> designing the Relativistic Heavy Ion Collider (RHIC). The
> collider, now under construction at Brookhaven National
> Laboratory, promises to be the world's most powerful
> smasher of heavy atoms and could quite possibly generate
> strange matter. Piet Hut put everyone's fears to rest. Applying
> the same logic his predecessors had used, Hut showed that
> innumerable cosmic particles collide with atoms on the earth
> and moon, creating conditions far more extreme than those
> of RHIC.[119]

However, the situation might merit some further commentary:

(1) Heavy nuclei in RHIC will reach collision energies of about
10^2 GeV. Hut and Rees estimated that in the cases of cosmic rays
consisting of heavy nuclei the highest energies so far observed are
'only 10^9 GeV, or $10^{4.5}$ GeV in the centre of mass frame of atmospheric collisions'.[120] Of these two figures, the second (which is the
square root of the first) is the relevant one, because we aren't now
concerned with what would have happened if two heavy nuclei
had suffered a head-on collision somewhere inside our past light
cone. Instead we are considering the situation when a heavy nucleus
hits Earth's atmosphere so as to be able, conceivably, to 'seed' a
strange-matter disaster. It seems, then, that an accelerator just
a few hundred times more powerful than RHIC could reach the
lower edge of a zone of energies which might just conceivably
be dangerous. Note that the Large Hadron Collider, presently
under construction, is expected to reach collision energies of about
1.4×10^4 GeV.

(2) Strange matter may perhaps continually strike the atmosphere
in small nuggets, ejected from colliding neutron stars or quark
stars. (Quark stars would consist largely or entirely of quarks.
F. Dyson, E. Witten and others have suggested that all alleged
neutron stars are in fact quark stars.) The nuggets might be responsible for some observed cosmic ray showers because hitting the
atmosphere could break any sufficiently small ones into very tiny

bits, each maybe consisting of just a few dozen quarks.[121] Any Earth-eating effects of a lump of strange matter might appear, though, only when it was both larger and slower moving. In effect, it might have to be a lump produced by physicists. (a) *Being larger* could be needed to give enough stability against, in particular, rapid radioactive decay. (We thus couldn't rely on an argument exactly parallel to that of Hut and Rees, reasoning that collisions of heavy-nuclei cosmic rays would long ago have caused any strange-matter disaster that was physically possible. Each cosmic ray collision could create only a very, very tiny lump of strange matter. Before such lumps reached the surface of our planet they could have plenty of time to undergo decay processes.) (b) *Being slower moving* could be important for the following reason. Quark nuggets rushing in from outer space would probably pass right through the Earth like bullets through a cloud if they weighed above a tenth of a gram.

The usual view is that any lump of strange matter, instead of attracting ordinary matter and converting it, would repel it ever more strongly the heavier it grew. Jaffe has written to me that all-attracting, all-consuming, negatively charged strange matter didn't occupy 'a favoured region of the parameter space explored by myself and Farhi': in other words, its existence could seem unlikely on grounds of the very same kind as made it seem possible. Also that if such matter were stable in bulk, then one would expect the same to be true of tiny lumps of strange matter which were instead positively charged. Such lumps 'would be rather easy to make in astrophysical processes' so that one might hope to find them on our planet, yet searches for them had been markedly unsuccessful.

All the same, F. Close could have been right in summing up the situation as follows:

> The theory of quark matter is very delicate and it is not certain whether it implies that strange matter exists. But it has at least made us aware that the observed stability of the familiar nuclei need not imply that we are made of the most stable forms of matter. It would be a bizarre joke if the most stable state for Nature was not realised somewhere. And if large amounts reach Earth someday, then . . . ?[122]

(3) An article by G. L. Shaw, M. Shin, R. H. Dalitz and M. Desai proposed bombarding a target with heavy nuclei to make drops of strange matter. The drops would immediately be passed through a linear electrostatic decelerator, made to grow very fast by absorbing neutrons from a tank of liquid deuterium, and collected in a magnetic bottle. The drops were to be grown as fast as possible in the hope of increasing their stability. The experiment might then produce strange matter in bulk when previous experiments and natural processes had all failed (with the possible exception of the processes creating ultradense stars). Very small initial drops would rapidly be given greater stability by a growth which increased their masses by over a hundred times, after which slow neutrons would be fed to them to push their masses and their stability to still higher levels.[123]

If the process described in the article could be made to work, it could form a superb source of energy: the drops would emit energetic radiation whenever more neutrons were fed to them. On the other hand – a topic on which the article is silent – the escape of a drop from its magnetic bottle might conceivably have the apocalyptic consequences which Farhi and Jaffe described. Jaffe's letter to me notes that if such drops could be grown to useful sizes 'then gravity would pull them out the bottom of any known confining device'.

Desai and Shaw elsewhere repeat the commonly accepted argument for feeling secure: if strange matter of the dangerous, negatively charged type were possible then a disaster would have been produced long ago, through a cosmic ray hitting Earth's atmosphere and creating a droplet of such matter.[124] But for the reasons I gave earlier, this argument's success is unclear. A cosmic ray could produce only a very tiny droplet. Perhaps this would decay long before it had any real chance to consume ordinary matter and grow.

We must, however, bear in mind the possibly immense benefits of the technology suggested by these authors. As a source of energy, it might solve a great part of the pollution problem, thereby considerably increasing the human race's chances of prolonged survival.

CREATING A NEW BIG BANG

What about producing a new, world-destroying Big Bang by mistake? While this, too, is a risk we may well find hard to take seriously, it might still seem worth discussing.

Cosmologists almost all accept the idea of early cosmic inflation.[125] When the Big Bang had proceeded for a very short while, there was a sudden burst of accelerated expansion. Like a rabbit population uncontrolled by foxes, a tiny initial blob doubled in volume again and again, exploiting the fact that the energy of a gravitational field *is negative*. A. H. Guth explains:

> Imagine two large masses, separated by a very large distance. The masses will attract each other gravitationally, which means that energy can be extracted as the masses come together. Once the masses are brought together, however, their gravitational fields will be superimposed. Thus, the net result is both to extract energy – and to produce a stronger gravitational field. If the absence of a gravitational field corresponds to no energy, then any nonzero field strength must correspond to negative energy.[126]

The remarkable outcome is that the energy density of the inflating cosmos would remain virtually constant. After each doubling in its volume, its every cubic millimeter would have virtually the same mass-energy as before. There would thus be no clear limit to the number of doublings it might undergo.

Linde suggests that when its inflation ceased the cosmos had grown by a factor of $10^{1,000,000}$ (one followed by a million zeros). A region originally stretching 10^{-33} centimeters (a billion-trillion-trillionth of a centimeter) would by then have grown immensely larger than the volume now visible to us: our cosmic horizon, set by the distance which light could have travelled towards us since the inflation ended, is only about 10^{28} centimeters away. So, Linde comments, there would be nothing problematic about 'the creation of all the matter in the observable universe (10^{50} tons) by gravitational forces operating inside a domain which originally contained less than 10^{-5} grams of matter'.[127]

Might human experimenters compress into a very tiny region, something like 10^{-33} centimeters across, the amount of matter which Linde contemplates, namely about a hundred-thousandth of a gram? And if so, might they start a new Big Bang? Linde writes that the idea 'is highly speculative, to say the least', but that we ought not to discard this possibility. A promising approach could be to compress a slightly larger amount of matter into a slightly larger region, and then rely on quantum fluctuations to trigger inflation. Simple estimates in the context of Linde's preferred 'chaotic inflation' scenario suggest that compression of somewhat less than one milligram of matter would be sufficient.[128]

Linde's 10^{-5} grams and 10^{-33} centimeters aren't chosen arbitrarily. They are roughly the Planck mass and the Planck length, quantities very important to physics and often considered to give the 'natural' mass and size of any newborn Big Bang situation. The Planck mass is equivalent to the energy consumed by an automobile between gasoline refills. While the most energetic cosmic rays may collide like rifle bullets, a collision which released this amount of energy would be like that of two small jet aircraft. Physicists speculating about creating a Big Bang in the laboratory have, however, been happy to imagine compressing mass-energy not just of some small fraction of a gram, but of several kilograms. Farhi and Guth wrote:[129] 'According to the inflationary model, the observed universe grew out of a region with a spatial size of less than 10^{-24} centimetres and a mass of less than 10 kilograms', making it natural to ask whether we ourselves could create a new Bang by compressing energy sufficiently. Although the requisite energy density, some 10^{76} grams per cubic centimeter, would necessitate a compression 'far too high to be provided by any known technology', the actual energy involved might be only the same as is released by a large H-bomb.

Further consideration, Farhi and Guth reported, seemed to show that no amount of compression would suffice. The equations suggested that a new Bang would have to start with a high-density bubble *which had no prior history* so that no laboratory could possibly have produced it. Still, 'a sufficiently weird bubble geometry' might overcome this difficulty. So might effects permitted by a quantized version of general relativity, a point developed in detail by a second paper by Farhi, Guth and J. Guven.[130] Its authors judged that Bang-creation at a GUT (Grand Unification of Forces) scale, with the newly created situation having a mass of 'about

10 kilograms' before inflating, was 'prohibitively unlikely'. On the other hand, the trick might well be possible 'at energy scales approaching the Planck scale'.

This last remark raises the question of whether the 10-kilogram figure, corresponding to an energy of around 10^{28} GeV, really is the right one. Calculations in the area, pursued further in another paper by S. K. Blau, E. J. Guendelman and Guth,[131] are extremely complex and far removed from well-established facts: at one point, for instance, these authors take a guessed energy density, square it, and then square the result. Besides, Linde has written to me that 10 kilograms is far too high a figure: 'it was obtained in the old inflationary scenario which is dead, then in the new inflationary scenario which I suggested in 1982 and which is almost dead. 10^{-5} grams appears in the chaotic inflation scenario which I suggested in 1983' – and which he and many others have defended ever since. It can certainly seem easier to understand the origins of our own universe if it commenced just as a 10^{-5} gram, 10^{-33} centimeter quantum fluctuation which then inflated, rather than as something a billion times larger and more massive. A. A. Starobinsky and Y. B. Zeldovich comment:

It is natural to begin with a closed universe whose radius is of the order of the Planckian one (10^{-33} cm), filled with some matter or quantum fields, whose density is of the order of the characteristic Planckian density. One needs the inflationary stage to develop from the Planckian size.[132]

Are there any real dangers here, even granted that the correct figure is 10^{-5} grams rather than 10 kilograms? Farhi and Guth state that any new Bang which we created would be merely the birth of a 'child universe' which expanded 'at no cost to the parent'. 'We would not be destroyed by a universe that we might create', for, thanks to 'the non-euclidean nature of the geometry', the new universe would expand into a space of its own.[133] To us it would appear only as a tiny black hole. Yet their paper is dotted with such disquieting phrases as 'we cannot be decisive', 'we have not excluded', and 'our entire discussion has been in the context of classical general relativity'. Heaven knows what surprises a quantized version of general relativity might perhaps have in store for us.

130

As explained further by Blau, Guendelman and Guth, the notion that we are safe is based on the idea that the child universe, *as seen from inside its parent*, would grow very rapidly smaller, despite how its volume *as seen from inside itself* would be growing at an ever-increasing rate.[134] No matter how much this may go against common sense, it can be acceptable in cosmology. Still, the topic is an extremely difficult one. Has anybody the right to be completely confident about it? Wouldn't there be at least some slight risk that the child would inflate into the innards of its parent?

Linde has drawn my attention to a seemingly very powerful ground for thinking ourselves safe. As he had written:[135] 'One cannot 'pump' energy from the new universe into ours, since this would contradict the energy conservation law.' An expanded version of the point might run as follows. We could create a new Big Bang only if its total 'energy cost' were zero or very small, as would be so if the (negative) gravitational energy of the newly created child universe were in exact or almost exact balance with all the other energy in it. But any such balance would be destroyed if the child universe had to do a great deal of work – which is what it would indeed have to do if it were inflating disastrously into its parent.

Regrettably, it isn't entirely plain that this line of reasoning succeeds. It is often said that the concept of total energy cannot be applied to a universe in any straightforward way,[136] or at least cannot be applied to a Big Bang universe at around the time of its creation, when its gravitationally induced curvature is extreme. It could seem, then, that there remained at least some slight risk that a new Bang, although we had created it at no great cost, might in its earliest moments come to have all the energy needed for destroying us.

3

JUDGING THE RISKS

—— .•. ——

This chapter makes a rough attempt to say which are the
most dangerous threats to the human race. It also identi-
fies general arguments that are relevant to evaluating the
threats: for instance, arguments about whether the world is
deterministic, which can be important to the force of the
doomsday argument.

GENERAL PROBLEMS OF RISK ANALYSIS

Analysing risks is a discipline with a large literature, including the
journal *Risk Analysis*: for a quick introduction see M. G. Morgan's
'Risk analysis and management'.[1] So far, though, the field's com-
plexities have made it only rather poorly developed. The fact that
smoking puts you in grave danger of cancer and other diseases was
doubted for quite some time by statisticians, yet the latest findings
from a forty-year study of British doctors indicate that one smoker
in two will die from the habit, a proportion much higher than
previously believed. Again, it has recently been discovered that the
strengths of many links between causal agents and risked disasters
have been systematically underestimated. Suppose you want to
know, for example, what increased risk of heart attack follows from
your high blood pressure. Well, those whose blood pressure is
usually high may have it measured when it is low, and vice versa.
Taking proper account of this, one finds that high blood pressure
is 60 per cent more of a risk factor than had been thought.

When such intensively studied medical risks, involving events
repeated in the lives of vast numbers of people, are so hard to
measure, it clearly won't be easy to get a trustworthy figure for

133

the risk, say, of nuclear war in the next ten years, let alone for the risk of extinction for everyone by the year 2400. To further complicate matters, ethical considerations enter into calling something 'a risk'. Suppose you considered that if humankind were to become extinct then this would be rather a good thing – or at least (see Chapter 4) that *merely possible lives*, lives which would in this case never be lived, couldn't have been in any ethically interesting sense 'lost to the world'. You might then refuse to speak of 'risks' of human extinction. And presumably you wouldn't accept that even a tiny chance of human extinction ought to be avoided at almost any cost.

This chapter will simply assume that human extinction would be a disaster and that any chance of it, tiny or great, would be something about which people ought to be warned. I don't buy the argument that talking of the risk of doom spreads despondency, thus increasing the danger. The argument is precisely what some powerful people want to hear, so that it can be business as usual, pollution as usual, and votes as usual for dangerous activities.

FACTORS IMPORTANT TO EVALUATING RISKS OF DOOMSDAY

Carter's doomsday argument

After what has just been said, it should come as no surprise that some centrally important principles of risk analysis have only lately been noticed and are sometimes violently resisted. Brandon Carter's doomsday argument is a prime example. As will be examined at greater length in Chapter 5, the argument exploits the fact that we ought to prefer (other things being equal) those theories whose truth would have made us more likely to find whatever we have in fact found. While this might seem fairly evidently forceful, many risk analysts have failed to reject Carter's argument only because they have never come across it. They haven't thought of asking themselves – and would positively refuse to ask themselves – where a human could expect to be in human history.

As explained in the Introduction, Carter is an applied mathematician who does ask it. He points out that if the human race came to an end within, say, the next two centuries, then quite a large proportion of all humans would have found themselves where you and I do: in a period of extremely rapid population growth which immediately preceded extinction (and probably helped produce it). If, on the other hand, the human race were to survive for another thousand centuries, then the late twentieth century would have been a period of human history occupied by (proportionately) hardly any humans at all: perhaps far fewer than 0.001 per cent of all the humans who would ever have been born. This ought to decrease our confidence that humankind will have a long future. Carter's reasoning may be controversial, but it is correct, as Chapters 5 and 6 will try to demonstrate.

Not just what might kill many people, but what might kill all of us quickly

Those influenced by Carter's argument could be interested in how long the human race might conceivably survive if it got past the next few centuries safely. They could want to consult such articles as Dyson's 'Time without end: physics and biology in an open universe', Frautschi's 'Entropy in an expanding universe', or Linde's 'Life after inflation',[2] or perhaps books like Islam's *The Ultimate Fate of the Universe*, Barrow and Tipler's *The Anthropic Cosmological Principle*, Tipler's *The Physics of Immortality* or Davies's *The Last Three Minutes*.[3] These discuss whether such things as slow decay of protons and the approach of 'heat death' (maximum entropy) would very obviously limit the future of all beings who might be counted as humans.

Still, there are several grounds for concentrating instead on the near future. One of them, mentioned in the Introduction, will in due course be examined in detail. It is that if humankind's future is *significantly indeterministic*, then Carter's argument cannot lead to any enormous revision of the estimated risk of Doom Soon, not even if Doom Delayed would mean enormously many trillion humans scattered through the galaxy.

Another is this. It could well seem that *only short-term dangers* could be much threat to the very survival of the human race or its descendant races. What can it matter if, for example, the sun will become a red giant and boil the Earth's oceans some five billion years down the road? If they had survived until then, humans or their descendants could be expected to have spread to Pluto, or to space colonies positioned at a comfortable distance, or to the neighbourhoods of other stars. Humankind's eggs would no longer be all in the one basket. Not unless, that's to say, a vacuum metastability disaster – see Chapter 2 – swept through the galaxy at virtually the speed of light. But the chances of such a disaster can seem tiny, while those of its happening in the distant future could be negligible: the necessary high-energy experiment would have been performed much earlier, or would have been banned.

Any good library can provide plenty of material on O'Neill cylinders each serving as a space habitat for up to ten million people,[4] or on ideas for making the atmospheres of Mars or Venus breathable at a cost of a few trillion dollars, or plans for pushing galactic colonization forwards at a sizable fraction of the speed of light, either with humans or with machines clever enough to be persons. Just on my shelves at home, there are fascinating discussions of all this in Barrow and Tipler's *The Anthropic Cosmological Principle*; in Brand's *Space Colonies*; in Close's *End*; in Davoust's *The Cosmic Water Hole*; in Dyson's *Disturbing the Universe* and *Infinite in All Directions*; in McDonough's *The Search for Extraterrestrial Intelligence*; in Rood and Trefil's *Are We Alone?*; in Sagan's *Cosmos*; in Shklovskii and Sagan's *Intelligent Life in the Universe*; in Sullivan's *We Are Not Alone*; and in Tipler's contribution to Rothman et al., *Frontiers of Modern Physics*.[5] Some of the suggestions in these and similar books involve speculative technological advances. For instance, they concern use of nuclear fusion or of antimatter in rocket engines, or accelerating a light-sail to tremendous speed with lasers, subsequently using it to deposit nanomachinery which manufactures braking-lasers to stop the massive passenger vehicles that follow.[6] But back in the 1970s G. O'Neill had persuaded many people that kilometer-long cylinders for ten thousand space colonists could be made quickly and inexpensively with the technology then already available. And the chemical-rocket technology of those days – let alone the small H-bombs of Project Orion, each accelerating a spaceship just a bit faster,[7] an idea studied intensively in the US until the treaty banning nuclear explosions in space – could itself conceivably have been used for sending space colonists to the neighbourhoods of other stars, albeit slowly: the Voyager spacecraft are travelling at a speed which could take them to the nearest star in forty thousand years.

Accelerated first by ground-based lasers and then by sunlight, and using the light of the target stars for deceleration, light-sails could today do the job at higher speed and smaller cost;[8] and there have been various further suggestions, some of them now quite old, for space travel using fairly low technology.[9] It could well seem, then, that the human race is sure to have become secure against imminent extinction, more or less regardless of whatever disasters thereafter hit the Earth, within five centuries from now, if only it manages to survive for that long. What is surprising is that so little has been done to develop Earth-based artificial biospheres to get us through whatever disasters those centuries may hold.

People were all too quick to criticize the poor science behind 'Biosphere 2' (see Chapter 1: oxygen levels dropped disastrously). What they tended to forget was that it had been left to a single individual, E. Bass, to provide the necessary $150 million in funding. If one-hundredth as much had been spent on developing artificial biospheres as on making nuclear weapons, a lengthy future for humankind might by now be virtually assured.

Always remember that for doomsday-argument purposes we aren't interested just in whether such things as a pollution crisis would mean misery and death for billions. Misery and death for billions would be immensely tragic, but might be followed by slow recovery and then a glittering future for a human race which had learned its lesson. What is crucial to the doomsday argument – and, I'd say, the issue most important from an ethical viewpoint – is whether anything could put an end to all humans.

Fermi's question

If we believe that interstellar travel would be easy for any civilization just a little more advanced than ours, we face E. Fermi's *Where are they?*: the question of why our solar system seems not to have been visited by extraterrestrials, while radiotelescope searches show no signs of them. If intelligent life is common in our galaxy, why didn't extraterrestrials colonize Earth long ago? Whereas the galaxy is in the region of ten billion years old, calculations suggest that once a civilization had begun space travel its spread from end to end of its galaxy would take a few million years only. Dyson was the first to publish a figure, giving roughly ten million years,[10] while other estimates have usually ranged between three hundred million and three million (although Tipler has argued for something as low as six hundred thousand).[11]

Ought we, then, to join the flying-saucer spotters who claim that extraterrestrials have in fact been seen? It could seem better to join Barrow and Tipler[12] in reflecting that Earth could easily be the one and only place in the galaxy where advanced life (or any life) had been going to evolve. It is little use arguing that we need to treat the intelligence-carrying planet on which we find ourselves as fairly typical until we get evidence to the contrary – for if there were instead only a single intelligence-carrying planet in the universe, where else could we intelligent beings find ourselves? Very possibly, almost all galaxies will remain permanently lifeless. Quite conceivably the entire universe would for ever remain empty of intelligent beings if humans became extinct. Very primitive life might itself arise only after chemicals in some primeval soup had combined in highly improbable ways.[13] The leap from primitive life to intelligent life could also be very difficult. And even if it were easy it might well not be made, because there was so little evolutionary advantage in making it. Think of the clever and curious animal putting its head into some dark hole and getting it snapped off.

In view of all this we have a strong duty not to risk the extinction of the human race, and above all not to risk it for utterly trivial benefits. As soon as it became fairly clear that CFCs were efficient at destroying stratospheric ozone, their use for spraying deodorants into armpits ought to have been banned outright and world wide.

Note, however, that our failure to detect intelligent extraterrestrials may indicate not so much how rarely these have evolved, but rather how rapidly they have destroyed themselves after developing technological civilizations. What strength we see in this point will depend, naturally, on how weak we think the competing suggestion that intelligent life evolves only very rarely. Suppose, though, that we do think it strong. This ought surely to affect our estimates of many risks discussed in Chapters 1 and 2 because presumably other fledgling technological civilizations would often face much the same risks as we do.

Other suggestions as to why we have detected no extraterrestrials in our galaxy are much less plausible, I tend to think. It can seem unlikely that extraterrestrials have spread right through the galaxy without our noticing it (perhaps because they treat our solar system as an untouchable zoo, or maybe because they are hidden in the asteroid belt); or that they have one and all been happy to stay at home; or that they haven't been travelling for long enough, since they developed advanced technologies only a little before us; and so forth. Very many such suggestions have been expertly defended none the less: see a fascinating review by G. D. Brin, 'The "Great Silence"'.[14]

Observational selection

Discussing how naturally occurring diseases had failed to push humankind to extinction, Chapter 1 commented that an observational selection effect might be involved. Suppose the universe has many planets inhabited by intelligent species, the pathogens 'winning' almost everywhere. Our planet must then be among the few where the pathogens have not triumphed, else we'd not be here to observe and discuss the matter. Again, our past light cone – the segment of space-time containing all the events of which we could yet have received news – couldn't have contained the kind of vacuum metastability disaster discussed in Chapter 2, because any such disaster would wipe out observers as soon as the news of it reached them.

Such *observational selection of an undisastrous past* could make it dificult to argue that we must be safe because nothing terrible has yet occurred, not even after millions or billions of years. H. B. Nielsen writes:[15]

> We do not even know if there should exist some extremely dangerous decay of say the proton which caused eradication

of the earth, because if it happens we would no longer be there to observe it and if it does not happen there is nothing to observe.

Presumably he has in mind some very rare decay-mode which sets off a vacuum metastability disaster. Might he then reasonably mean that the non-occurrence up till today of any such disaster inside any region, its boundaries leaping forward at virtually the speed of light, which would by now have engulfed our planet, *should count for nothing*? Might this make specially good sense in an infinitely large universe containing countless life-bearing planets, or in a finite universe which (see Chapter 2) had inflated enormously at early moments, a universe of which we can see only a very tiny fraction?

Compare how H. P. Moravec is impressed by a story in which a powerful new particle accelerator repeatedly fails to start up, always through seemingly atrocious luck: a fuse blows, a janitor trips over a cable, a little earthquake triggers an emergency cutoff, and so on. Moravec asks himself whether many-worlds quantum theory could throw light on the affair. On this theory the universe, and every observer in it, keeps branching into more and more versions. In most cases the accelerator does start up, causing a vacuum metastability disaster. Observer-versions can, however, detect only universe-versions in which luck has prevented this.[16] Now, could *that* make sense?

The right approach is as follows, I think. We must first ask how confident we are in the theories which make past disasters *not* to have been expected. (1) Suppose our confidence in them is great. We can then more or less disregard the suggestion that the absence of past disasters is a sign of observational selection. (2) But what if our confidence in those theories is instead low? We should in this case take the idea of observational selection seriously, *provided that* it seems reasonable to believe in a realm of actualities – for instance many actual planets carrying intelligent beings and their pathogens, or many actual branches of the branching universe described by many-worlds quantum theory – inside which observational selection could operate. (The principle being used here is 'No Observational Selection Effect Without Actual Things from which to Select'. Imagine that all the marksmen in a fifty-man firing squad have missed you. Don't just comment that if they hadn't all missed then you wouldn't be considering the affair – unless, that is to say, you really believe in billions of firing squads and potential victims. Ask the janitor to steer clear of the cable and keep trying to start up the particle accelerator – unless you think that the many worlds of many-worlds quantum theory actually exist, instead of being mere useful fictions.)

Suppose, now, that we are trying to make sense of the fact that Earth hasn't been hit by an asteroid big enough to wipe out all intelligent life. We ought to give some force to the point that observational selection could be operating. The notion of many other Earthlike planets inhabited by living beings, all exposed to asteroid bombardment, mustn't simply be dismissed. But first, there are various reasons for doubting the existence of such other planets. And second, it seems that asteroid impacts roughly follow the law that impacts which are ten times larger occur ten times less frequently: calculations may then suggest that an impact big enough to destroy all life on Earth *wasn't* to have been expected. Those would be two grounds for doubting that observational selection was at work.

How about the case of naturally occurring diseases? Chapter 1 suggested that pathogens 'take care' not to wipe out their hosts. Since this gives a plausible explanation of why our ancestors weren't wiped out, we should once again hesitate to speak of observational selection. We ought not to reject the very idea of it, however. Whether by little or by much, it certainly should reduce our confidence in a long future for humankind.

New risks

The fact that the human species has survived past diseases might (as Chapter 1 pointed out) be unimpressive in view of today's new conditions: the population crisis, megacities, pollution, international travel and trade. The risk that the entire species would be wiped out by disease might thus be classified as 'largely new'. In contrast, the danger of asteroid impacts appears unlikely to have increased just when the population began to grow enormously. Asteroid impacts would therefore seem to present a risk that is 'old'. The fact that all our ancestors have survived it can suggest strongly that you and I will survive it too.

Would it be of much help to inquire how long biological species in general, or mammalian ones in particular, have survived in the past? I think not, because humans form such an unusual species. No minor heatings or coolings of the planet, no slight changes in natural vegetation, are likely to make humans extinct. They needn't fear some new predator species, come to gobble them all up.

Is it important to ask whether previous human population explosions have ended in disastrous crashes? Once again, today's situation might seem so novel that the past couldn't be much guide to what we might need to fear. Still, both Carter – writing to me in 1989 – and Brin[17] point to the case of Easter Island, 'for so long isolated as to be virtually a separate planet' (Carter), 'as much like an interstellar colony as any place in human history, when settled around AD 800' (Brin). The island's inhabitants underwent a population explosion, utterly destroyed the virgin ecosystem, and were very nearly pushed into extinction in the resulting wars.

Risks largely neglected in this book

Trying to examine the main threats to the survival of humankind, I have left a host of apparently minor ones undiscussed. For example, I was silent about the idea that people might bring back some deadly germ which had survived on Mars after most of the Martian atmosphere and water were lost. Yet astronauts returning from the moon, a far less likely habitat, were treated with disinfectants just in case. And I failed to mention the recent successes (well verified) of R. Cano and M. Borucki in reviving 25–40-million-year-old bacteria and fungi from inside insects entombed in amber. Their tests for novel antibacterial, antifungal and antitumour effects are said to have had promising results, but might ancient diseases be resuscitated, against which modern organisms had little resistance?

Again, I didn't discuss Moravec's idea that the universe 'is prowled by stealthy wolves that prey on fledgling technological races'. The wolves 'may be simply helpless bits of data' – perhaps carried by radio waves – 'that, in the absence of civilizations, can only lie dormant in multimillion-year trips between galaxies'. Whenever, though, 'a newly evolved country bumpkin of a technological civilization' stumbles upon one and acts on its instructions, enticed perhaps by 'blueprints for a machine that promises to benefit its hosts', it engineers 'a reproductive orgy that kills its host and propagates astronomical numbers of copies of itself into the universe'.[18] Brin likewise speculates about 'deadly probes', self-replicating machines that destroy 'any unrecognized source of modulated electromagnetic radiation' such as the radio waves of *I Love Lucy*, which have spread 'well past tau Ceti by now'.[19] Moravec and Brin suggest that such killers could arise by evolutionarily successful mutation, so to speak: their ancestors might have been designed to spread benefits through the galaxy. Sorry, but these are scenarios I do not take seriously.

I might, however, find it hard to say exactly why not: there may well be many dangers I dismiss too quickly. And there must be others mentioned in the literature which I have failed to discuss simply through not having heard of them, the field being such a wide one.

There are also risks which haven't been mentioned on the grounds that I know so little about them or that (like the risk that a disaster will happen because there is no single individual who can be sued or sacked[20]) they are rather hard to classify. Could some mind-destroying chemical be so addictive that, introduced into tapwater by would-be drug barons, it caught all of us in its net? And how much danger is there of a world-wide economic collapse caused by the huge US governmental, commercial and household debt, twice the size of each year's gross national product?[21] Might human extinction actually spring from something like that? Or from stock-market trading in 'derivative securities'? This trading, most of it unregulated, has an annual volume approaching the combined gross national products of the United States, Europe and Japan, so that, P. Wallich reports,[22] 'observers have begun to worry that a major misstep could vaporize financial markets'.

Again, with crime now a global industry whose annual turnover is of roughly a trillion dollars, an amount almost equalling that spent on military activities,[23] and with more than a million convicts in US prisons, should we take seriously the old warning that a civilization plagued by just 1 per cent criminality would return to Stone Age conditions? Or could a single extremely rich hater of humankind represent a still greater threat?

Something of which I may have said too little is the difficulty of persuading people that various acts are evil. Computer hackers can think it good, clean fun to try to break into systems controlling nuclear weaponry. In the Second World War, great Allied statesmen saw little wrong with the firestorm in Dresden, a city of not the slightest military value and crammed with women and children. The scientists developing the atomic bomb contemplated poisoning half a million Germans with strontium – radioactive and accumulated by living bone – if the bomb itself couldn't be produced. ('There is no better evidence anywhere in the record of the increasing bloody-mindedness of the Second World War than that Robert Oppenheimer, a man who professed at various times in his life to be dedicated to *Ahimsa* ("the Sanscrit word that means doing no harm or hurt", he explains), could write with enthusiasm of preparations for the mass poisoning of as many as five hundred thousand human beings', R. Rhodes exclaims.[24]) In a world in which one-fifth of the people have four-fifths of the wealth, making the distinction between terrorist and freedom fighter so difficult to draw, this kind of historical background can be frightening.

Still, I don't want to suggest that deliberate acts of producing firestorms in German cities, or even the atomic bombings of Japan, were very obviously and very purely wicked. The argument that the war was thereby shortened, and millions of lives saved, cannot be rejected out of hand. Being influenced by the long-term benefits to be expected from one's actions can be a lot preferable to following always some primitively simple, stubbornly inflexible set of moral rules while mouthing virtually meaningless words such as 'The ends don't justify the means.' (When a surgeon says he is causing some pain to save a life, is this 'using ends to justify means'? Whether or not it is, there's nothing wicked in it.) Remember that disaster can be brought to us not only by the vicious but also by those who self-righteously deny obvious facts. Those, for instance, who claim that schizophrenics aren't really ill (and so shouldn't be kept away from nuclear weapons?), or that censorship (perhaps of instructions for filling water supplies with deadly viruses?) always has bad results, or that democratic decisions are always best – despite how a committee of three rational people can vote that A is better than B, which is better than C, which is better than A.[25]

COMPARING THE RISKS, AND TRYING TO GUESS THE TOTAL RISK

Let me now make some guesses about the seriousness of the various threats.

Even after taking the doomsday argument into account, there remain many grounds for hope and none for absolute despair. For a start, there's the fact that the doomsday argument could be much weakened if the world were indeterministic, which is what many people think it to be. This will be discussed in just a moment.

Next, it seems that supernova explosions, solar flares, mergers of black holes or of neutron stars, large-scale volcanism or impacts by asteroids or comets are very unlikely to kill all of us in the near future. Now, as was said earlier, it is probably only the near future that we need consider, because humans can be expected to spread throughout the solar system fairly soon. They could thereafter survive in great numbers regardless of whether all Earth's inhabitants were destroyed.

How about natural diseases? Megacities, air travel, etc. do tend to make them more dangerous, yet this could be more or less counteracted by advances in medicine. Even if not, the diseases appear unlikely to kill absolutely everyone.

It seems still less likely that a collapse of banking systems, or systems (perhaps computer-controlled) for distributing food, water or electricity, would exterminate one and all, although the results could well include famine and anarchy.

Ozone layer destruction, greenhouse warming, the pollution crisis, the exhaustion of farmlands and the loss of biodiversity all threaten to cause immense misery. Yet they too might well appear unlikely to wipe out the entire human race, particularly since people could take refuge in artificial biospheres. Now, a few surviving thousands would probably be a sufficient base from which new billions could grow. The same can probably be said of global nuclear warfare. Artificial biospheres could maintain the human race if the remainder of the planetary surface became uninhabitable.

Advances in nanotechnology might be very perilous. However, there is every hope that they wouldn't be made before humans had moved far enough towards a single world government to be able to insist on safeguards. Furthermore, colonization of the entire solar system, and perhaps even of other star systems, would probably be progressing speedily when the nanotechnological revolution arrived – so that, once again, destruction of all humans on Earth wouldn't mean the end of humans as a species.

Risks from high-energy experiments – the most important one would be of upsetting a metastable vacuum – seem to me unlikely to materialize despite my confidence (which only a few physicists share) that extremely high energies are likely to be had in the next three centuries. I expect it will be found, either by theoretical investigations or because no disaster in fact occurs, that the vacuum state which we inhabit is fully stable, while strange-quark matter can exist only in ultradense stars.

All the same, the above-discussed dangers can be impressive enough to destroy complacency. And I think the chief risks have yet to be mentioned. Genetic engineering seems to me one of them, particularly because of its possible uses in biological warfare or in the hands of criminals. Another is that intelligent machines will come to replace humans – although, at least if the machines exploited quantum effects in achieving unity of consciousness (see Chapter 2), it perhaps isn't clear that this would be a disaster. Finally, we may well run a severe risk from something-we-know-not-what: something of which we can say only that it would come as a nasty surprise like the Antarctic ozone hole and that, again, like the ozone hole, it would be a consequence of technological advances.

I nevertheless feel inclined to say that the probability of the human race avoiding extinction for the next five centuries is encouragingly high, perhaps as high as 70 per cent. Also that if it did so, then it would be likely either to continue onwards for many thousand centuries or else to be replaced by something better.

Still, it's extremely hard to be sure. Mere expressions of confidence in the resilience of human beings, the cleverness of scientists, the wisdom of our elected representatives, strike me as sickeningly glib. Although the imminent extinction of humankind is the constant theme of crackpots, it might conceivably be very likely. In words which Brin applied (with far less excuse) to another matter: aversion to an idea, simply because of its long association with crackpots, gives crackpots altogether too much influence.[26]

To end the chapter, let us take a closer look at how risk estimates are affected when we see force in Carter's doomsday argument.

DETERMINISM, INDETERMINISM AND THE DOOMSDAY ARGUMENT

Although Carter's argument gives grounds for re-evaluating the danger of imminent human extinction, these grounds would (as the Introduction noted) necessarily be weakened in an indeterministic world. Indeterminism would mean that there wasn't yet any suitable 'firm fact of the matter', in theory available to anybody who knew the present situation and the laws of physics in sufficient detail, concerning how many humans remained to be born before humankind became extinct: compare the fact that exactly this or that many names remain in an urn after your own name has been drawn from it. Carterian efforts to re-estimate the risk of Doom Soon – to attach a probability to the prospect, for instance, that no humans would be alive after the next five hundred years – would be hindered by this.

Just how much would they be hindered? Perhaps any indeterminism might be considered unimportant. It might be believed that 'the number of names still to come out of the urn', the number of humans remaining to be born, was already virtually settled to within a few billion because, for instance, the world was so polluted that Doom Soon was virtually inevitable, or because the only serious threat was from comets or asteroids whose movements were deterministic.

However, it might be believed instead that indeterministic factors had considerable importance. Carter's argument would then serve mainly to reduce extreme confidence in humanity's chances – the

147

kind of confidence which leads some people to say that a long future for the human race is *as good as determined.*

Is the world in fact indeterministic? Do we have clear signs that events, as well as being very largely unpredictable by, say, gamblers in casinos, are radically undetermined? Imagine another universe which was today precisely like ours, right down to its tiniest details. Might it develop very differently from ours in future years?

Here it is crucially important to distinguish *radical indeterminism* from *unpredictability by us.* As discussed in Chapter 2, workers in the fast-growing discipline of chaos theory can point to numerous examples of 'the butterfly effect'. Many chains of events develop in ways very delicately dependent on their starting-points. Could it be important whether a particular butterfly flapped its wings in Australia at a given moment? Perhaps it could, for it might conceivably decide whether Florida was ravaged by a hurricane a few months later. But this, crucial though it is for many purposes, is a matter quite distinct from whether the world is radically indeterministic. Take two worlds to which chaos theory is markedly applicable. A tiny difference between them today – maybe a difference in something as small as the radioactive decay of a single atom – would make these worlds develop differently enough to change the number of people living fifty years later. But if the worlds are in fact *precisely the same* and *entirely deterministic,* then they will develop in precisely the same way for as long as they remain in existence.

In short: the phenomena noted by chaos theory, while they render it much harder to arrive at initial estimates of the risks, aren't by themselves enough to affect Carter's grounds for revising those initial estimates. Carter's point is weakened if the number of people who will ever have been born hasn't yet become settled by the laws of physics and the situation at the present moment; but if the world is deterministic, then this number has indeed been settled by these things. Like the date of the next major earthquake in California it is knowable 'in theory' (i.e. by Laplace's demon of vast calculating powers who perceives today's world in all its details without in any way disturbing it) despite our own inability to know it. A butterfly's wings may influence it, but the wings will then be influencing it in ways which were determined ever since the Big Bang.

People are led to believe in indeterminism by two main arguments which we must now examine. One is that quantum physics demands that they believe in it. The other is that complete determinism would make humans unfree.

(A) *Does determinism destroy freedom?* The word 'free' behaves in a very complex fashion, often under a heavy load of philosophical and theological theories. A much-disputed matter is whether determinism would make people unfree in ways affecting the justifiability of blame and punishment. 'If misdeeds were fully determined from the beginning of time', it may be asked, 'where would be the justice of punishing? What good could it possibly do?'

It certainly strikes me as very unfair to send a murderer to hell in an afterlife for deeds which it had been determined that he would commit – so that if the world could somehow be rewound like a clock, he would commit them anew. And it might next be thought that the same would apply to punishing the murderer here and now. If the murder had been part of a fully deterministic pattern, then the punishment would be wildly unjust, on this view of the matter. But be that as it may, punishing the murderer here and now could definitely do some good. In a fully deterministic world, the movements of billiard balls could still be influenced usefully by such things as the movements of other billiard balls. The fact that a ball's movements were determined wouldn't enable it to go on its merry way, no matter what other balls did. Likewise: in a fully deterministic world people's actions could still be influenced usefully by praise and blame, reward and punishment. The fact of a murderer's imprisonment could deter other people from murdering.

I myself happen to have been converted by the arguments of the thousands of philosophers, 'compatibilists', who see no real conflict between freedom and determinism. Determinism wouldn't involve predictability of a simple kind. If determinism made humans into 'machines', then their machinery would be every bit as complex as the machinery of the weather – and this, remember, is something which a butterfly's flutterings could make unpredictable, at least by any forecaster who lacked divine powers. Further, even a divinity might be powerless to predict *to a man himself* how he would act, for the man could be obstinately resolved to do just the opposite of whatever was predicted. (Very simple machines can mimic this. A child could construct a device whose red light went on when you pressed the key marked 'Green light will go on', and vice versa.)

Some determining factors do, of course, erode freedom. Determinism involving stone walls and iron bars can keep you in prison, unfreely. Determinism involving drug addiction or a brain tumour, or guns pointed at your head, can reduce freedom or destroy it utterly. At a first approximation, being free is being able to make up your own mind about how to act. Imprisonment, drug addiction, etc. may put this beyond your control. In contrast, today's primitive chess computers do, I think, make up their minds about how to act, in some fairly important sense.

Now, it is tempting to say that being a free person *just is* being the sort of person who, because of being able to make up his or her own mind, can properly be blamed and punished for bad actions. Many philosophers think that blame and punishment, because of being able to do a great deal of good by deterring murders etc., could be *morally right* in a deterministic world. Others are attracted by the argument that anybody could be free only to the extent that he or she acted deterministically: the sole obvious alternative to determinism is randomness, they say, and you surely wouldn't consider yourself free if you thought of your decisions as random. Yet the issues involved here are difficult, and this book is not the place for long discussion of them.[27] Further arguments for the compatibility of freedom and determinism are developed by David Hume, John Stuart Mill, J. L. Mackie, D. Odegard and I. Tipton.[28]

(B) *Is quantum physics indeterministic?* Quantum theory is often thought to deliver a clear message: that the world's very smallest events are governed by statistical laws only. Seeing large numbers of these events together, we discover largely predictable regularities. Compare how we would find (almost always) just about exactly five tons of heads and five tons of tails, when ten tons of coins had been tossed. But whereas the way in which a particular tossed coin was about to land might be knowable, perhaps by a physicist with superbly efficient detectors and a super-fast computer, there might be absolutely no fact of the matter about exactly when a particular uranium atom will decay, or exactly where the very next quantum of radiation will be emitted from a heated filament. Not even God could know these things, it is often said. J. von Neumann actually claimed to give a firm proof that quantum theory's uncertainty relations – they connect time, position and energy – characterized reality itself, instead of just setting limits to what humans can know.[29] Standard quantum theory could thus never be supplemented by a more complete theory which described underlying deterministic mechanisms.

Philosophers tend, however, to be suspicious of such attempts to 'prove a negative': to show, that is to say, that something is non-existent instead of merely being hard to find. Reacting to von Neumann, W. C. Salmon wrote that in the interests of achieving a thoroughly deterministic theory 'the present quantum mechanics could be replaced – not merely supplemented'.[30] In *The Mysterious Universe* Sir James Jeans told a story about worms which felt sure that raindrops sprang into existence at random. Moving only over the Earth's surface, the worms knew nothing of the weather's three-dimensional machinery. Mightn't we be like them, ignorant of some important dimensions of the real?

Physicists speculate about 'hidden variables' which determine precisely how events happen at the quantum level. Experiments inspired by J. S. Bell have established that 'local' hidden variable theories cannot be right. Even when quite far separated in space and in time, particles can have properties correlated in ways which cannot be explained by supposing that each particle had been carrying some record of a decision about how to behave, a record formed when they were last in contact and consultable ('locally') when the time came for the decision to be carried out. But as Bell himself was quick to say, 'non-local' hidden variable theories, for example the one defended by D. Bohm, can survive this difficulty. According to such theories, far separated events can have a connectedness permitting them to influence one another deterministically and instantaneously.

Would such instantaneous linkage conflict with Einstein's theory of relativity? No, for it couldn't be controlled, and so couldn't be used for faster-than-light signalling.[31] It is as if, seeing a coin landing heads in New York, we were blessed with immediate knowledge that its partner tossed in London was landing tails, yet knew also that we couldn't in any way have influenced how the coins would land.

Bohm's views are particularly interesting because they represent a dramatic change of mind. His *Quantum Theory* of 1951, for long the subject's standard textbook, had strongly defended indeterminism. In coming round to attacking it instead, Bohm made great use of the idea that the quantum potential (a factor central to all quantum mechanics) could be interpreted as a force whose effects depended only on its form, not on its intensity, so that it could act across considerable distances. While rather hoping that the world included some element of absolute randomness, Bohm suggested that apparently undetermined happenings might in fact be products of a determinism so complex that we couldn't possibly keep track of it. 'Non-local' effects – instantaneous linkages between systems maybe at great distances from one another – could easily bring about complexity of this sort.[32]

T. Boyer and H. Puthoff have developed another way of replacing standard quantum theory by a refurbished classical and deterministic physics.[33] Their 'stochastic electrodynamics' takes classical physics and adds a background of ever-fluctuating zero-point fields. 'Zero-point' is an adjective torn from the term 'zero-point motion'. This refers to a jittering which particles would have (according to quantum physics) at temperatures right down to zero. Puthoff suggests that zero-point fields drive the motions of particles throughout the universe, these motions in turn giving rise to the fields 'in a self-generating feedback cycle'.[34] Calculations based on such an approach are in good agreement with experimental findings.

These ideas by no means exhaust the possibilities. Whether the world is radically indeterministic is therefore very much an open question. True enough, we are sadly ignorant of what individual particles are about to do, and our ignorance cannot be explained in any straightforward fashion. (In the famous double-slit experiment, opening a second path down which a particle might travel *decreases* our ignorance of where it will end its journey. Just try explaining that straightforwardly! The mere fact that *interrogating a particle about its present movements involves disturbing it in unknown ways* won't do your job for you.) All the same, the future may contain nothing which hasn't been settled by the past.

COMBINING ESTIMATED RISKS WHEN USING THE DOOMSDAY ARGUMENT

The estimated total risk of Doom Soon cannot possibly exceed 100 per cent, no matter how greatly it is magnified by doomsday-argument considerations. It is therefore very wrong to apply these considerations to risks taken individually. We need to consider the entire packet.

Suppose, for example, that we started by thinking that the risk associated with high-energy experiments stood at 1 per cent, the only other cloud on the horizon being a 9 per cent risk associated with pollution. The doomsday argument might then perhaps encourage us to re-estimate those risks as each eight times greater than they had initially seemed – but certainly not as thirteen times greater, because this would mean estimating the total risk as 130 per cent.

If, on the other hand, we started by thinking that the sole risks were a 2 per cent risk associated with pollution and (just as before) a 1 per cent risk associated with high-energy experiments, then there would be no logical absurdity in re-estimating each of those risks as thirteen times greater.

4

WHY PROLONG HUMAN HISTORY?

—— •◆• ——

This chapter attacks various philosophical doctrines, remarkably popular nowadays, which cast doubt on any real ethical need to keep the human race in existence. (1) Many philosophers think it quaintly out of date to believe that ethical needs, ethical requirements, are 'elements of reality' like geographical or mathematical facts. They interpret all talk of such needs as mere expressions of emotion; or they say that calling acts of certain types 'ethically needful' is just prescribing that everyone is to perform such acts; and so on. (2) Other philosophers have doubted whether the human race should be encouraged to survive if even a small proportion of lives were unhappy. (3) Again, there are those who suggest that duties are always towards people who now exist, or whose existence is more or less inevitable. There can therefore be little call to bring happy people into being unless already existing folk happen to want it.

REAL NEEDS

The possible dangers of denying that good and bad are real

In view of all the threats confronting the human race, very vigorous efforts could well be needed if it is to survive long. Can we tell people that they truly ought to make these efforts? That this is quite as much a matter of *what really is so* as the fact that three fives make fifteen?

155

Many modern philosophers deny that ethical needs involve realities of that sort. I myself find their doctrines profoundly depressing. What if I suddenly became converted to them? I'd inevitably continue to prefer some things to others, and no doubt I'd find myself recommending things to other people. But I think I'd see no real point in painful efforts, or in doing without what I happened to like. From my present viewpoint at least, *real point* looks to be tied to how some things are better than others as a straightforward matter of what's real, of 'the fabric of the world', as an eighteenth-century writer might say, without which all that we could have would be *being really motivated* to seek some things rather than others, which is altogether different. Selfishness itself could have any real point only if various things which selfish people could get for themselves had a goodness which was part of the world's fabric – so I am not saying that being converted to the depressing doctrines would make me see real point only in getting what I liked. I am saying that it would make me see no real point *anywhere*.

Are those remarks tediously autobiographical? John Leslie may be sickened by the idea that nothing is ever 'as a matter of reality' any better than anything else, but he knows many extraordinarily energetic and kind people who accept it. These people often struggle hard to help others to have pleasant lives. Can they fully believe what they say? Aren't they perhaps poor at introspection, or expert at what George Orwell called 'doublethink'? Well, many of them are very intelligent philosophers in the analytic tradition, highly trained to distinguish one idea from another. And they can certainly look to be doing their best to be honest about themselves.

Possibly what all this illustrates is that people can like or dislike just about anything. As Hume remarked, "'tis not contrary to reason to prefer the destruction of the world to the scratching of my finger' – Hume's point being that, at least on one common use of the word 'reason', using reason in deciding how to act is just a matter of such things as not taking poison when you happen to want to improve your health, or not preferring apples to black-berries *and* blackberries to cherries *and also* cherries to apples. There is seemingly no limit to what people can find tremendously unacceptable or tremendously motivating. In ancient Rome, fans of chariot-racing teams enthusiastically murdered the supporters of rival teams. More recently, there have been those whose chief aim in life was to spit tobacco juice as far as possible, while many a man would rather have died than be seen wearing green shoes. Today, some people's idea of supreme self-fulfilment is lying motionless in the sun like crocodiles. Etcetera.

Still, H. Putnam was exploring an interesting point when he wrote these words:

> Imagine a poor peasant boy. Let us suppose he is offered the opportunity to become a member of the Mafia. If he accepts, he will do evil things – sell terrible drugs, run prostitution and gambling rackets, and even commit murders; but he will also live comfortably, have friends and women, and, perhaps, even enjoy a kind of respect and admiration. If he refuses, he will live a life of almost unimaginable poverty. . . . This kind of sacrifice is one that millions of people, millions of the poor, make and have always made. Now I ask you, would anyone make such a sacrifice if he believed that the thing which was impelling him to make it was, at bottom, just a desire to impress (some of) his neighbors, or even in the same ball park as a desire to impress the neighbors? It is all very fine for comfortable Oxford philosophers and comfortable French existentialists to wax rhetorical about how one has to 'choose a way of life' and commit oneself to it (even if the commitment is 'absurd', the existentialists will add). But the poor person who makes such a sacrifice makes it precisely because he does not see it that way.[1]

Mind you, Putnam is notorious for vacillating over what 'reality' means. ('A moving target', he has called himself.) Further, I have just now been suggesting that his attempt at psychology may be faulty. Some people, I strongly suspect, lead self-sacrificing lives although they believe, even 'deep down', that any betterments which they bring to the lives of others couldn't be real in the way that Africa is real, or in which it's real that two and two make four. And, of course, other people are instead convinced that such betterments could be real like that, but have no inclination whatever to produce them. There clearly is a difference between (1) believing in straightforwardly real goods and evils, and (2) being motivated. R. M. Hare, a main defender of the 'prescriptivism' to be discussed in a moment, has repeatedly sworn that he simply cannot understand how his enthusiasm for the things he calls good, i.e. prescribes to himself and to everybody else, could be affected if he came to believe that their goodness was straightforwardly factual. However, people like Hare may be rare outside philosophy departments.

Who would I prefer to have loose on the streets: the man enthusiastic about doing things I consider good, or the one who brings equal enthusiasm to deeds I think evil? The first man, to be sure. I'd prefer him even if he truly believed, deep down, that calling things good was doing nothing more than prescribing them to himself and to everybody. I'd still prefer him even if he held that calling them good simply meant that some very powerful being had commanded them, or that one had a personal liking for them, or that they glowed in some strange fashion which only saintly persons could detect. If you deny that keeping the human race in existence would be good *as a matter of reality*, no doubt this may not matter all that much. The world might run more smoothly if you kept quiet about it, yet it won't make you ipso facto a major menace to humankind. You may still be passionately in favour of keeping the human race in existence.

All the same, let me now mount brief attacks on some of the doctrines I find so disheartening.[2]

Relativism; emotivism and prescriptivism; naturalism; contractarian 'internalization' or 'invention of values'

(a) *Relativism* suggests that being ethically required is rather like being called for by etiquette. Just as correct etiquette varies from country to country, so goodness varies between Mr Smith's world (i.e. the world relative to Mr Smith – or to Mr Smith 'and his society', whatever those vague words mean) and the world of Mr Jones. A thing can be both good and bad: good relative to Adolf Hitler's sincerely adopted moral standards, perhaps, and bad relative to those of Winston Churchill. The case is as with mustard's nastiness or niceness. A blob of mustard cannot have nice-tasting-ness just in itself, in the way that it can be spherical or with a volume of a cubic centimeter. Mustard's being nice-tasting might perhaps be called 'a reality', but this would mean only that it really does taste nice to the people who like it.

An ethical relativist might even state such things as that burning babies alive for fun is absolutely wrong. All the same, there is said to be something entirely relative here. Yes, 'absolutely wrong' *in the sense that* absolutely everybody would be wrong to burn babies for fun, but *not* in the sense that its wrongness is 'out there in the world'. It is wrong simply in relation to standards of rightness and wrongness which our ethical relativist happens to accept. 'But don't you think it very wrong to reject those standards?', we ask. 'Yes indeed', comes the reply, 'but rejecting them still isn't in the least like thinking that Africa is a fiction, or that two and two make five.'

Most philosophers agree that this position utterly fails to capture the ordinary use of ethical words. For one thing, there seems to be nothing odd about the humble statement that one's own present ethical standards (or those of one's 'society', defined somehow or other) contain no actual self-contradictions *but might perhaps be wrong* – yet ethical relativism is unable to make much sense of any such statement.

Note: the relativism which is here in question is quite different from such sensible views as that surgery without anaesthetics may be good relative to a situation in which anaesthetics simply aren't available. Also, the philosophers who argue for it are sometimes no fools. They can avoid woefully idiotic arguments: the argument, for example, that since one can never be sure of what's good and what's bad 'it must all be just a matter of taste' or '*good* can only mean *what I personally think good*'. (Here one reason for saying 'woefully idiotic' is that what you personally think good, or what is to your taste, are precisely the kinds of thing of which you *can* often be sure.)

(b) *Emotivism, prescriptivism and suchlike.* Philosophers often hold that calling something good doesn't describe any reality concerning it: instead it expresses an emotion towards it, or prescribes that everybody, oneself included, shall favour it, or 'grades' it in a manner which doesn't portray any fact about it, and so can't be correct in the way that a geographical or mathematical claim can be correct. (Emotivists, prescriptivists, and those who talk vaguely of 'grading' do very often say such things as that giving food to the starving 'is correctly described as good' or that it's 'a fact' or 'true' that burning babies alive is bad. However, they regard this as just a matter of adopting common speech habits. *The correct analysis of* 'Baby-burning is bad' would still, they say, be something like 'Boo to baby-burning!' or 'I prescribe that nobody is ever to burn babies', rather than 'A complete and accurate map of Reality would show baby-burning's badness.')

Like relativism, these doctrines face the problem of how one could ever say humbly that one's own present ethical standards, even if fully self-consistent, might conceivably be mistaken. A prescriptivist, for instance, can defend calling something 'good' by showing that it really does fit his or her standards, standards which prop one another up by forming a consistent set. Yet declaring that the consistent set which you had accepted on Monday *was wrong*, and that Tuesday's new set *was right*, would simply be saying something like 'I prescribe that everyone is to accept Tuesday's set, not Monday's.'

Another difficulty confronting prescriptivism – but not emotivism, so that this, the 'Boo–Hurrah' theory, as its critics sometimes call it, may actually be marginally the better of the two – is that all sorts of matters could be thought good although no sense could be given to *prescribing them* or to *prescribing acts which favoured them*. Mightn't it be good that the law of gravity continued to hold, or that the universe continued to exist, and yet how could we be prescribing anything here? (Are we prescribing *to God* that he keep the law of gravity operating? What if God doesn't exist, then?) Or mightn't there have been something good about freedom's initial appearance in the world? Yet to whom could we be prescribing what, in this case, even if we rather queerly allowed our prescriptions to apply to people who have long been dead? Before freedom had made its appearance, who could have freely chosen to follow any prescriptions?

What about the torments of animals trapped in forest fires at times long before evolution had produced free beings, beings intelligent enough to follow prescriptions? Couldn't those torments have been genuinely bad?

(c) *Naturalism, and contractarian 'invention of ethics'*. Although doctrines such as prescriptivism can seem very severely inadequate, it is easy enough to understand why philosophers have felt driven to them. You have only to look at the defects of ethical naturalism, the theory that attaching labels like 'intrinsically good' or 'intrinsically bad' to things (objects, events, situations, acts) is a straightforward affair of describing their intrinsic natures, so that 'really being good' means really having these or those *constitutive properties*: the property of being pleasant, for instance, which helps to make some state of mind just what it is. There are two main problems with any such theory. *Problem (A)*: the sorts of things which people often label 'good' form a very ragged collection: knowledge, blessed ignorance, a peaceful state of mind, wild excitement, self-indulgence, self-denial, joy, aesthetically elegant sorrow, respect for tradition, originality, etc., etc. Trying to define real goodness in terms of *properties generally called good*, you can therefore quickly get into a dreadful mess. If you attempt to bring some order to the situation by talking of 'fundamental human wants', then you have to face the fact that many people's lives are founded on wanting appalling things. But to refuse to call something 'really wanted' unless you consider it really needed, i.e. *genuinely good to have*, is of course of no help in deciding where genuine goodness lies. Again, emphasizing how various things are needed *if the human race is to survive* raises the difficulties (1) that many other things could also be considered good, and (2) that Schopenhauer made no very obvious mistake when he held that life's miseries were inevitably so great that annihilation would be preferable. I think Schopenhauer very seriously mistaken – and therefore not trivially mistaken, like the foreigner whose poor command of English makes him say he doubts whether all wives are married. *Problem (B)*: even the goodness of pleasure is non-trivial. People could doubt it without making any merely linguistic error, or perhaps any error at all. When, for instance, pleasure is had through stimulation of the brain's pleasure centers with electrodes, what's so good about it? As this last example illustrates, it looks as if we are faced with two quite separate questions when we ask about intrinsic goodness: the sort of goodness, that is to say, which something can have just through being what it is (in contrast to the goodness of, for example, undergoing

161

a painful operation which is the sole means of saving your life). The first question concerns what a state of affairs is like: is it a pleasant state of mind, perhaps? The second concerns whether a state of affairs *like that* ought to exist. Ethical naturalists can seem to confuse these questions. They appear not to see that while situations can, of course, be *made good* by the properties which make them what they are, 'being good' isn't itself just a synonym for 'having such and such properties' or even for 'having properties drawn from such and such a loosely connected group' (as in the case of being a game, or being a fruit). It instead means *having an existence which is ethically required.*

When a thing has ethically required existence, what is required is, of course, the existence of exactly that thing, and not of another thing. And yes, the thing is made exactly what it is by having various properties: by being, perhaps, a state of mind both exciting and pleasant. But you cannot think that its ethical requiredness is itself one of those properties, or any connected group of them. Not unless you are radically confused about the idea of goodness enshrined in ordinary thought and language.

Now, this point about ordinary thought and language is currently accepted by quite a few philosophers, but often only when in company with another point which strikes me as thoroughly unfortunate: namely that it's quaintly old-fashioned to believe that the real world contains any instances of ethical requiredness as here imagined. The notion that something could have ethical requiredness *in itself* is looked on as 'queer', like the notion that mustard in itself has nice-tasting-ness. The only plausible story, it is urged, runs as follows. People's aims very naturally tend to differ. Codes of behaviour have evolved to minimize the resulting conflicts. The strong social pressures to stick to these codes can make life stressful for individuals unless they 'internalize' them. And they do this most successfully when they come not only to share the wishes of society, but also to treat violators as offending against demands which are in some mysterious way *absolute*. Any suggestion that all that's involved here is *internalized social pressures* will then be indignantly rejected – except, that is to say, by the philosophically sophisticated few, who can tell the difference between convenient fictions and realities.

Military training could provide an illustration. Repeated rewards and punishments gradually instil a burning desire to present a solid front to the enemy, and a contempt for all who run away. But there is more here than mere contempt. There is profound indignation, the conviction that running away is a crime against the nature of things. Suppose Tom and Dan are soldiers manning two nearby strong-posts. With the enemy approaching, each would like to run if he decently could. He will do better for himself by running, no matter what his companion does. But (so a well-developed contractarian story runs) he is held to his post by fictitious bonds which he has come to regard as real. He feels he 'must' support his comrade instead of leaving him to face the enemy alone. He sees 'an absolute called-for-ness' in the act of adhering to a ghostly contract, so to speak: a contract not to run just whenever it would suit oneself. Of course, no actual contract has been signed between Tom and Dan, or between both of them and all their fellow countrymen; yet not even a signed contract could carry much weight. Duties to adhere to contracts couldn't be mere matters of those contracts having signatures on them, not even if the very first of them contained the words 'I contract to adhere to all contracts bearing my signature.' What holds Tom and Dan to their posts is something better: a conviction that helping each other and their country is absolutely demanded. Instead of seeing sergeant majors, military police, and so on as doing the requiring, Tom sees sticking by Dan as having *required-ness in itself*. Tom's error may be virtually as great as thinking that mustard in itself has nice-tasting-ness, but it is a very common error, and traditional ethics is founded on it.

Notice that this goes beyond the simple thesis that individuals come to want what others want of them. Tom may desperately want to run away. It is the belief in absolute requirements which keeps him from running.

In his *Ethics: Inventing Right and Wrong*,[3] which includes the story of Tom and Dan in its fifth chapter, and in his long and generous treatment of my markedly different views in chapter thirteen of his *The Miracle of Theism*,[4] J. L. Mackie discusses this area with extraordinary forthrightness. The quotations which follow will be from these two books. Attacking 'the assumption that there are objectively prescriptive values', cases of 'objective ought-to-beness', Mackie 'can find no actual contradiction implicit within it' yet claims that it involves 'a very strange concept'. 'We should hesitate to postulate that this strange concept has any real instantiations' because our inclination to use it can be explained 'in a manner that Hume has indicated'. Ethics concerns 'systems of attitudes developed particularly by interactions between people in societies', and 'the concept of intrinsic requiredness results from an abstraction of the requiring from the persons that really do the requiring'. This is 'much more acceptable than the rival view that things or states of affairs actually have such objective requiredness'. With an 'argument from queerness' Mackie dismisses objective values: they would be 'utterly different from anything else in the universe'. Surely, he writes, there can be nothing 'in the fabric of the world' that 'backs up and validates the subjective concern which people have' about this or that: feeding the starving, or stopping a man from burning babies alive for his amusement, or anything else you care to name. Conscience, taken at its face value, often does declare that there is 'a to-be-done-ness or a not-to-be-done-ness' involved in some action, 'in that kind of action in itself', yet it is 'overwhelmingly plausible' to view this as resulting from 'mere introjection into each individual of demands that come from other people': 'inventing of moral values' can readily be accounted for sociologically since it allows us to 'live together without destroying one another'. Yes, 'the main tradition of European moral philosophy' has favoured objective values. Belief in them has 'a firm basis in ordinary thought' and in 'the basic, conventional meaning of moral terms'. But a calm consideration of what is probable shows that no act could ever be 'wrong in itself'. Statements about what is to be done or refrained from 'are not capable of being simply true'. No situation could have 'a demand for such and such an action somehow built into it': 'notions of what is intrinsically fitting or required by the natures of things' are merely 'very natural errors'.

In opposition to all this, some main things can be said. (1) While Mackie himself managed to be a thoroughly upright, warm-hearted, self-sacrificing human being although believing these things, it may be that few are capable of such a feat. (2) Mackie is very honestly conceding that his own use of words like 'good' and 'bad' isn't the usual one. In effect, if his theories are correct, then there can be no good *in the ordinary sense of the word* in anything at all, let alone in believing them correct. (3) As I am going to argue next, there is in fact nothing too 'queer' in good and bad as ordinarily conceived. In contrast, it could well be thought odd to believe that nothing, not even burning babies alive for your amusement, was 'wrong in itself'.

A defence of intrinsic ethical requiredness

'In calling something good', Mackie concedes when discussing my position, 'we do commonly imply that it is intrinsically and objectively required or marked out for existence, irrespective of whether any person, human or divine, or any group of persons, requires or demands or prescribes or admires it.' Well, what could be so very queer in this?

One thing which troubles Mackie is the supposedly necessary link between a thing's ethical requiredness and its other properties. Remember, though, that he finds 'no actual contradiction' in the idea of intrinsic ethical requiredness. Now, this certainly sounds like saying that intrinsic ethical requiredness is a logically possible property of the things commonly thought to possess it. Does Mackie therefore think that such things don't possess it in our world, while other things exactly like them might possess it in other worlds which were, in all other respects, exactly like ours? In other words: that it *just happens to be a property absent from these things in our world*? What nonsense this would be; and Mackie rejects it, for he praises Plato's denial that goodness or badness could be added to things by arbitrary divine decrees. However, if a property's absence is neither a matter of logic nor a matter of chance, then it must be a matter of what philosophers call *synthetic necessity*: necessity which is absolute but not provable, as logical necessities are, by appeal to the very definitions of words or other symbols. Now, I happily accept synthetic necessities. I think they can be found, for instance, in experienced colours: those, say, of the 'after-images' produced by bright lights. If you have first an experience of red, and second an experience of orange, an experience of a third colour may be such that it is *necessarily nearer to the second experience than to the first*; for it may be an experience of yellow, and orange (as experienced) lies between red and yellow, necessarily. Yet here the necessity isn't like that of every bachelor's lacking a wife. It isn't a product merely of definitions. Cavemen without language could appreciate it, and so could modern children who had never considered defining the word 'orange' to mean 'colour between red and yellow'. It is a synthetic necessity. Where I differ from Mackie, apparently, is in thinking that in ethics the thing which is synthetically necessary is not *the absence* but *the presence* of real ethical requiredness.

Suppose, to steal an example from Dostoevski, that a soldier wants to have a little fun by tossing a baby girl upwards and catching her on a bayonet. Thinking of the real ethical need to stop him – the categorical demand that he be stopped – as 'necessarily built into the situation' strikes me as every bit as plausible as thinking, as Mackie seems to, that it is necessarily walled out of the situation.

Outside ethics, there is at least one case where philosophers meet the idea of categorical demands which aren't logically demonstrable. In the case in question, almost all of them agree that the demands can indeed be real. It is the case of rational inductive reasoning. Almost all philosophers hold that mere logic can never tell us that, for instance, gravity will operate tomorrow much as it does today or that boiling water will still hurt any feet which are plunged into it – yet they believe that situations of wondering about such things, of asking yourself whether various regularities found in the past will continue into the future, have the need for particular conclusions built into them. The state of mind of thinking that boiling water would continue to hurt your feet has its own brand of intrinsic requiredness, they would say. They would scorn the suggestion that the requirements of inductive rationality are on a par with those of etiquette, or with 'requirements of irrationality': the requirement, for instance, to believe that boiling water *won't* hurt your feet tomorrow. There is much more here, they would insist, than the fact that certain ways of thinking are required of a person *if* the label 'rational' is to fit that person, just as it is required of you that you have a red nose *if* the label 'red-nosed' is to fit you.

The very natures of certain possible things can, I am arguing, provide authoritative grounds for their existence or for their non-existence. In the case of ethics, in contrast to that of thoughts about tomorrow's boiling water, they can sometimes be grounds for acting to bring things into existence, or to keep them in existence. Sometimes, again, they are grounds for acts which destroy existing things (states of suffering, for example) or which keep things out of existence. Still, if ordinary ideas about goodness and badness are on the right lines, then there are also some ethical grounds which go beyond all moral grounds for action – because, as was said during the attack on prescriptivism, some things ordinarily thought good or bad are things which no actions could affect.

Elsewhere all this has been developed in detail.[5] Here there is room only for the following three main points:

(1) The central idea is that various things are *marked out for existence in a non-trivial way.* The ethical requiredness of what's good isn't comparable to the 'thermal requiredness' of whatever makes the world hotter or the 'diabolical requiredness' of torture, and mere whims can't be the source of the requiredness. Its authority is *absolute* in some crucial fashion. (That much, at any rate, is correct in Kant's doctrine of 'the categorical imperative'. Where Kant went astray was in thinking – if he ever did really think this – that every ethical demand is absolute in a fashion guaranteeing that no other ethical demand will ever overrule it.) It may be hard to get a really good grip on the notion involved, but if the notion makes no sense whatever to you then, sorry, you haven't got as far as square one in understanding what Ethics is all about. Nevertheless, this isn't to say that human likes and dislikes are ethically unimportant. When Mr Bloggs detests music, there may well be no absolute ethical demand that he should listen to music. Nor is it being suggested that moral laws such as 'Don't tell lies' have absolutely no exceptions, or that if a thing is intrinsically good then it should absolutely always be favoured. Alternatives, after all, could have greater intrinsic goodness. (A thing can possess length intrinsically without being longer than everything else. Why on earth should possession of intrinsic goodness behave differently?) Sometimes, too, an intrinsically good thing ought to avoided because of its evil consequences. A man's enjoyment of music could be *good in itself,* in the sense that its existence all alone would be better than the existence of nothing,

but perhaps he ought not to be enjoying music if the house is on fire.

(2) Believing that good and bad are 'objective', in the sense of being 'out there in Reality', doesn't automatically make you a 'cognitivist' or 'intuitionist' who thinks that ethical truths can be detected in reliable ways: perhaps by some wondrous searchlight implanted in our minds by God. You may instead simply join me in believing that it really is true, a genuine fact, that it's right to do such things as feeding hungry people and stopping others from shooting them for fun. If we could never go beyond mere moral beliefs – if we could never have anything worth calling *moral knowledge* – would this then mean that we *would know that it was moral* to tolerate shooting people for fun? Of course not.

Professional philosophers tend to place severe restrictions on what can count as 'knowledge'. As one of them, I hesitate to say that I truly know that anything is ever better or worse than anything else. Might not good and evil be utterly illusory? This doesn't seem to be an affair about which we can be completely sure. Still, I'd label a man 'mentally diseased' if he declared that shooting people for fun had really nothing bad about it. After all, there can be diseases of ideas (neuroses) just as much as of brain cells (psychoses), and 'diseased' doesn't just mean 'abnormal'. 'Diseased' is a word carrying ethical weight. Mathematical genius is very abnormal, but isn't a disease.

Dropping my standards for knowledge just a little, I could very well claim to know all sorts of moral truths – much as I might claim to know that boiling water would hurt my feet tomorrow. I might even claim to know that Schopenhauer was wrong when he wrote that our planet would better have remained as lifeless as the moon.

(3) The ideas of *ethically required existence* and *ethically required non-existence* are ones which I take with great seriousness. Ethical truths would continue to be true even if the universe vanished. In an absence of all actually existing things it could be ethically required, for instance, that this empty situation *not* be replaced by a world consisting merely of people being burned alive. If you refuse to accept this, how could you believe that any such world would be *in itself bad* in the ordinary sense of 'bad'? Goodness and badness aren't just matters of the praiseworthiness

or blameworthiness of moral agents! They are robust enough to survive in the absence of people whose duty is to do this or that. The coming into existence of a thoroughly evil world perhaps couldn't be counted as *a moral disaster* unless some moral agent was responsible, but this would just go to show that some things can be very bad without Morality and Duty entering in.

Such an approach to good and bad can be called platonist. In mathematics, platonists think that the truth of 'Two and two make four' is independent even of the existence of objects to be counted, let alone of people to count them. If the entire universe of existing things were to vanish, two and two would continue to make four: it would continue to be true, a matter of genuine reality, that if there were ever in future to be two sets of two things then there would be four things. Platonism in ethics is very similar. Plato's 'Form of the Good' was something which 'transcended Being'.

Plato also seems to have thought that the Form of the Good was itself responsible for the existence of the universe. Although his words about this (see Book VI of the *Republic*) are rather obscure, the theme was taken up by such neoplatonists as Dionysius, and later by P. Tillich and H. Küng. Also by some analytically minded philosophers: A. C. Ewing, for instance, who used it in trying to understand God's existence in particular. I have repeatedly tried to defend it,[6] insisting that goodness isn't just a quality added to other qualities like an extra coat of paint. *Being marked out for existence* in a non-trivial way is what goodness *is*, and this means that goodness is at least a reality of the right sort – 'in the right ball park' – to act creatively. True enough, there's a sense in which no ethical need for a divine person or for a universe could ever *as such* carry responsibility for the existence of that person or that universe; but bear in mind that there's also a sense in which no *cows as such* are brown, although they are female. Neoplatonists needn't be blind to how words behave.

Still, the study of how words behave cannot compel you to join the neoplatonists. It might force you to treat ethical requirements 'platonically', as unconditionally real, if you believed in such requirements at all, but this couldn't thrust you into neoplatonism. Ethical requirements could create a universe *necessarily* without the necessity being one which anyone could prove. It would be a synthetic necessity, and synthetic necessities can be very hard to establish. (As was argued above, the reality of any ethical requirement whatsoever, let alone the reality that the universe owes its existence to an ethical requirement, is only synthetically necessary and therefore easily disputed. Reasonable people can disagree considerably on which things are intrinsically good.)

What's more, even those converted to neoplatonism may find their ethics entirely unaffected. Neoplatonists can think that the best sort of world for ethical requirements to have produced would be a world governed by natural laws, not a world as disorderly as a drug addict's happy dreams. They need therefore have no difficulty in accepting that nuclear bombs, for instance, really are unpleasantly dangerous. They aren't forced into the ridiculous belief that absolutely all ethical needs – for example (a) the need for people to have freedom and (b) the need for people not to use their freedom by exploding nuclear bombs above cities for fun – will always be satisfied simultaneously. And they can reject the notion that we are equipped with moral searchlights which make it easy to tell what's good and what's bad. In spite of my being a neoplatonist, I think Mackie right about where I got most of my ethical beliefs. They were produced by social pressures, and no doubt quite a few of them are wrong.

WHY NOT EXTINCTION?

Could it be a fact that Earth was sadly underpopulated, if the human race had become extinct? Philosophers who reduce all ethical facts to moral duties, obligations to act in various ways, would have to answer No unless some moral agent (God, or some extraterrestrial?) remained in existence, so that he or she or it could have a duty to improve the situation. And many further philosophers would say that the fact that humans had died out couldn't be sad, a pity, something less than ideal, unless there were somebody to contemplate and evaluate it. Why, even the process of causing the dying out, or of just letting it occur, would be one in which many of them would see nothing unfortunate *unless people were actually made unhappy by it*. In their view there is nothing essentially wrong in leaving a merely possible happy person in a state of non-existence because, they explain, moral duties are only towards actually existing people.

Other philosophers go so far as to suggest that the dying out of the human race would be *fortunate* because at least a few human lives are unhappy.

All such views seem to me mistaken. If people listened much to philosophers, then views of this kind could be very dangerous. Besides discouraging efforts to keep the human race in being, they encourage putting its survival at risk, for instance during nuclear brinkmanship. ('Could the human race become extinct if I now ordered nuclear missiles to be made ready for launching? So what? Philosophers assure me that the merely possible human lives which then wouldn't be lived *can carry no ethical weight*. I can omit them from my calculations of what I'd be risking.')

In trying to show that mistakes really are being made here, the next pages will be drawing on things I have written earlier.[7] Throughout they will follow the long-established philosophical practice of taking 'happy' lives to mean lives which are worth having, rather than simply ones which are enjoyed. The life of Vlad the Impaler, filled with joy in acts of torture, could therefore be a very poor example of a happy life.

Could Schopenhauer's gloom have been right?

Suppose some political leader becomes able to create planet-wide nuclear explosions just by pulling a lever. Given sufficiently many explosions in a sufficiently short period, nobody would suffer pain or disappointment. Living normally at one moment, we should all be gas and ashes at the next. What could be unfortunate here?

Schopenhauer argued that every human life is inevitably miserable on the whole. Humans, he wrote, concentrate not on such things as the general health of their bodies, but on 'the one spot where the shoe pinches'. Imagine that the political leader agreed with this. Would it necessitate Schopenhauer's gloomy conclusion that lives aren't worth living?

The correctness of this gloomy conclusion couldn't follow in any logically provable way. Attacking ethical naturalism, I argued that it would be a mistake to think 'good' had the sense of 'pleasant'. The notion that 'bad' has the sense of 'miserable' would be equally mistaken. Being born into the world can seem an adventure every bit as great as travelling to the moon. Might it not be an adventure which was worth having despite being disliked? After all, many people feel gladness at having had various experiences, although they did not like them at all at the time. Could it greatly matter whether someone's dying moments were filled with this sort of gladness? Perhaps not.

Still, if ethical naturalism fails then Schopenhauer's gloomy conclusion could have no logically provable incorrectness, either. Without committing any conceptual blunder, the political leader could consider lever-pulling a duty, and start to pull.

Could it be right to interfere? Certainly. If only a burst from a machine-gun would do the job, then I wouldn't blame whoever fired it. Remember, an inability to prove ethical *oughts* cannot *prove* that we *ought* always to be tolerant. And although I think it almost always bad to kill people, and particularly political leaders who are doing what they see as their duty, I recognize no 'inalienable right not to be killed'. (Insane people are to be pitied, not blamed, but if a madman were reaching out to push a button and thereby start a nuclear war, then I wouldn't classify failure to shoot him as 'keeping one's hands clean'. I'd think of it as getting one's hands very dirty indeed – as committing a crime of inaction which the madman himself would be the first to condemn if he could suddenly be cured.) None the less, I might feel considerable respect for the lever-pulling leader. Trying to annihilate the human race could be the act of a thoroughly decent person who *not unreasonably* thought that human lives were seldom or never worth living. Discussing whether the universe was created by a benevolent deity, philosophers regularly point out that our world might be considered an ethical disaster, something of negative value, because of all the misery it contains. It is severely inconsistent of them when, leaving philosophy of religion and entering the field of ethics, they blithely assume that life is usually worth living.

It could be just as well that they assume it, though. While Schopenhauer is making no immediately evident mistake, I think of him as very seriously mistaken. It's a good thing that – when doing ethics – today's philosophers almost all see things my way. Despite this, their books and journals are often filled with arguments for wiping out the human race, or at least for denying any duty to keep it in being. Let us next see why.

Should our dominant concern be for the miserable?

To begin with, it is quite often argued that our chief duty is to help the unfortunate. Resources which could make five thousand fairly contented people very happy should instead be used for making five rather miserable people fairly contented. People ought never to buy their pleasures with other people's miseries.

At times there are efforts to sell this view by asking: 'If you were behind a veil of ignorance, not knowing which role you'd have to play in life, wouldn't rationality motivate you to ensure that the least desirable role was as pleasant as could be?' (In his *A Theory of Justice*[8] J. Rawls is strongly inclined to answer Yes.) But this is poor salesmanship, for you could reasonably reply that, for example, eight chances of becoming a slave seemed a fair price to pay for twenty-eight of living in comfort while slaves did all the work. Yet how about *knowing* you were a slave-owner, and that this wasn't as the result of some roulette game which you and your slaves had willingly played? Oughtn't *that* to trouble your conscience? What gives such strong attractions to 'attempting to maximize the minimum' – trying to ensure that even the least fortunate individuals have lives which are as good as possible – isn't, so to speak, that nobody can bear the thought of risking being bottom dog. Instead it's that decent people find it hard to bear the reality of being top dogs.

However, placing great emphasis on minimizing misfortune can lead straight to this: *that we ought to work towards the extinction of humankind.* At least occasionally, humans have lives which could plausibly be thought so little worth living that their value was negative. Children are sometimes born with defects which lead to an early, painful death. While medical advances might eventually make this sort of thing very rare, it could presumably never be prevented entirely. Sometimes, too, painful death must occur by accident soon after the first glimmerings of consciousness have appeared in a foetus. If human life is allowed to continue, happy lives will continually be being purchased at the price of there being miserable ones. You simply couldn't have the ones without the others. Yet isn't it the contrast between happiness and misery which gives most charm to the idea of 'maximizing the minimum'? Few would be much tempted by this idea if nothing were at stake but differing degrees of bliss. It would be preposterous to ask people to put enormous resources into making a single slightly happy individual a little more happy, if they could instead be used to make a billion marginally happier individuals intensely happy. In contrast, the notion that we ought to favour the extinction of humankind *because human lives are inevitably of negative value sometimes* can look rather attractive. Anyone who saw absolutely no force in it would be callous.

Nevertheless, think twice before accepting it.

No duties towards merely possible people?

Suppose lives were known to be always well worth living. You would continue to meet philosophers who denied any clear duty to save humankind from extinction.

A position occasionally adopted is that our duty towards others is only to avoid hurting them. So if life could be seen as a gift which we could give to future generations, we'd still have no obligation to give it. In fact, even when somebody was in danger of drowning, there would be no duty to throw a lifebelt. Duty would be satisfied so long as one didn't throw a rock. Luckily, however, most people can see that this is devilish, making it safe to disregard it. What isn't safe is to lose sight of various other positions which are often considered right by folk whose moral views are in other respects admirable. First comes 'average utilitarianism', a position to which philosophers can feel driven if thinking of morality in terms of an implicit contract between people: actually existing people. Good acts, it is alleged, are ones which raise the average value of human experiences – or possibly *human and animal* experiences, for 'contractarians' sometimes try to bring dolphins, dogs, etc. into the *mythos* of contracting. It follows that we could have no grounds for doubling population size if this left the distribution of happiness and misery precisely as before. (Rawls notes this in sections 27ff. of *A Theory of Justice*, without in any way acknowledging that it shows the wrongness of his contractarianism. His indifference to population size doesn't depend on the fact that some people are miserable. He would be indifferent to it even if everybody were immensely happy.)

Admittedly, supporters of average utilitarianism don't recommend *just any* acts which raise the average. They would shy away from shooting the merely moderately happy, whether or not this would increase the average degree of happiness. Yet they appear forced to accept that human (or human-and-animal) life ought to be allowed to become extinct if the existence of later generations would necessitate any lowering of the average, no matter how slight. This would be so even if it were known that the universe would thereafter be permanently empty of intelligent living beings. The prospect of giving rise to billions of happy descendants couldn't justify reducing the happiness of a hundred people, perhaps sole survivors of a nuclear war, unless the billions could be expected to be on average happier.

A sterner variant leaves out the 'unless . . .' clause. It says that the average value of lives which had already begun, or whose coming into existence was more or less inevitable, should never be lowered, regardless of whether lowering it would lead to a much higher overall average through allowing billions of utterly blissful new lives to enter the world.

Another variant runs as follows. Facts about happy lives which might be lived couldn't set up duties to produce such lives, but producing them could be *permissible* even at the cost of some lowering of the values of lives which already existed, or whose existence was more or less inevitable. Now, this can look excessively odd. If there are no strong moral grounds – some philosophers write 'no moral grounds whatever' – for producing a life likely to be happy, how could it be permissible to produce it *at the risk that it would be unhappy*? Oughtn't we to conclude that our duty was to stop producing children? But leaving this last point aside, why in heaven's name are all these various theories saying that facts about the happiness of billions of possible lives can't set up forceful obligations to produce those lives?

The chief reason lies in what M. Black called *horror possibilitatis* when he met it among writers on probability theory.[9] Just as it used to be declared that Nature 'abhorred a vacuum' since evacuated space would be too empty to be real, so it now tends to be held that the goodness of merely possible happy lives can't give rise to real duties because a mere possibility is something as empty as you can get.

J. Narveson[10] and J. Bennett are two main defenders of this view. Following what he terms Narveson's 'excellent lead', Bennett holds that philosophers are confused when they deplore the situation where – as he chooses to express the point – some possible happiness 'lacks a person'. The question 'of whether *Homo sapiens* should be allowed to continue' shouldn't, he says, be influenced 'by any such thought as: We ought to perpetuate our species because if we do larger amounts of happiness will be had than if we don't.' Suppose he learned that some region of the universe was filled with intelligent beings whose lives were happy. This would, he says, be 'good news' for him, but only because (a) all beings who are intelligent must be *instances of rich organic complexity* and (b) these particular beings *weren't markedly unhappy*: 'happiness is relevant only in that the extra organic complexity would not be very welcome if the organisms were desperately miserable'.[11]

It presumably follows that if Bennett had been able to make the lives in question extremely happy, instead of just *not miserable*, then he'd have felt no obligation to do it, not even if all that had been asked of him had been the lifting of a finger.

Such reasoning isn't a mere invention of the twentieth century. Consider the theological problem of evil: the problem of how a good divine being could possibly have created a world with as many miseries as ours. A time-honoured attempt to minimize the problem involves reasoning that God *had no duty to create any beings at all*, because beings who for ever remained *merely possible* would never actually exist to complain about anything, let alone about not having been created. It would, of course, follow that God had no duty to create any blissfully happy beings. If he created less happy ones instead, then these might thank him, while the others couldn't reproach him. Yet isn't this altogether too weak an argument? Why, after all, begrudge a devil the fun of creating lives miserable enough to have negative value? Suppose we reasoned that a merely possible being 'wouldn't be there to have any right

176

not to be created'. Isn't this quite as forceful as the former argument? Of course miserable beings, once created, would actually be there to bear grievances. Yet happy beings, once created, would actually be there too – and that they wouldn't be there bearing grievances seems relevant only if (as on the 'Just make sure you don't throw a rock' approach) avoiding hurting people were all that duty could involve.

Can it matter that possible people of the future *have no definite identities*? Imagine that somebody has a plan to store radioactive waste in a manner fairly sure to kill billions of people in distant centuries, if the human race survives for that long. Would you dream of arguing that because the world was indeterministic (for reasons of quantum physics, perhaps) it followed that any people who might live in those centuries hadn't got definite identities, and that therefore the plan was morally quite OK?

To be sure, whatever duties we have towards possible people are surrounded by philosophical mists, and the mists become particularly thick in the cases of those possible people who won't ever become actual. Can such individuals have definite identities? My own answer is Yes, because completely detailed descriptions can in theory be given of them. Suppose, though, that I'm wrong here. T. Parsons would then have been mistaken when he dedicated his book *Nonexistent Objects*[12] 'to his parents, but for whom he'd have been one of them'. (Where would any identifiable *he* have been?) And Bennett would be correct in writing that failure to beget a child couldn't have a wrongness stemming from any fact that 'one deprives *it* of something'.[13] (Compare Narveson's insistence that 'it makes no sense to say that one has done some kind of damage to a possible person by refusing to make that possibility actual'; 'we cannot sensibly say that a possibility is worse off for remaining one than it would be if realized' since '"possible persons" are not persons'; '"one" who was never born in the first place has no identity at all'.[14]) But, as D. Parfit has pointed out,[15] we could always write that being born had been good or bad for an individual, and better for some individuals than for others, even if there were some conceptual confusion in writing that so-and-so would have been worse off or better off if non-existent. Now, fancying that duties can be set up by the need *for there not to be miserable individuals, for whom being born would be bad*, yet that it would be conceptually muddled to see them as set up by a need *for there to be happy individuals, for whom being born would be good,* is itself a wonderful example of conceptual muddle.

Just as a planet of utterly miserable people could be worse than nothing, so also a planet of happy people could be better than nothing. If a philosopher had a chance to create the first planet simply by lifting a finger, then prima facie the finger oughtn't to be lifted, regardless of whether there's any fine conceptual difficulty in saying that finger-lifting would be 'disregarding a duty towards possible miserable people, the duty not to give them miserable lives'. Similarly with the second planet. Assuming that creating it wouldn't produce harm elsewhere, it ought to be created, no matter what conceptual niceties we find when trying to translate the words 'the planet ought to be created' into talk of duties towards anybody in particular.

If necessary, let's just say that there can be many duties which (like duties not to bury radioactive waste in ways which would ruin the lives of any people of the far future) *aren't* towards anybody in particular. Or let's talk of duties based on what would happen to describable possible people who *would in due course be* real people, uncontroversially identifiable people, *if* we did this or that.

How, then, are we to treat the notion that letting the human race die out would be morally acceptable if having children came to be viewed as tedious? The correct reaction, I suggest, is the one which tends to be taken for granted in the Far East, where it is considered shameful to enjoy one's own life while feeling absolutely no call to give lives to others. The only possible excuse for letting humankind die out would then be that future humans were thought likely to be miserable, and/or it was assumed that other intelligent beings would quickly evolve to occupy the slot which humans had filled. Yet it could be very unwise to assume any such thing. Humans could easily be the only intelligent living beings who would ever have evolved in our galaxy, or in all the galaxies observable by our telescopes.

Concessions

(a) In a world as overpopulated as ours is now, there could be a duty not to produce children.

(b) It can be wrong to send food parcels to distant places when your own family is hungry. For one thing, the parcels may never get there. Similarly, it could often be wrong to ask for large sacrifices from today's actually existing people, in the hope of bringing benefits to future people.

(c) As mentioned during the attack on ethical naturalism, a main reason for denying that there can be a logical proof of the intrinsic goodness of anything, pleasure, for instance, is that this would trivialize the affair. It would make it on a par with the marriedness of wives. Now, we'd be involved in similar trivialization if we defined the rightness of any actions, for instance actions to keep the human race in existence, in terms of their ability to maximize good results. Pleasure could be good, and actions aimed at increasing the total amount of pleasure by bringing pleasant lives into existence could be right, without any of this being provable by conceptual analysis. If the word 'right' *had the sense of* 'producing maximum goodness' (or trying to produce it, or trying to do what is reasonably judged likely to produce it while having little likelihood of producing evil) much as 'puppy' has the sense of 'young dog', then it would be just a linguistically guaranteed fact that it was right to produce maximum goodness (or to try to produce it, etc.). Yet this seems far too like supposing that 'right' has the sense of 'commanded by God', so that if God were to command torture for everybody, then torture would automatically be right. One trouble with *that* is that 'God commands what is right' could be taken as a compliment to God, something which could inspire moral people to do God's will, only if it said something more than 'God commands the things which God commands.' Similarly: 'Right acts are those which maximize good results' can be inspiring only if it says something more than 'Acts which maximize good results are acts which maximize good results.' The point was recognized by W. C. Kneale.[16]

The philosophical literature of this area is vast and tangled. Rough ways of labelling my own position would be 'utilitarian' or 'ideal utilitarian' or 'non-hedonistic utilitarian' or 'total utilitarian', or 'consequentialist' or 'anti-Kantian' or 'rejecting deontology'. Like two very well-known philosophers, G. E. Moore and J. J. C. Smart, I never have managed to see why it would be my duty to do something which I knew would make the world *really and truly worse* than something else I wanted to do. (Smart is famous for insisting on this simple point and refusing to accept that alleged counter-examples disprove it.[17] This has led to an easily guessed pun about outwitting the opposition.) It would be nice if people who think like Moore and Smart could be treated merely as mistaken, instead of as 'showing a corrupt mind',[18] when they urge that opposing doctrines are needlessly complicated; but in ethics there's no master formula for establishing who is right. Morally fervent folk, long trained in philosophy, might therefore think we had practically no duty to keep the human race in existence, regardless of how much happiness future humans could be expected to have. No firm logical proof could establish their wrongness. As will next be argued, however, there are extremely powerful reasons for thinking them wrong.

The story of the windowless huts

Although denying that logic can prove a duty to bring happy lives into being, I think two points very forceful. First: human lives, or at any rate most of them, can reasonably be thought worth living even today, and are likely to become happier than ever before if humankind manages to survive for long. Second: anybody who denies all duty to increase the number of new and happy lives is in a wildly paradoxical position.

For a thorough defence of the second point, go to D. Parfit's *Reasons and Persons.*[19] Here, I shall defend it quickly with the aid of a story that reflects various elements of Parfit's reasoning. It may sound rather a fantastic story, yet this doesn't worry me. The story is intended to show the plausibility of a principle, not the likelihood of some imagined state of affairs. The idea behind it is this. It can surely be ethically required to bring happy people into existence in order to make a situation *which would otherwise be very bad* into a good situation. Now, why wouldn't it be equally

180

required to bring them into existence even if the situation *wouldn't* otherwise be bad?

Many philosophers – let's call them the theorists of Sweet Sufficiency – think that some largish number of happy people would be quite enough, morally speaking. For the sake of my story, let's say the number is seventy-seven billion. Imagine, then, some future time in which seventy-seven billion happy people exist. Suppose there are ninety trillion islands somewhere. Using harmless means – magic spells, if you like, since my story isn't intended to be realistic – you can populate each island with a hundred thousand happy people. Now, every island carries a windowless hut. The hut might perhaps already be inhabited by somebody, in which case he or she would have a life whose loneliness made its value negative. The hut is 'windowless' in a philosopher's sense: it has no doors either, and absolutely nothing can be done to decrease the misery of any people in it. Nothing happening outside the hut is detectable inside, and vice versa.

A further island, Undisastrous Island, already carries a hundred thousand happy people plus a windowless hut. As its name suggests, the island presumably isn't an ethical tragedy. Surely it is remarkably good, regardless of whether its hut is inhabited. If you denied this, then you'd have fairly strong grounds for thinking it right to annihilate the human race in some quick and painless fashion. In the foreseeable future, the human race seems sure to contain at least one miserable person per hundred thousand.

Presumably, too, it wouldn't be tragic for there to exist ninety trillion islands like Undisastrous Island. For how could ninety trillion islands be tragic when each would have been very good, had it existed all alone?

On the other hand it *would* be tragic, immensely tragic, if the universe contained ninety trillion people each on a separate island and in a windowless hut, miserably lonely people with lives of negative value, and only seventy-seven billion happy people. Wouldn't there be a moral need to replace so tragic a situation by the non-tragic one in which there were a hundred thousand happy people on each island in addition to its miserable person? Surely there would. The need could safely be assumed to be immensely strong. For one thing, creating the happy people would in no way harm the miserable ones since the huts are windowless.

It follows that theorists of Sweet Sufficiency must defend the conclusion that whether the moral need to populate each island with a hundred thousand happy people was (1) immensely strong or (2) entirely absent *would depend on whether the huts were inhabited* – despite their being so firmly windowless that any people inside could never know about the happiness of any people outside, so as to get some generous pleasure from the thought of it. Yet isn't such a conclusion wildly implausible? How could a duty to create happy people outside huts depend on what was inside, when outsides had no detectable influence on insides and vice versa? Sweet Sufficiency must be a badly mistaken theory – and those who think of *zero* as sufficiency ('No Moral Obligation to Give Actual Existence to Even One Possible Happy Person') must be still worse mistaken.

True, I've supplied no logically watertight proof that a mistake has been made. I said only that in certain circumstances an immensely strong moral need 'could safely be assumed'. But the act of replacing an ethically disastrous situation by an undisastrous one, without in any way harming anybody, surely gets very, very near – as near as could reasonably be demanded – to being self-evidently right.

No, there is nothing callous in this line of reasoning. It isn't being denied that every additional life whose value was negative would be an additional tragedy. All that's being said is that a world could be ethically undisastrous despite including such lives. If even one miserable life per hundred thousand strikes you as too much, then alter the story so that you can create ten million happy people on each island, or ten trillion trillion trillion trillion. Wouldn't you now accept that the islands could be made ethically undisastrous? If you still wouldn't, then notice that to refute Sweet Sufficiency we need only assume the following: that islands each carrying one miserable life are, if not actually good, then at least *less disastrous* when huge numbers of happy people exist on them as well.

My argument doesn't run: 'Rather than try to help the miserable, let's leave 'em in their misery and create adequately many happy people to swamp 'em!' Instead it asks what our duty would be in a situation where absolutely nothing could be done to help the miserable, no matter how hard we tried. Situations like this aren't logically impossible. They aren't particularly unrealistic either.

There's often little to be done to help miserable individuals: those, for instance, who are born so ill or crippled that efforts to help tend just to prolong their misery.

It might be protested that all this has nothing to do with real life, our planet being so heavily populated that adding more people would result only in misery for everyone. However, it seems to me that real life could soon present us with a moral question interestingly similar to that of whether to populate those ninety trillion islands. If the human race manages to survive for the next couple of centuries, it will quite probably be in a position to start spreading right across its galaxy. It could have a very strong duty to do so. If the story of the windowless huts has any force, then, so long as they aren't interfering with one another's happiness, the more happy people the better.

Some philosophers are prepared to accept this conclusion only if positional restrictions are placed on it. If groups of happy lives could succeed one another for ever and ever, these philosophers would feel horror at the idea that *from such and such a position in time onwards* the universe could decently be allowed to become lifeless, because sufficiently many happy lives would by then have been lived. Yet they think very differently about matters *from any position in space sideways.* They fancy that if the universe contained, say, seventy-seven billion happy people at any time, then this would be sufficient for that time. But the supposed preferability of lives when they are scattered through time, not through space, strikes me as merely magical. No matter whether its islands are separated temporally or spatially, the story of the windowless huts works just as powerfully.

Some opponents of utilitarianism

As indicated, I defend 'utilitarianism' in a fairly strong sense. I accept a fairly firm link between the praiseworthiness of any action and the goodness of its probable results, although bearing in mind such things as (a) that even a minor risk of producing a very unfortunate result, for instance the extinction of the human race, could justify very major sacrifices, and (b) that an agent may simultaneously deserve a pat on the back for following the guidance of

conscience, and a kick in the pants for having a misguided conscience. Remembering always that when asking whether a life is
'happy' one needn't be asking simply whether it is filled with pleasure (though pleasure could be very important), I think no limit
can be set to how much happiness we ought to struggle to bring
into existence. Just let's beware of struggling so very hard that we
all become unhappy, or of demanding that individuals should work
for the happiness of others by making sacrifices much larger than
can be expected of ordinary mortals.

Astonishingly many professional philosophers oppose all ways of
thinking which are even vaguely on the above lines. Scores of them
recognize no moral call to keep the human race in existence: if
waving a hand were enough to guarantee the existence of a trillion
happy galaxy-colonizing humans, they would see no duty to wave.
And scores of others imagine that by rejecting utilitarianism they
are somehow *strengthening* the case for keeping the human race
in existence. They allege that the utilitarian who urges us to try
to maximize benefits has a theory which is paralyzed whenever
moral certainties aren't available, or which can't care whether it is
criminals or honest folk who enjoy benefits, or which encourages
us to put the happiness of future generations at tremendous risk
in exchange for various minor present-day advantages, maybe
actually 'discounting' the future at such a rate that a million deaths
a few centuries from now can have no more significance than a
single death tomorrow.[20] Having thereby dismissed utilitarianism
with suspicious ease, they find all manner of curious reasons for
trying to produce benefits for posterity: benefits which anyone
favouring mere maximization of benefits would supposedly be
uninterested in producing! Some base their concern for future
generations mainly on the need to respect the wishes of the dead.
Others emphasize that love for one's grandchildren can be logically
linked to a wish that they too should have the joy of having grandchildren. The idea that those later grandchildren themselves could
somehow benefit from being more-than-merely-possible is classified
as sheer confusion.[21]

The upshot should come as no surprise. Obligations to keep the
human race in existence may sometimes be recognized in theory,
but are then eroded by a thousand considerations: uncertainty
about what future people would be like; loving concern for those

already in existence; the reflection that things like pollution control might have to be imposed undemocratically or in defiance of 'rights' which manage to be 'genuine' or 'taken seriously' only because they must never be overruled; and so forth. Sometimes it is declared that any considerable prolongation of human history would be 'valueless repetition'. Torture would be worse and worse, the more people there were who suffered it, but any additions made by happy lives to the goodness of the universe would somehow have reached an upper limit in the early twenty-first century. The conclusion that we ought therefore to work hard to end the human race (its continued joys being worthless duplications of what had come before, whereas each new instance of misery added negative value) is unlikely to be stated explicitly – yet it's tempting to draw it, isn't it?

J. Glover was, I believe, right when he reached quite the opposite conclusion: that to end the human race 'would be about the worst thing it would be possible to do'.[22] But while he and a handful of others are very encouraging exceptions, the general run of philosophers who have contributed to this field have done so in unfortunate ways. Consider, for instance, T. H. Thompson's disgusting statement[23] that 'we are not obligated to future others' – so that there would be nothing essentially wrong in, for example, placing unwanted hydrogen bombs in a huge concrete-covered dump which was bound to explode after a couple of centuries – together with his bizarre effort to support this by proving that nobody can feel sympathetic concern for people who haven't yet been born. Besides being almost as silly as trying to prove that nobody really likes beer, this is an instance of a disease well diagnosed by R. and V. Routley.[24] Why, they ask, do so many contemporary theorists deny strong obligations towards the people of any future which stretches at all far? It's because these theorists picture obligations as 'conditional on doing or failing to do something (e.g. contracting) or having some characteristic one can fail to have (e.g. love, sympathy, empathy)'. If such theorists are right, then how easy it is to get rid of an ethical requirement! Just declare that you've no interest in the matter.

5

THE DOOMSDAY
ARGUMENT

—— •••• ——

This chapter develops the Carter–Leslie 'doomsday argument' outlined in the Introduction. It can be read in isolation,
though, since it includes all the main points made earlier,
much expanded. It also makes many further points in the
argument's defence. Several of them work smoothly only if
our world is a deterministic world, or at least a world whose
indeterminisms are unlikely to have much influence on how
long the human race will last.

THE STORY OF THE CAT

Prima facie, we should prefer theories which make our observations
fairly much to be expected, rather than highly extraordinary.
Waking up in the night, you form two theories. Each has a half-
chance of being right, you estimate. The first, that you left
the back door open, gives the chances as 10 per cent that the
neighbour's cat is in your bedroom. The second, that you
shut the door, puts those chances at 0.01 per cent. You switch on
the light and see the cat. You should now much prefer the first
theory.

Consider next your observed position in time. If the human
race is going to last for at least a few thousand more centuries at
its present size, let alone at the much larger size to which it would
grow if it spread through its galaxy, then you are very exceptionally early among all the humans who will ever have been born,
perhaps among the earliest 0.01 per cent. But if the race is instead
due to end shortly – which, when one thinks of the ozone layer,

H-bombs, etc., can seem not particularly unlikely – then you are fairly unexceptional. Because of recent population growth, roughly 10 per cent of all humans who have been born up to date are still alive today. Now, shouldn't this influence you? Mayn't the rather unexceptional position which you'd have occupied in human population history, if that history were soon to end, give you some grounds, reinforcing those got through considering the ozone layer and H-bombs, for thinking it will indeed end fairly shortly?

The answer would seem to be Yes. If the world is deterministic, then the grounds can be disturbingly strong. If it is radically indeterministic, on the other hand, and if its indeterminisms are of a sort likely to have much influence on how long the human race will survive, then they may be quite a bit weaker, yet still worrying. In either case they could be *reinforcing grounds* even if they had no power by themselves. For, as will be explained in a moment, they could magnify any risk-estimates that were reached by considering such things as H-bombs and the ozone layer.

Although many find it paradoxical that you could learn anything in this way from your own observed temporal placement, the 'doomsday argument' which I have just sketched can seem natural to people accustomed to 'anthropic' reasoning in cosmology.[1] In fact it was first sketched by Brandon Carter, the Cambridge mathematician who invented the phrase 'anthropic principle'. Carter has, however, written asking me to speak of 'the Carter–Leslie doomsday argument', at least from time to time, to share 'not only the credit but also the blame, which will not be in short supply'. As we both know from experience, the argument often provokes cries of 'Rubbish!'. In a way that's odd, because probability theory, inside which this particular argument is firmly situated, is so difficult a field that little is obvious in it. In a way it isn't odd at all. People are frequently at their most aggressive when it is hardest to see who is right.

THE ARGUMENT'S ANTHROPIC
AND BAYESIAN REASONING

Anthropic arguments

As first stated by him, Carter's anthropic principle is 'that what we can expect to observe must be restricted by the conditions necessary for our presence as observers'.[2] Carter has since insisted that the anthropic principle was poorly named. It can be applied to observers throughout the universe, not just to *anthropoi*, humans. It can remind us that organisms intelligent enough to be observers can expect that their own places and times do not exclude intelligent life. Although this is as trivially true as that wives must have husbands, it can encourage interesting theories: for example the theory that our spatiotemporal location is unusual because in most locations life cannot exist. Observations may be possible only in unusual circumstances.

The idea had already been used by R. H. Dicke. The large number 10^{40} (which is one followed by forty zeros, or ten thousand trillion trillion trillion) enters into several cosmologically important equations. Noticing this, A. S. Eddington developed his physics around it, and P. A. M. Dirac then imitated him. *The universe's present age* stands to *gravity's measured strength* in a relationship into which the large number enters. Dirac suggested that the relationship held at all times, necessarily. If so, then gravity would be varying. It would be growing weaker and weaker as the universe aged. But Dicke protested that the only necessity in this area was an observational necessity. Observers could expect to find themselves at times sufficiently late for heavy elements – carbon above all – to have been formed inside stars and then scattered when those stars exploded. Again, they could expect to see skies filled with stars which hadn't burned out, because stellar radiation would very probably be essential to life. Dicke calculated that at these times gravity's strength, if unvarying, would nevertheless have to stand in Dirac's relationship.[3]

A more ambitious use of the anthropic principle occurs in J. A. Wheeler's writings.[4] Wheeler pictures an oscillating cosmos. Each of many Big Bangs is followed by a Big Squeeze and then a new Bang as the crushed material rebounds. At the moments of greatest

189

compression, the cosmos loses all memory of its earlier properties. It then explodes with properties which are settled randomly. The number of its particles may differ from cycle to cycle. So may its expansion speed. So, too, may the ratio between the strengths of (say) the nuclear strong force and electromagnetism, or the extent (if any) to which the proton is heavier than the electron. It might be only during very rare oscillations that the resulting mixtures of properties were life-permitting. An observational selection effect would ensure, however, that living beings found themselves in the life-permitting eras only.

Probabilistic uses of the anthropic principle

The preconditions of observership may never be entirely firm. Consider the 'Hawking radiation' of black holes. According to S. W. Hawking, black holes emit particles of all kinds in a quantum-mechanical, random way. In a huge enough collection of black holes, a television set would be emitted occasionally. So would Charles Darwin – by which Hawking of course means not Darwin himself but someone just like him, someone who'd be observing all that Darwin would be, if Darwin were flying out of the black hole.[5] Yet obviously observers could only very rarely find themselves in circumstances like these. In its most useful formulations, the anthropic principle considers *where one is at all likely to find oneself* rather than *where finding oneself isn't utterly impossible*.

Suppose that some intelligent beings exist during the Big Bang's first few minutes, at the margins of black holes out of which they come flying like Darwin. In a huge enough cosmos they really would. Nobody can yet set limits to how huge the cosmos is. It should still come as no surprise to me that I exist in a much later epoch. Observers can most expect to find themselves in the spatiotemporal regions where most of them are found.

Again, suppose that almost all intelligent life is based on water and exists on planets when numerous stars still shine. (Dicke's argument against Dirac would fail if it had to assume that absolutely no life-encouraging stars would be shining at late times.) It should then come as no surprise to us that we are on a watery planet and see a starry sky.

Compare the case of geographical position. You develop amnesia in a windowless room. Where should you think yourself more likely to be: in Little Puddle with a tiny population, or in London? Suppose you remember that Little Puddle's population is fifty while London's is ten million, and suppose you have nothing but those figures to guide you. (You don't recall ever having been in either place; you have no theory that the mists of Little Puddle induce amnesia; and so on.) Then you should prefer to think yourself in London. For what if you instead saw no reason for favouring the belief that you were in the larger of the two places? Forced to bet on the one or on the other, suppose you betted you were in Little Puddle. If everybody in the two places developed amnesia and betted as you had done, there would be ten million losers and only fifty winners. So, it would seem, betting on London is far more rational. The right estimate of your chances of being there rather than in Little Puddle, on the evidence in your possession, could well be reckoned as ten million to fifty.

If you are in London, then of course this fact will have resulted from countless particular causes which made *exactly you* be in that city. But the correctness of an explanation in terms of those particular causes is compatible with the reasonableness of saying, 'Many more people are in London, so that's where I could most expect to find myself.' Compare the following cases. (a) You throw two dice together, just once, and fail to get a double-six. A full explanation of why you got something else, perhaps a four and a two, would involve countless details of particular causes: initial positions and velocities, wind speeds, table roughnesses and so forth. But you can shed light on your failure to get a double-six if you say that double-sixes occur only one thirty-sixth of the time when two dice are thrown repeatedly. (b) Blessed with seven children, you find not all of them are girls. Can't you view this as altogether to be expected, without actually being given a causally detailed tale showing precisely how it came to be true? (c) If you want to know why a square peg won't fit into a round hole with the same cross-sectional area, you needn't wait for full details of quark and electron movements. Rather similarly: if you want to know why you haven't caught a fish measuring 33.84 centimeters more or less exactly, you needn't wait for the full life history of the one fish which you did catch.

What if your amnesia gives you doubts about whether London's population is the larger? Finding yourself in London should reduce the doubts. With the larger population, London would be prima facie where you'd be more likely to find yourself. And if London and Little Puddle were the only places in which you could be, then finding yourself in Little Puddle could suggest strongly that London was a fiction, so long as its fictitiousness had no great initial improbability.

We could use similar reasoning when considering *Where are they?*, the famous question posed by E. Fermi. Why, that is to say, do we see no signs of extraterrestrial intelligent beings? Might there be very many technologically advanced civilizations in space-time as a whole, but only very few, and those ones unusually small, at the early time at which I am living? Just conceivably this scenario is correct. But an observer in a technological civilization would be far less likely to be in an early period, a period when such civilizations were small and few, than in a later one when they were huge and many. I therefore have grounds for thinking the scenario wrong. This could mean that my technological civilization wasn't among the very earliest: many others had developed previously without making their presence known to us humans, probably because they quickly became extinct. Alternatively it could mean that only a very few technological civilizations will ever have developed, in the entire history of the universe.

True enough, my technological civilization might be the very first in the universe. Some technological civilization would be in that position even in a universe whose temporal entirety contained a trillion trillion trillion technological civilizations. But please don't ask me to believe I am like this: *in the earliest technological civilization among immensely many.* Not unless you can give me very strong grounds for believing it.

Carter's disturbing point

As Carter noticed in about 1980, we can make a slight extension to such reasoning, an extension which comes as a shock to almost everybody. Although 'anthropic' reasoning is typically concerned with where you'd be likely to find yourself, granted only that you were an intelligent life form of some kind, there is nothing to prevent our applying it more narrowly, asking about human life in particular. Where, then, would a human be likely to find himself or herself, inside the temporal spread of the human race? In an early period when humans were comparatively few, or in a later one when they were immensely many?

Carter describes this question as introducing 'an application of the anthropic principle outstandingly free of the questionable technical assumptions involved in other applications' and 'obviously the most practically important application'. Yet instead of finding those words in his published work, I have had to take them from a letter in which he reacted to various writings of mine.[6] I had sent him these in the hope that he would say whether their reasoning was, as rumour suggested, essentially *his* although he had never developed it in print.

Neither, apparently, had anyone apart from me – though Carter's letter confirmed that the reasoning really was his. 'You seem to be the first', he wrote. But Andrei Linde has since drawn my attention to somewhat similar reasoning published by H. B. Nielsen at virtually the same time.[7]

A main cause for Carter's failure to go into print, he explained, was that 'with a few notable exceptions' the people he had spoken to were 'even less willing to take in this particular application of the anthropic principle than other applications'. (It is astonishing how much opposition the anthropic principle provokes. Who would have thought there was anything terribly controversial in the point, insisted on by David Hume and Immanuel Kant, that the situation in which we find ourselves could be very untypical of the cosmos in its entirety? Who would have predicted you would meet with real anger if you dared suggest, for example, that intelligent life quite probably arises only on planetary surfaces, or that our Big-Bang universe would have been lifeless if it had recollapsed within a year or two?) In a lecture of 1983 which emphasized how anthropic reasoning could be applied to circumstances in which observers *are at all likely* to find themselves, Carter had introduced the doomsday argument, adding that nuclear submarine commanders would do well to think about it. Yet the printed version of his lecture only hinted at it, saying that 'something like a man made ecological disaster might well be discussed with reference to the anthropic principle'.[8] Since then he has confined himself to mentioning it in seminars, particularly when faced with the objection that the anthropic principle leads to no predictions.

Let me insist, not for the first time and not for the last, that the doomsday argument *does not* announce firmly that the human species will soon die out. At most it suggests that the risk of its soon dying out is probably greater than we suspected, and very possibly a lot greater. Suppose we started off extremely confident in a long future for humankind. The doomsday argument, even if we accepted it fully, could then leave our confidence largely unshaken. Again, the argument *cannot* run really smoothly *if* the world is radically indeterministic, *unless* the indeterminism is of a sort unlikely to have much influence on how long the human race will survive. These points will need to be repeated again and again. People find it extraordinarily difficult to remember them. No doubt the label 'doomsday argument' – I got it from Frank Tipler, who first told me of Carter's ideas on the subject and knocked down the 'obvious refutations' which I at once threw at him – is in part to blame. But 'anthropic argument suggesting that we have systematically underestimated the risk that the human race will end fairly shortly' would have been far too lengthy as a label.

The chief theme of Carter's lecture of 1983 was that when a process (for instance throwing a triple six once or many times with three fair dice) involves one or more very improbable events, and so is very unlikely to be completed inside the period available (such as thirty throws), then it has most chance of being completed after something roughly approaching that period. Carter reasoned that this gave the best explanation for the rough equality between the time taken for evolution to produce the human race and the period separating Earth's formation from the date, a few billion years in the future, at which our sun will become unstable. The associated 'anthropic prediction' was that races of humanlike intelligence are rare. Even given very many life-bearing planets, such intelligence would almost never evolve quickly enough. This argument was very different from the one which the printed version of his lecture only hinted at, the worrying argument discussed in this book.

Whereabouts in time, Carter and I ask, would a human observer be likely to find himself or herself? If the human race is going to survive for very many millennia without any population decrease

– and particularly if it is actually going to increase hugely by colonizing the entire galaxy, a process which might take only a few million years – then you and I could plausibly be in the earliest hundredth of 1 per cent of all humans, or even the earliest 0.00001 per cent. Suppose, though, that the race will instead come to an end shortly, maybe because of nuclear war or environmental poisoning or perhaps (as was discussed in Chapter 2) through experiments in high-energy physics which upset a space-filling scalar field which is in a merely metastable condition, so that a bubble of fully stable field is created and then expands at nearly the speed of light, killing everyone. You and I are rather ordinary humans on this scenario, granted that something like 10 per cent of all humans who have so far been born are alive at this very moment. (If the human race met its doom tomorrow, then you and I wouldn't be very unusually late, for roughly one in ten of the whole race would be as late as we were. If I arrive in a town of unknown size and see a tramcar marked Tram No. 179, then it could be odd of me to suppose that there were only 179 tram-cars in the town, but thinking that the human race will meet disaster during my lifetime is nothing of this sort.)

Surveying space-time, we can say firmly that human observers have found themselves at points since the earliest beginnings of their species until roughly the end of the twentieth century. On the other hand, we have no firm assurance that any will find them-selves at later points. How should we react to this major difference – so far as concerns what is known to you and me – between people existing at or before roughly the end of the twentieth century, and any who will exist later? The Carter–Leslie suggestion is that Bayes's Rule of the probability calculus could apply here, acting to increase any estimate of how likely it is that the human race will end fairly shortly.

Compare how you could argue if you got first, second or third prize in a lottery. No matter how many names beyond three were contained in a lottery urn, somebody or other would win first prize, second prize, third prize – just as, no matter how long the human race lasted, some people would be born earliest. Still, if your name is among the first three drawn from the urn, then this can support your suspicion that only a few names remain in it.

Only someone who had in fact won a lottery could be in a position to inquire, 'How is it that I've won? Am I simply very lucky or did my friend at lottery company headquarters arrange it, or were there just a few names in the urn?' Such queries aren't foolish, though. They don't, for example, take the probability that the winner has won and confuse it with some other probability. The suspicion about the friend at headquarters is no mere idiotic reaction to a question which only a fool would ask, such as 'What's the chance that whoever actually won did in fact win?' The suspicion that the urn contained only a few names isn't idiotic either.

Here is a true story. A publisher organized a raffle whose prize was $300-worth of books. In view of the length of the form which raffle-entrants had to fill in, my suspicion was that few would bother, so I filled it in myself. Two weeks later, $300-worth of books arrived on the doorstep. My suspicion was supported.

A suspicion of this kind would have been supported even if I hadn't known of the raffle before winning it. What if someone else had got the raffle ticket on my behalf? The case would be unaffected provided it had been guaranteed that I'd sooner or later learn the ticket's fate, regardless of whether it had won. This is a significant proviso, of course. If I first hear of a raffle by learning that I've won it, then this supports the 'few tickets' theory more strongly than if I learn just that someone has purchased a ticket for me – but only if the losers, too, would be sure to learn the fates of their tickets at some stage or other. That's important. If nobody but the winner could ever come to know that the raffle had been held, then nothing could be deduced from hearing how very successful one's own ticket had been; one could not possibly have heard instead that it had been unsuccessful.

On the other hand, it would make no difference that the losers hadn't learned about their losses when I learned that I had won. To think that everything would hang on whether the winner learned before, after or simultaneously with the losers is a case of replacing probability theory by a belief in magic.

It would make no difference, either, if the ticket had been got on behalf of some third party, so long as it was guaranteed that (to take the simplest case) the fate of just this one ticket would be made known to me. Any probability calculations I carry out in this area mustn't be made magically dependent on my being the actual beneficiary, let alone on my being exactly me and nobody else. While it's wrong to adopt a 'God's-eye view', protesting that somebody or other has to win every raffle, it's equally wrong to think that my my-ness can have any relevance *in itself*. It can be relevant only because of being linked to my not being God, i.e. to the limitations of my knowledge. God may know exactly how many raffle tickets were sold, but I am trying to guess it. I may know only of my own ticket, and that I was guaranteed to learn its fate. But suppose I additionally knew just this: that Susan had bought a ticket on her own behalf, and that I had been guaranteed to learn its fate whether or not it had been the winner. The fact that Susan's ticket had won the raffle would then support the 'few tickets' theory just as strongly as if my ticket had won.

If ignorant of how many names were in the urn, every winner of a lottery has, by the sheer fact of having won, increased reason for suspecting that there were only a few. Every loser has increased reason for suspecting that there were many. There is nothing paradoxical here. For a start, losers know that the urn contained more than one name. The winner of the first prize may not. In getting the $300-worth of books, did I benefit from the luck of the draw? I doubt it. My hunch is that mine was the only raffle entry.

Imagine that the Devil knows there were a thousand raffle entries. Because of his 'God's-eye view' of the situation, he laughs at me. He tells himself that whoever had won could have used exactly my reasoning. But what does this show? Simply that the Devil likes arguing unfairly. My reasoning isn't poor reasoning, since I don't share all the Devil's knowledge. Now, I have to estimate probabilities on the basis of my own evidence, not his. For imagine that, fearful of being misled, I was no more eager than before to believe that mine had been the only name in the urn. Then, if the raffle were repeated, my knowledge of how it had turned out earlier ought not to affect me: if I won again on the second occasion, I ought to use exactly the same reasoning as on the first occasion, making no change in my estimate of the probabilities. Likewise, even winning thirty times in a row ought to give me no extra reason to doubt that the urn was always being filled with hundreds of raffle tickets. But surely fear of the Devil's laughter shouldn't be allowed to lead to a conclusion so ridiculous – so bizarrely hostile towards efforts to learn from experience.

Bayesian reasoning

Bayes's Rule is a mathematical one. It says that the probability, in view of evidence *e*, that hypothesis *h* is correct, grows or shrinks in proportion to any extra or lesser likelihood that you'd have got such evidence if the hypothesis were indeed correct. This is common sense, very widely applicable. The evidence can be that you have won a lottery or have been hit by an arrow or bitten by a dog, or that an observed car is red, or evidence in virtually any other field. The hypothesis, too, can be from virtually any field. It could be the hypothesis that there were few names in the lottery urn, or that there were many; that the arrow was aimed, or that it was shot at random; that many cars are red, or that few are.

No doubt we could get a long way without using any mathematical formula. We could simply bear in mind two considerations:

1 that *we ought to have some tendency to prefer theories when their truth would have made us more likely to make various observations which we've in fact made*; and

2 that, all the same, *some theories are so utterly silly, or so badly at variance with all evidence collected previously, that we ought to continue to put little trust in them, despite how much their truth would have increased the likelihood of those observations.* If, for instance, you had a fairy godmother, then she might well have contributed a million dollars to your bank account, but seeing the million dollars is insufficient reason for believing in a fairy godmother.

We might just make points (1) and (2) to ourselves, in a commonsense way. Still, it can be useful to have a mathematical procedure for judging the interplay between point (1) and point (2). And in case after case, Bayes's Rule seems to be what we need.

In some cases, ones involving such things as lottery urns, the Rule's usefulness is very firmly provable. In others it can merely seem very plausible, or at least plausible enough to suggest that applying the Rule will be quite as reasonable as appealing to (1) and (2) in a mathematically unsophisticated fashion.

In one of its simplest formulations, Bayes's Rule states a relationship between four things: $P(h, e)$ and $P(h)$ and $P(e, h)$ and $P(e)$. The first of these things is the probability that hypothesis h is correct, in view of evidence e. The second is the 'prior probability' that the hypothesis is correct: its probability of correctness prior to taking evidence e into account. The third is the probability that you would have got evidence e if hypothesis h were in fact correct. The fourth is the probability that you would have got it one way or the other: in other words, with the hypothesis right or with it wrong.

What Bayes's Rule states is that the first thing equals the second multiplied by the third and then divided by the fourth. And this amounts to what I said a moment ago: that the probability, in view of evidence e, that hypothesis h is correct grows or shrinks in proportion to any extra or lesser likelihood that you would have got such evidence if the hypothesis were indeed correct. In other words: 'Take account of the extent that you would have been more likely – or else less likely – to see what you did see, if such and such a theory had been right.'

As this book isn't a treatise on mathematics, let's simply write down a slightly more complex version of the Rule, considering how it applies in particular cases. $P(h, e)$ equals

$$[P(h) \, P(e, h)] \div [P(h) \, P(e, h) + P(\text{not } h) \, P(e, \text{not } h)]$$

in this more complex version.

What that means could be illustrated as follows. Suppose there is a 98 per cent probability that a lottery urn with my name in it contains one thousand names, and a 2 per cent probability that it contains just ten. These 'prior' probabilities are my personal estimates – maybe superbly well grounded or maybe not – of how likely the two alternatives are, before the drawing of any names. (Perhaps I actually watched my name being put into one hundred identical urns, noting that in 99 cases a further 999 names were added; etc.) What if I next find that mine is among the first three names drawn from the urn? Bayesian calculation gives me a new estimate. The 'posterior' probability of there having been only ten names in the urn is

$$[2\% \times 3/10] \div [(2\% \times 3/10) + (98\% \times 3/1000)],$$

which is approximately 67 per cent. An estimated probability of only two out of a hundred has grown into one of over two out of three. Whereas I used to be very confident that the urn contained a thousand names, I should now think it quite a lot more likely that it contained just ten – so that there are very few names still waiting to be drawn.

Calculations on similar lines can suggest that the risk that the human race will end soon has been regularly underestimated, perhaps very severely. All depends on whether the case of one's name coming out of the urn is sufficiently similar to the case of being born into the world: similar enough, that is to say, to make Bayes's Rule a useful guide. If there were a thousand names in the urn, then a name which was drawn among the first three would have been drawn very, very exceptionally early. If there were many trillion humans scattered through space-time, then a human who had been born before roughly the end of the twentieth century would have been born very, very exceptionally early. Can we be guided by similar reasoning in each case?

'DOOMSDAY ARGUMENT' CALCULATIONS

Remember, there's no absolute need for Bayesian mathematics in this area. In fact the kinds of simplification introduced to get the mathematics working – the use of crude 'two-bin' approximations, for instance, in which complex ranges of possibilities are replaced by just a couple of alternatives between which we are asked to choose – might be quite a good reason for preferring unmathematical common sense to Bayesian manoeuvres. We can make much progress by considering some basic facts about inductive logic: the logic of learning by experience. We could never learn from experience unless we tended to prefer theories whose truth would have made our actual experiences more likely. If you were bitten by a dog, you should view this as increased reason for suspecting that the dog quite often bites. Hit by an arrow, you should consider its stopping-place as supporting the theory that it was aimed at you. If you see a red car coming round the corner, you should treat the event as reinforcing the hypothesis that quite a few cars are red. The baby who keeps crawling into the fire, because unwilling to develop new confidence in the notion that fires are causes of pain, is an incompetent baby. And so on.

All this is common sense. While we could dress it up in Bayesian mathematics, there'd be no real need to do so. Non-mathematicians can have an excellent grasp of the area.

None the less, let's look at various actual Bayesian calculations which the doomsday argument inspires, just to get some idea of how greatly our risk-estimates could be shifted by the argument. (To say that *the risk that the human race will end shortly is n%* is equivalent to saying that *the theory that it will end shortly has n% probability of being right.*)

Simplifying greatly, let's say that the sole alternatives are a race-annihilating catastrophe by AD 2150 or else survival, at present population levels or above, for a few thousand centuries; and further, that the world isn't radically indeterministic (for indeterminism could complicate matters considerably, in ways to be discussed later). Should doomsday be judged likely to arrive soon? Yes, unless the 'prior probability' of Doom Soon – i.e. its probability as estimated before we take account of our own observed position in time – is very low. Bayesian calculation supports this.

Suppose, for instance, that the chance of a human's finding himself or herself alive at the same time as you and me is *one in ten* in the case of the short-lasting human race, while in that of the long-lasting race it is only *one in a thousand*. Suppose you start by thinking that the risk of Doom Soon, the probability that the race will end by the year 2150, is merely 1 per cent, while the probability of Doom Delayed for a Few Thousand Centuries is 99 per cent (since we're simplifying matters by allowing only these two alternatives). That is to say, 1 per cent and 99 per cent are your estimates prior to taking account of your position in time. You now take account of it. If you can use Bayes's Rule exactly as before, then the revised estimate of the risk of Doom Soon is

$$[1\% \times 1/10] \div [(1\% \times 1/10) + (99\% \times 1/1000)],$$

which is slightly over 50 per cent. So, from thinking that Doom Soon is only 1 per cent likely, you shift to thinking that there's a good half-chance of it.

What if it is instead assumed that the human race, if it passed the year 2150 safely, would spread so widely beyond the solar system that the figure of *one in a thousand* ought to be replaced by *one in a million*? Well, the estimated risk of Doom Soon now rises much further, to almost exactly 99.9 per cent. Naturally these figures are only illustrative. They are presented just to indicate how huge a 'Bayesian shift' you might reasonably give to your estimates, if you suddenly came to accept that the doomsday argument worked smoothly.

There may be little need to apologize for choosing AD 2150 as the date dividing Doom Soon from Doom Delayed. There are fairly strong grounds for thinking that the next one and a half centuries will be a period of grave danger, and that if we manage to escape disaster during this period then there will be an excellent chance that the human race will survive for very many further millennia, quite probably growing to an enormous size through galactic colonization. Yet the significance of Carter's mathematical argument could well be only slightly affected by choice of some date other than 2150, and of other plausible figures for the percentage of all humans living nowadays on the two competing scenarios (Doom Soon, Doom Delayed). The crucial point is that large Bayesian shifts could be reasonable if the argument worked at all.

The point survives even when one's mathematics becomes covered with approximation signs, 'at least' signs, signs standing for ranges of figures rather than single figures, and so on. Compare how the report that your name has come out of a lottery urn 'in something like the tenth draw', or 'between the sixth and the sixteenth draw', can act powerfully against the suggestion that there are 'at least a thousand other names' still waiting to be drawn, or 'from one to two thousand other names'. (No single figure for the size of the human race in its temporal entirety – the number of humans who will ever have lived – has much chance of being *exactly right*, to be sure. And of course the difficulty of guessing exactly the right figure could increase enormously if the right 'ball park' were composed of gigantic figures. You've a far better chance of guessing precisely how many coins there are in a friend's pocket than of getting exactly the right figure for how many atoms there are in the sun. But the doomsday argument doesn't demand accurate figures. Approximations and ranges can fit its purposes admirably.)

Don't protest too vigorously that the 'two-bin' approach cannot take account of the vastly many conceivable futures: for instance that the human race will end in the year 2150, and that it will end in the year 7257, and that it will end in the year 94183, and that it won't end for a very long time but will collapse to a population of just a few thousand in the year 54323 and then remain there. For although such a way of protesting does have some force, it has no overwhelming interest. The big question is instead whether we have any right to treat *being born at a particular point in human population history* as at all analogous to *having one's name come out of an urn at such and such a stage.*

What if the analogy worked rather well? Carter and I wouldn't see this as a message of despair. For remember, all that the doomsday argument involves is a Bayesian shift – (or if you dislike Bayesian mathematics, then just *a shift*, a shift produced by the commonsense consideration that we should be somewhat inclined to think of our situation as rather ordinary, instead of highly unusual) – in any estimate of how likely it is that the human race will end shortly. Prima facie, there could be seem to be little risk of destroying the entire race by a nuclear war, and within a few centuries after such a war we might well expect population levels to be back where they were before. Prima face, the risk of irrevocably upsetting a metastable scalar field by high-energy experiments could well be tiny: cosmic ray collisions have attained energies far higher than humans will attain by any readily developable technology. Carter's reasoning could suggest that these and other risks should be re-evaluated as threats to human survival many times greater than they at first seemed to be, but we could then, of course, try to compensate for this by taking greater care. We might ban attempts to attain extremely high energies, for instance. Yet if we find that the risks continue to look tiny even after the Bayesian shift, then we may simply shrug them off – saying to ourselves that it seems far more likely that we are very unusually early in the career of the human race than that this career will end soon.

The point is that the Carter–Leslie argument doesn't generate risk estimates *all by itself.* It argues for Bayesian shifts which magnify any risk-estimates that have been reached by other means. It isn't an armchair proof that the human race would be likely to end before the number of humans who had ever been born grew much larger than it is today. (It's unclear whether H. B. Nielsen properly appreciated this point when he presented Carter's reasoning, or something somewhat like it.[9] If he didn't, then all that he presented was something somewhat like it, although 'doomsday argument' was his label too.) A philosopher's ontological argument for God's existence may try to get to real facts from Pure Reason, but Carter doesn't. A Bayesian shift can magnify a risk-estimate only when something is already there to be magnified.

We thus have to look seriously at, say, the effects of CFCs on the ozone layer, asking whether humans are willing to ban CFCs. We have to consider such facts as that scientists are clever at warding off catastrophes, that species quite often undergo population explosions without disaster, and that very many humans have managed to die peacefully in their beds. If various risks were initially estimated to be very, very small, then even after a Bayesian shift which made them look a thousand times larger they could still look small. If they came to look great, however, then we could change the data to be put into our Bayesian calculation by taking stern measures such as banning all CFCs.

In short, the Carter–Leslie reasoning isn't a doomsday argument in the sense of telling us we are doomed regardless of what we do. The 'doomsday clock' of the *Bulletin of Atomic Scientists* has hands which are justifiably pushed further from midnight whenever some heartening development takes place: for instance the apparent end of the nuclear arms race. And there could actually be general grounds for putting the clock hands further and further from midnight – where 'hands near midnight' means 'high probability that humans will soon become extinct' – as time went on. The sheer fact of having survived a threatening situation for many years would tend to show that its threats were really rather small. Carter has never denied that humans would have grounds for growing more and more confident, the longer the human race had survived the dangers confronting it in the twenty-first century, and the further it had spread through the galaxy.

It is wrong to protest, as I did when first introduced to Carter's reasoning, that any ancient Roman who had used the doomsday argument could have been led to conclude mistakenly that human numbers would soon decline to zero. (1) A first reply is: 'So what?' It isn't a weakness in any merely probabilistic argument if it leads someone very improbably placed – someone very early in time, maybe, or someone who has thrown a dozen dice with eyes shut and expects (but unfortunately, since a dozen sixes are in fact on the table) not to see a dozen sixes upon opening them – to a mistaken conclusion, a false conclusion, the conclusion of somebody who is *misled* about the actual situation. A conclusion can be misleading, false, without being *unwarranted*, stupid, the result of poor reasoning. (2) A second reply is that any Roman might well have been right in thinking that the human race would end fairly shortly. If it ended by the year 2150, this would be fairly soon after Roman times. The doomsday argument needn't take the form of saying that the human race will probably end tomorrow. (3) A third reply is that no immense population explosion was taking place in Roman times, or was readily predictable. (4) A fourth is that any Roman might have had insufficient grounds for attaching more than a very tiny 'prior probability' to the imminent extinction of humankind. It is then an interesting question whether in view of environmental poisoning, nuclear bombs, diseases which spread world wide within days because of air travel, etc., our own case is different.

Throughout the universe, mightn't intelligent races master scientific laws in ways which made huge population explosions virtually inevitable, while seldom taking adequate precautions against the risks coming from those explosions themselves or from other aspects of science? Of intelligent beings, mightn't most find themselves in rapidly expanding races which would rather quickly die out? Perhaps so. But always remember that the doomsday argument could be important even without telling us that Doom Soon *was likely*. Both today and for any Roman who had thought of it, it might be important just through suggesting that Doom Soon *was more likely than one would otherwise have estimated*.

OBJECTIONS TO THE ARGUMENT

Given twenty seconds, many people believe they have found crushing objections to the Carter–Leslie approach. Here are some, collected into four groups. The objections of Group IV, centering on the fact that the world may be markedly indeterministic, are clearly important and will be discussed in Chapter 6 as well.

Group I

These objections raise general doubts about whether a Bayesian approach, or anything like it, can justify the suggested conclusion.

(Ia) Everybody is unusual in many respects. It's therefore wrong to favour theories which make our position ordinary.

My reply is that, yes, everybody is of course unusual in many respects; but this is insufficient reason for viewing ourselves as very unusual when there exist fairly plausible theories whose rightness would make us rather ordinary. Look at the risks of ozone depletion and so forth. An imminent end to the human race can well seem fairly plausible.

It was, I now think, wrong of me to have said in the *Philosophical Quarterly* that Carter's argument was 'not straightforwardly inductive'.[10] Any respectable inductive argument – any well-constructed argument from actual experience – must take account of the plausibility or implausibility of various hypotheses, and Bayes's Rule often shows how to do so. For these purposes, the hypothesis that you and I could quite have expected to find ourselves as early as this *because there just won't be all that many humans at later times* can be much like any other hypothesis. Inductive reasoning is seldom entirely straightforward. The Bayesian reasoner will, of course, have little interest in utterly implausible theories: fairy-godmother theories, the theory that iron nails are in love with magnets, the theory that the human race will end within the next thirty-five seconds, the theory that it will end during the next century because of fluoridation of tapwater, and so forth. True enough, zillions of those theories are such that their correctness would greatly have raised the likelihood of our seeing what we did. But their silliness gives them a 'prior probability' of correctness *so low* that their chance of being correct remains extremely small even after their 'success at predicting what we actually saw' has been taken into account in Bayesian fashion. (Besides, the more of them there are, the less their individual attractions must be. As a matter of logic, there cannot be zillions of theories which compete – if one's right then the others are wrong – and which all have non-negligible chances of being right.)

When the doomsday argument considers the possibility of your being an extraordinarily early human, it of course doesn't deny that you are rather late and ordinary among all humans existing *up to the present moment*. The matter which the argument exploits is that whereas you are fairly ordinarily placed in human population history up to today, since maybe 10 per cent of all the humans who have so far been born are still alive now, your ordinariness won't continue – it won't be ordinariness inside the career of the human race in its temporal entirety – if the race is going to survive for many more millennia at its present size, let alone if it is going to spread throughout the galaxy.

Just why, though, could it be unacceptably odd if we were very exceptionally early in the total temporal spread of the human race? In response to this one needs to insist (not for the first time, not for the last) that Carter and Leslie aren't claiming as the starting-point of their argument *that it definitely would be unacceptably odd*, nor need they claim this even at their argument's conclusion. If, before considering the doomsday argument, you thought the prob-ability of Doom Soon very low – the mere fact that the population was expanding perhaps making you confident that the human race was hard to kill – then you could perhaps continue to think it low *even after* the argument's Bayesian manoeuvres. Still, a reason for fairly strongly suspecting that something, for instance our position in time, specially needs to be explained instead of being dismissed as 'how things just happen to be' is that a fairly plausible expla-nation comes to mind; and Doom Soon may indeed be fairly plausible. We have, in effect, to be guided by what can be called the Merchant's Thumb principle.[11] When does a dealt hand of cards call for explanation by something other than chance? It quite probably calls for it when cheating is easy, when this particular hand is certain to bring great profit to the dealer, when the dealer is in sore need of great profit, and so forth. A poker hand which at first looks worthless, not specially calling for explanation, can come to be thought very special indeed when it's realized that a million dollars are at stake, that poker has many variants, and that in the variant actually being played this apparently valueless set of cards which the dealer has dealt to himself is a powerful hand. When, again, is there a fairly clear need to explain – other than by appeal to 'mere chance' – why an arch collapsed precisely as you were passing under it? Perhaps when you see that your rival in love is lurking in the nearby bushes. And why is there anything 'special' in the placement of the thumb of a merchant as he exhibits a silk robe? Every thumb must be somewhere or other, yet the merchant's thumb is covering a hole in the silk and he hopes to make a sale.

Ultimately it is the Merchant's Thumb principle – a principle that can be dressed up as Bayes's Rule but that is in any case programmed into our brains in a way making us see it as 'merely common sense' – which explains why we shouldn't just shrug our shoulders and say that we have to exist at some point or other in time, and that some people or other have to be born earliest. Sure enough, we might in the end have little need to fear that the human race will become extinct shortly. It might in the end be most reasonable to conclude that we do just happen to find ourselves markedly early in humanity's spatiotemporal spread. But Carter's argument definitely must lead us to think Doom Soon *more likely than we would otherwise have thought it*. If we paid no attention to how various fairly plausible theories could throw light on why we experienced what we did, then experience could never teach us anything.

'What's so special', it may be protested, 'about coming out *as early as we did* from the imaginary urn of all humans, past, present and future? How could earliness be anything special? Being drawn in the first ten would be no more special than being drawn somewhere among draws 767,421 to 767,430.' The answer to any such protest is that your name coming from an urn in the first ten can be 'special' when you have some viable theory, for instance that there were only about fifteen or only about a hundred names in the urn, instead of about a million, which makes being drawn in the first ten specially much to have been expected, or at least not very unlikely. Surely there's nothing too strange and difficult in this idea.

(Ib) Urn analogies are inappropriate. We weren't given our birth times by a deity who pulled out souls from an urn at successive seconds and put them into human bodies.

This objection seems faulty. Urn analogies are relevant to many statistical calculations. For example: (1) Jim and Mike drive cars equally frequently in the same city. Jim has had twenty accidents and Mike not a single one. Are they equally good drivers? Consider an urn filled with two balls, one marked 'Jim' and the other 'Mike'. Balls are drawn again and again. In each case the drawn ball is put back in the urn, which is then shaken. Would it be likely that the 'Jim' ball would be drawn every single time? (2) You are hit by an arrow while walking around on a small island. Was this bad luck, or was the arrow aimed at you? If only luck was involved then this would be (at a rough approximation) as if the grid references of every square foot of the island had been put on slips of paper in an urn, your name being written on just one of them, etc.

Quite how could any urn analogy be used by the doomsday argument? Look again at your amnesiac self as you try to say where you are more likely to be, in London or in Little Puddle. You have nothing but population figures as a guide. To simplify things suppose that, much as all human observations must occur either before or after the infinitely brief first instant of AD 2150, so also all humans must find themselves in Little Puddle or else in London, and you know it. You know, too, that the populations are fifty and ten million, respectively. An appropriate model of the situation is an urn containing fifty balls marked 'Little Puddle' and ten million marked 'London'. But now, what if you knew instead that your only possible location was either fifty-bodied Little Puddle, which definitely existed, or else ten-million-bodied London, which might be fictitious? Suppose you were markedly uncertain whether

London was real. This, Carter and I suggest, can be interestingly comparable to knowing there have been humans before AD 2150, while being unsure that there will be any afterwards. Your situation now invites comparison with that of a man with an urn which he looks on as having, for instance, a 63 per cent probability of containing ten million 'London' balls in addition to the fifty marked 'Little Puddle' which he knows it to contain. If you next discover that you're in Little Puddle then you should react as if you'd drawn a 'Little Puddle' ball in such circumstances, which would give excellent grounds for believing that the 'London' balls were imaginary. You have powerful new reasons for thinking London unreal.

(Ic) No suitable 'prior probabilities' are available, so we've nothing to feed into a Bayesian calculation.

This objection might be forceful if the sole 'prior probabilities' which could be used were ones *known to correspond to facts* in some strong way. Suppose you had watched a hundred urns being filled. You therefore knew for sure that your name was in every urn and was joined, *in two of the cases*, by just nine other names, and *in all the other ninety-eight cases* by 999 names. Suppose the urns looked identical and were shuffled around while your back was turned. Then you'd have a strong excuse for saying you'd known entirely firmly, prior to drawing a single name from one of the urns and finding it was your own, that the probability that the urn contained a thousand names was 98 per cent. But what if you'd lacked this kind of knowledge? What if you'd instead seen two urns being filled, the one with just nine and the other with 999 names in addition to yours, and had been merely *rather confident* – you thought you remembered but weren't quite sure – that the left-hand urn of the two contained more names? Forced to give a figure for your degree of confidence, you would have said 98 per cent. You then drew a single name from this urn, and it was yours. What difference does it make that you'd started with '98 per cent confidence' rather than with 'a known 98 per cent probability'?

Some would reply: no difference whatever. Bayes's Rule, they would say, could be applied in exactly the same fashion in the two cases. But let's not get into a dispute about whether they would be right. Instead, let's simply note that there is no massively important difference between the two cases. In the second case just as in the first, finding that yours was the very earliest name drawn from the urn should lead to a large reduction in your confidence that the urn contained a thousand names.

It is certainly true that in estimating the probabilities of the two scenarios, Doom Soon and Doom Delayed, and the probable population sizes associated with those scenarios, we are engaged in much guesswork. What isn't in the least true, though, is that we can have no interesting reasons for guessing as we do, and no excuses for basing actual actions on our guesses. What if a man guessed that the chance that human history would come to an end in the next hundred and fifty years was only 0.000000000000000000000000000001 per cent? I wouldn't claim firm knowledge that he was wrong. But couldn't I quite reasonably say that he seemed far too optimistic, too irresponsibly unworried by the dangers confronting us? Without being any sort of idiot, couldn't I say, prior to considering Carter's argument, that the chance of Doom Soon struck me as about 5 per cent? And if so, exactly why should I refuse to put the figure of 5 per cent into a Bayesian calculation?

I don't want to suggest that a Bayesian calculation would be very obviously appropriate here. We'll later be looking at reasons, based on the world's possible indeterminisms, for doubting its appropriateness. But what seems fairly plain is that the sheer fact that the figure of 5 per cent would be 'guessed' rather than 'known' would be rather a weak reason for refusing to enter it into any calculation. For one thing, the entire distinction between guessed and known probabilities is itself very unclear.

When you try to estimate how many humans will be born from now onwards, even rough figures for the probabilities of various numbers or ranges of numbers (such as 'three hundred billion, give or take fifty billion') are difficult to derive. They are got with the help of much guesswork. But they aren't pulled out of thin air – as if they were 'prior' in the sense of 'a priori', i.e., reached without bothering to look at any actual evidence. Many fairly sensible folk believe they have quite good evidence, quite apart from any argument of Carter's, for the view that the human race has at least a 5 per cent chance of ending fairly shortly because, for instance, the air it now breathes is thick with pollution, or because bacteriological warfare is possible. And I know people with fairly attractive grounds for expecting it will colonize the galaxy if it survives the next few centuries. That's one reason why they are eager to make efforts to ensure its survival for those centuries – efforts which they'd view as unnecessary if the risk of Doom Soon appeared very low.

Politicians untroubled by such things as thinning of the ozone layer have, it seems, made rather a confident guess that the human race will survive without much difficulty. Let's please not leave all the guesswork to folk like them.

(Id) The reference class is wrongly chosen. Instead of being just human observers, it should be the class of all conscious or intelligent organisms.

I reply that, for predictions about human survival, the only evidently relevant names in any urn would be those of humans; we would seem to have a right to disregard any others. If so, we needn't consider pterodactyls, wise elephants or Martians. (Later pages will return to this point.)

Group II

These objections concern the fact that you and I can be sure that we (and maybe also all others like us) are in existence now, regardless of what will come later.

(IIa) The far future cannot kill us. That's an obvious truth.

Unfortunately (for it would be a great relief to find that the doomsday argument didn't work) this truth could undermine the Carter–Leslie position only if it were assumed, ridiculously, that present-day evidence for future events must be evidence *caused by* those events. Which would be as if you argued, on seeing an

212

avalanche tumbling towards your village, that this could be evidence of an imminent disaster only if the disaster in question were somehow causing the tumbling.

A similar objection runs: 'How could the fate of the entire human race depend on little me and my position in time?' You might almost as well protest: 'How could havoc wrought by the avalanche depend on little me and my position?' Carter and Leslie might perhaps be wrong in the conclusions they draw from their temporal location, yet at least they have grasped that the Fates won't attack the human race soon after AD 2150 'just to make sure that not too many humans live after Carter and Leslie, making them too unusually early'. There is no new 'doomsday argument mechanism' which threatens the human race, in addition to the mechanisms provided by ozone layer destruction, research into bacteriological warfare, mighty rocks rushing in from outer space, and so forth. The doomsday argument is simply an argument for re-evaluating the risks associated with those mechanisms, on the basis of our observed position in time. Observations can suggest this or that future catastrophe without having to be potential causes of it. Movements of clock hands may be mere indications that a bomb is about to explode, rather than being parts of a triggering process.

However, bear in mind also that a human race which had too many members born too soon after Carter and Leslie might pollute its environment calamitously. Population growth could enter our reasoning *both* as something affecting whether our temporal location was fairly ordinary *and* as a likely cause of disaster in the next few centuries. The fact that humankind has survived many earlier population increases can give us little confidence in our new, planet-polluting situation. We might be interestingly like recipients of a chain letter. Each copies the letter many times and posts it to others, until it can spread no further. It then dies out. Suppose each new generation of recipients is three times larger than the previous one. I get the letter. Where am I likely to be? In the last generation, it would seem, since more people would be there than in all previous generations lumped together. My observing the letter wouldn't cause its dying out; it would merely help to indicate its probable dying out. But the letter's previous rapid spread could be both an indication and a cause.

(IIb) We cannot move around in time as we do in space, so temporal position can't be treated as analogous to spatial position. The comparison with the cases of London and Little Puddle therefore fails.

To this objection, a first reply is that our ability to move around in space is strictly limited. We cannot, for instance, move to regions so distant that only faster-than-light travel could get us there inside our lifetimes. Yet surely we can apply 'anthropic' reasoning to such regions – for instance, to ones we can call Region 1 and Region 2. Surely we can say that if our own region had many million observers in it for every one observer in Region 1 or Region 2, then observers with nothing but this fact to guide them should expect to find themselves in our region rather than in either of the others.

A second reply is that nobody, no matter how free to move around in space, can have chosen the place where he or she was born, yet this doesn't block probabilistic reasoning about the birthplace of one's very own self: for example, about whether it was London or Little Puddle. Likewise, the fact that nobody can choose the time of his or her birth cannot block similar reasoning. You have forgotten your birthday: are you likely to have been born on July 4? Prima facie, the odds are against it.

Suppose you found that your birthdate was August 19. Notice how odd it would be to claim that probabilistic argumentation should never have been applied to this, because anyone born on some other day wouldn't have been *exactly you.*

(IIc) It's trivial that people now discussing Carter's argument find themselves alive today, not many thousand years in the future. But nothing non-trivial follows from a triviality. Since no humans of the far future are yet alive, it isn't in the least surprising that we aren't among them. We couldn't be fair samples of a pool of people unless all its members currently existed. Our calculations ought to assume that what happens 'after sampling' is irrelevant. The doomsday argument can therefore prove only that doomsday hasn't yet occurred.

My reply is that Carter doesn't try to squeeze information from such trivial truths as that bachelors are wifeless or that people alive now must all find themselves alive today, neither does he deny that people of future generations can't yet have found themselves anywhere. What Carter's calculations use is our awareness of *where today is*, that is at roughly the end of the twentieth century, and of how large the population in that period looks by comparison with the later populations which could plausibly be anticipated, were the human race to survive for much longer.

The objection that we couldn't possibly be anywhere earlier or later than roughly the end of the twentieth century, because roughly-the-end-of-the-twentieth-century *is now*, misses Carter's point. He doesn't dispute that roughly-the-end-of-the-twentieth-century is now. What he asks is how likely it would have been, against the backgrounds of competing scenarios, for instance (1) Doom in the Twenty-Second Century from Ozone Layer Destruction and (2) Doom Delayed Until AD 500,000 or Later, that a human would find himself or herself in a period when roughly-the-end-of-the-twentieth-century *was now*. This is a question whose answer depends straightforwardly on how humans are distributed in time on those competing scenarios – very much as if the issue were how likely a human would have been to be born in some small village rather than a mighty city. Carter can ask the question without fancying that babies are really first born in heaven, then travelling to their earthly birth-dates in time machines which have more chances of arriving in epochs in which humans are more plentiful.

Similarly, Carter needn't imagine souls hoping to enter human bodies and occasionally getting good luck, 'non-null results', the success rate reflecting how many bodies are 'currently available' instead of being in the past or in the future. The fact that people could never get the answer 'No' if asking *whether they currently existed* doesn't prove that all humans ought to treat themselves as utterly biased samples of the human race's temporal distribution, samples which could suggest nothing of interest. All it proves is that humans who do exist at such and such a date can't correctly judge that they exist at some other date instead. If the world had been fated to be one in which the large majority of all humans ever to be born would be alive in AD 2000, then finding yourself in AD 2000 could help to indicate this truth – instead of being 'merely finding yourself where you, as somebody of AD 2000, which is *now*, are 100 per cent biased to find yourself'. (Note: Existing as a human of AD 2000, you would yourself be a sample of the human race's temporal distribution. It isn't as if you would *first* come into existence at that date and *thereafter* attempt to sample the distribution, quite probably meeting with failure, 'a null result', because the person you were trying to select as a sample wasn't alive yet, or wasn't alive still.)

The objection that, when the human race ends, at least some humans will of course have existed at roughly the end of the twentieth century again misses the point. In asking how likely 'a' human would be to find himself or herself at about that time, Carter isn't asking how likely it would be for at least one human to occupy such a position. Asking how likely it is that a person who knows Latin will know Greek too, you aren't merely wondering whether anybody at all knows both.

Yes indeed, we can be just as certain that we live near the end of the twentieth century, no matter what theory we have about how many people will exist later. But what does this prove? Observations *logically compatible with* two theories can still support the one theory rather than the other. Suppose you toss a thousand successive heads with a coin. While logically compatible with the coin's being a fair one, this result can add force to the theory that it's double-headed, can't it? (Consider a critic arguing as follows: 'Imagine two lists, one – let's call it the Doom Soon list – with just twenty-three names, and the other – call it the Doom Delayed list – with a great many names. Suppose the first twenty names on the two lists are the same and that, taking a list and starting at the top, you read out twenty names. What if mine is among them? I still won't have any idea as to which list is being read from. Hence the doomsday argument fails.' Well, this is almost as strange as saying, 'Imagine two lists. One gives the results of tossing a double-headed coin twenty or more times; the other, those of tossing a fair coin, it just so happening to land heads the first twenty times. Take a list and, starting at the top, read out twenty entries. All are heads, regardless of which list is being read from. Therefore getting twenty heads with a coin in no way tends to show that it will fall heads in future because of being double-headed.' Carter doesn't deny that *if* your name were in the first twenty on a list then it would be in the first twenty whether or not the list continued onwards lengthily. He doesn't deny, either, that it might be surprising to find your name on a list at all, if those of most other people were left off it. What he has noticed, though, is that if there were a list naming everybody who would ever have been born, then, prima facie, you wouldn't expect your name to appear very unusually near the top. Yet the critic is asking us to assume that his own name's appearance in an analogous position would be in no way specially unlikely. For does he picture the choice between his story's two lists as made with the help of dice, the longer list – the one where his name is indeed very unusually near the top – being chosen only if the dice fall in some very improbable way? Not at all. Perhaps without being fully conscious of it, he is instead treating the two lists as put into an urn which is then well shaken so as to guarantee that each becomes *precisely as likely as the other* to be the list taken out and then read from! Otherwise, of course, he *could* have an idea as to which list was being read from.)

It is absolutely no refutation of Carter to say that, since we are alive near the end of the twentieth century, we cannot find ourselves alive in any later period instead. It's equally no refutation to say that our presence near the end of the twentieth century would be just as much a reality, and we should be just as certain of it, no matter what theory we had about how long the human race would survive. Bayes's Rule encourages people to change their estimates of various probabilities when particular evidence is considered. If a red car enters your visual field, the Rule can encourage greater confidence in the theory that 10 per cent of all cars are red, as compared with the theory that 0.01 per cent are. Suppose you argued that you *knew* you were looking at a red car; that you would be equally certain of this, even if you thought all other cars in the world were blue; and that therefore this particular car could add no weight to the theory that 10 per cent are red. You would be blundering. Experience could scarcely teach much to people who argued so strangely. Applying Bayes's Rule, you might indeed speak of 'the likelihood of a car's being red if 10 per cent of all cars are'. This could be ambiguous, but what would be intended is the likelihood of *a car's turning out to be red* if 10 per cent of all cars are red ones – and not the likelihood (which is 1, or 100 per cent) that *a car which has in fact turned out to be red*, as you personally know because you are looking at it, *really is red*. Now, a similar point applies when one asks where one would have been likely to find oneself inside the total temporal spread of the human race, (a) on the assumption that the race is going to last only until, say, AD 2150, and (b) on the assumption that it will last for many hundred thousand more years, perhaps colonizing the galaxy. It would be absurd to say, 'I know for sure that I exist at about the end of the twentieth century; it's because I exist there, not later, that I know that the human race got that far safely, but am uncertain about future dates; and therefore my existence no later than about the end of the twentieth century couldn't possibly be in any way surprising.' When Carter suggests that being alive near the end of the twentieth century would be being alive *very surprisingly early* if the human race were going to last for many more millennia, he isn't for one moment *doubting* that he exists near the end of the twentieth century and collects his evidence then. He's instead asking where in human population history he could at all have expected to find himself.

If we let ourselves be impressed by the truth that anybody discussing anything now has to be alive exactly now – instead of being, say, somebody not alive yet, perhaps because even the necessary ancestors haven't yet been born, or else not alive still, perhaps because of being dead for centuries – then we could never apply the anthropic principle to our position in time. We could see no force in Fermi's argument that we'd not be likely to be members of the very earliest intelligent species in a universe which was going to include numerous such species. Such an argument would fail at once, on the grounds that if one were actually in the first such species, then the others *wouldn't yet exist*. But surely this is far from enough to destroy Fermi's point. We might equally well refuse to apply the anthropic principle to our position in space, on the grounds that people discussing things *here*, where we are, have indeed to be *exactly here* and not elsewhere.

Two points still need to be considered in this connection:

(1) The 'Old Evidence' objection. A difficulty is that people are too often impressed by what they call 'the problem of Old Evidence'. It is thought, for instance, that if you've long known you live in Little Puddle then you cannot use this fact to support any theory – for example the theory that London is a fiction. Yet

isn't this a very curious thing to think? ('Dear Mr Newton: What's all this nonsense about deriving a new physics from the fall of an apple? Surely you've long known that apples do fall.') Consider the case of Dicke's argument against Dirac. Dicke felt that there would be only few observers at any much later times, and that this could help show that Dirac's theory wasn't needed. It is a blunder to protest, 'Dr Dicke, it's a sheer triviality that you exist when many life-giving stars are still shining. You have always known it!' Whether he has long known his position in time is plainly irrelevant. What's relevant is just whether he had previously taken account of this item of evidence when considering Dirac's theory. When old evidence is evidence you haven't yet taken into account, it can be just as good as new.

Imagine a man who had long known he had won a lottery, but who had just said to himself that somebody or other would have to have won, even in a lottery with a trillion participants. Introduced to Bayes's Rule, he is invited to conclude that his win did provide some reason for suspecting that there were only a few participants. Surely his prolonged disregard of the fact that he won cannot now be used as a good excuse for continuing to disregard it. The 'prior probabilities' which enter into Bayesian calculations *are not* defined as probabilities prior to observations *which have only recently been made.*

Keeping all this in mind, picture a girl raised to adulthood in a windowless room and in total ignorance of its spatiotemporal position. In neutral, 'tenseless' language – neither the language of the historian nor that of the commentator on contemporary affairs – she is now told of late-twentieth-century threats to the human race. Contemplating how any race which managed to survive such threats and begin colonizing its galaxy might well have a lengthy and very heavily populated career thereafter, she estimates that, despite the fact that in the late twentieth century 10 per cent (let's say) of all humans who had been born up to that period wouldn't yet have died, the probability that she lives in the late twentieth century is extremely small. Nuclear bombs, environmental poisons and other late-twentieth-century hazards don't impress her. But she next learns that Earth in the late twentieth century is where she is. Would it be reasonable of her to comment, 'This merely suggests that all but a very tiny minority of humans will live later

219

than I do'? Wouldn't she have some grounds for revising her earlier confidence in how safe bombs and environmental poisons can be? Yet if she can have such grounds, why cannot we?

Why couldn't we take account of our positions in time, without having to be raised in windowless rooms to avoid our long knowing about those positions? – or without having first to hit ourselves on the head to induce amnesia, so as to be able to discover the positions anew?

(2) The irrelevance of the B-theory of Time. I can say all that I've just said without being committed to the view of Time known as 'the B-theory' – the view that temporal now-ness is just as relative as spatial here-ness, so that when trying to picture the whole universe we ought to join Einstein in thinking 'of a four-dimensional existence, instead of, as hitherto, the evolution of a three-dimensional existence' (which is how he expressed the point in appendix 5 to the fifteenth edition of his *Relativity, the Special and the General Theory*). Like many other philosophers, I share Einstein's liking for the B-theory; yet what if it had to be rejected? There would still be no force in the objection (which, please note, is altogether different from objections based on the world's supposed indeterminisms) that any humans of the future *haven't yet* had an opportunity to consider their temporal positions; that they cannot be considering them *now*; whereas you and I, contemplating our position at present, are definitely contemplating it now and not a minute earlier or later. Sure enough, one *doesn't* exist somewhere different from where one actually is, either in space or in time. Yet there remains the question of whether one would have been at all likely to find oneself there.

Recall the story of the emeralds as told in the Introduction. Knowing that many more people were to get emeralds in a later century than in an earlier one, and lacking any further relevant evidence, it's in the later century that any emerald-getter should most expect to be. If that century were still in the future, then, true enough, the people in it wouldn't be alive yet, but this truth is irrelevant to you as an emerald-getter when you try to guess whether it's still in the future. And it remains irrelevant even when you don't know that the later century was to contain the most emerald-getters, but are instead asking yourself whether to

believe it. All this is so, no matter what you think about Einstein
or the B-theory.

*(IId) People like us are to be found only nowadays. Our character-
istics force us to occupy this era and not another.*

My reply is that the Carter–Leslie doomsday argument isn't
concerned with the question to which such an objection might be
relevant, namely 'Is it really true that we live at roughly the end
of the twentieth century?' – a question which we might perhaps
answer by finding, say, that we had some 'genetic signature' typical
of that time. Very possibly there are such genetic signatures,
constantly changing, so that anyone knowing enough about typical
DNA patterns near the end of the twentieth century could tell,
on examining the DNA extracted from my tomb at some far
future date, that I had lived at around that time. And presumably
there was no real chance that anyone *recognizably me* could have
existed at any very different time. The brand of English I speak,
the prejudices clouding my mind, my areas of knowledge and of
ignorance all show that I'm not a sixteenth-century or even a
nineteenth-century human. But when arriving at the doomsday
argument Carter wasn't in any doubt about *where he really was* in
time. He rightly chose not to ask himself the maximally specific
question of where someone with exactly his characteristics – which
might well include not only a mind remembering twentieth-century
parents, but also genes common in the twentieth century and never
found very far from this period – would have been likely to be.
Instead he asked what the likelihood was that, as a human observer,
one would observe oneself to be in the twentieth century *and
hence* with genes, memories, linguistic habits, knowledge and
ignorance such as are found there.

'If you do have such and such genes', the objection runs, 'then
how could you have been in the shoes of somebody who had
to have different ones because of living in some far distant era?'
If the objector's line of argument succeeded, then it would ruin
not only the doomsday argument but almost all 'anthropic'
reasoning. It would, for instance, ruin this reasoning: that one
would more probably find oneself to be based on chemistry, rather

than on forces governing the plasma inside a star, if chemical life evolved more often than plasma life. The objection would now run: 'Observers based on chemistry couldn't possibly have found that they were plasma-based instead. Being based on chemistry is incompatible with being based on plasma!' Yet surely no such objection can be forceful.

Similarly, the objector would argue that an extraterrestrial belonging to a lemming-like species, a species constantly undergoing population explosions and collapses, couldn't rightly ask itself (if it didn't already know its temporal position) whether it was *more probably* in one of the huge generations immediately preceding a population collapse, or in one of the tiny generations near the start of a population explosion. It couldn't ask itself this, supposedly, because of the point that it couldn't possibly have had just the genes which it had, if existing elsewhere in the population cycle. Without at all knowing what those genes were, it could use this point to make nonsense of the query 'At which stage in the cycle am I likely to be?' Yet the query wouldn't in fact be nonsense, would it?

Think once again of Fermi's question of why we see no signs of extraterrestrials. Surely it could be improbable that our species was the very first to develop a technologically advanced civilization, in a universe which was going to contain numerous such civilizations. It mustn't be protested that if our species really were the first, then, having the genes which we do have, we couldn't possibly be in some later species, perhaps of six-legged beings.

If still unconvinced, consider a variant on the Introduction's story of the emeralds. A firm plan was formed to rear humans in two batches: the first batch to be of three humans of one sex, the second of five thousand of the other sex. The plan called for rearing the first batch in one century. Many centuries later, the five thousand humans of the other sex would be reared. Imagine that you learn you're one of the humans in question. You don't know which centuries the plan specified, but you are aware of being female. You very reasonably conclude that the large batch was to be female, almost certainly. If adopted by every human in the experiment, the policy of betting that the large batch was of the same sex as oneself would yield only three failures and five thousand successes. Clearly you mustn't say: 'If I'm in the first, smaller batch, then those of the second batch *won't yet* have become observers. Someone observing things *now*, as I do, will have to be in the small batch. Hence I can have no special reason to think I come from the large one instead.' And it's surely every bit as clear that you mustn't say: '*My genes* are female, so I have to observe myself to be female, no matter whether the female batch was to be small or large. Hence I can have no special reason for believing it was to be large.'

More simply, suppose you are a woman and that you like it. Could you have had remarkable luck in being born female? Surely it makes sense to answer, 'No, for roughly half of all humans are female. As a human, one could quite have expected to find oneself as a female.' It would be thought odd if someone then protested that you couldn't possibly have been you, if you'd been male.

None of this denies that being *exactly you* results from immensely complicated causal sequences, with much linkage between your genetic heritage and the details of the world around you. None of it conflicts, either, with a fully deterministic world-picture in which everything has to happen exactly as it does, so that there are – in some sense – absolutely no true matters of chance, not even ones involving tossed coins or radioactive decays. For present purposes I simply do not care whether a maximally specific description of the world at this very moment would tell a highly intelligent demon not only where I was in time but also everything I'd ever have thought or heard or seen. For remember, specific causal sequences which make it true, for example, that a particular fish caught at a particular instant has precisely this or that length, or that a particular coin is about to land heads, are compatible with a general understanding of the world which allows us to call it highly improbable that the fish you've just caught is more or less exactly 33.84 centimeters long, or that the coin you're about to toss ninety times will fall always heads and never tails. Probabilistic reasoning must be given its due, whether or not the universe is fully deterministic. What if I did indeed have to experience everything which I do experience? I can apply probabilities to my experiences none the less.

Before leaving this general area, consider the objection – somebody actually raised it – that the doomsday argument has the following fatal defect. You and I cannot be treated as if we'd been drawn at random from the entire temporal spread of the human race, because we have the mathematical sophistication needed to understand the argument: sophistication which no caveman, for instance, could possibly have had. I can see three ways of replying to this objection. (1) The first is to insist once again that the right question for our purposes can be 'What would be the probability of a human observer finding that he or she lived at a time when genes, intelligence, use of language, mathematical sophistication, etc., etc., were of the varieties you and I find ourselves to have?' The doomsday argument's 'reference class' can indeed be *human observers* instead of *human observers able to pass exams on the calculus of probabilities.* How uninteresting most 'anthropic' arguments would be, if they could be applied only to mathematicians! (2) The second involves repeating that you don't need mathematical sophistication to understand the argument's main outlines. The mathematically unsophisticated, too, can hope to grasp the idea that they should be suspicious of theories whose truth would make them immensely early in the career of the human race. (3) The third is this. The doomsday argument insists that even people born *as late after the cavemen* as you and me would have been born unusually early if the human race continued for many millennia. But it could at most *help* the argument, not hinder it, if the cavemen could be disregarded, the appropriate population clock having started to tick only when humans became mathematically sophisticated. For then, by that clock, you and I would have been very exceptionally early indeed, if the human race survived for a few thousand years beyond the twentieth century. Not just the cavemen, but a great many later men as well, would have become unable to reduce our degree of earliness. They would have lived before the clock started ticking.

Group III

The objections in this next group revolve around the notion that there are more chances of existing in a large human race.

(IIIa) The bigger our race is in its temporal entirety, the more opportunities there are of being born into it. This counterbalances the greater unlikelihood of being born early.

This seems to me false. In the cases of many ordinary lotteries, no doubt, the sheer fact of having a ticket might well suggest that many tickets had been sold or thrown to an eagerly expectant crowd. Suppose that, because a friend bought the lottery ticket on your behalf, you first learn of a lottery through learning that you've won it. Your win can give you grounds for suspecting that the lottery urn had only a few names in it, but you should also bear in mind that a large, widely publicized lottery would be more likely to have attracted your friend's attention. Notice, however, that you'd have existed whether or not the friend had bought the ticket for you. In our cosmological situation, on the other hand, we cannot say that we'd have existed in numbers which remained constant regardless of whether we ever had the luck to be born. It seems wrong to treat ourselves as if we were once immaterial souls harbouring hopes of being embodied, hopes growing with each increase in the number of bodies to be created. Again, we mustn't imagine that we had risked finding out that we were unconscious collections of atoms, the risk being reduced by the existence of each additional human. If only ten people ever had been and ever would be born, could any of them have cause for surprise at finding themselves among those few? Not at all. Among all conceivable people, only those who are born can find themselves as anything.

Even, therefore, if there is a strange sense in which the human species, if very long lasting, would ipso facto provide 'very many more opportunities' of being born into it, the only thing relevant to a twentieth-century human considering the doomsday argument would be the probability of finding oneself in the twentieth century *granted that* one had in fact been born into the human species. One's likelihood of observing oneself to be in existence in the twentieth century could only be *decreased*, never increased, by 'extra opportunities of existing' which were just opportunities of existing afterwards. Struggling to swallow the idea that you're very unusually early in human history, you cannot be helped by being told that people would in this case have very many chances of finding themselves later!

Mayn't it be merely silly to argue as if a human's chances of being before AD 2150, which would be 100 per cent if the human race ended by AD 2149, would be in no way reduced if the race instead continued for a million more years?

Consider L. S. Marochnik's idea[12] that there is a distance from the galactic center at which a density wave orbits at almost the same speed as the stars; that our sun is at this distance; and that the material of the solar system would thus have undergone unusually prolonged compression – which, he proposes, is essential or nearly essential to the formation of planets. What if he turned out to be right that unusually prolonged compression occurs at the distance in question? Surely his theory connecting such compression with the formation of planets ought then to be seen as getting support from the fact that, sure enough, we did find ourselves on a planet which was at that particular distance. Few would dream of using the argument that if planets could form readily throughout the galaxy (and therefore in greater numbers), then this would have given us a far larger chance of being born into the galaxy than if they were almost all confined to a narrow band; that the greater size of this chance would compensate for the lesser chance of being born inside such a band rather than elsewhere in the galaxy; and that in consequence Marochnik could draw no support from our finding ourselves precisely where his theory suggested! Yet remarkably many people bring forward a very similar argument as soon as position in time is in question, and not spatial position.

In effect these people argue that finding oneself alive at roughly the end of the twentieth century would have been highly improbable, no matter how long the human race was going to last: either (1) highly improbable because one was very unusually early in a long-lasting human race, or else (2) highly improbable because one was in a short-lasting human race, missing the very many additional opportunities of existence – opportunities of existence at late times – which would have been provided by a long-lasting one. But this argument of theirs, that our temporal position is queer *no matter what*, is itself queer. The quick answer to it is that if the human race were short-lasting, then there would in fact be *no* 'opportunities for a human to exist at late times' which the humans of earlier times would have 'missed'.

Imagine that you had absolutely no observations to tell you your probable temporal position and how many members the human race would be likely to have had when its history ended. Suppose you now considered two possibilities: five trillion members, and only half a trillion. Would you treat the larger figure as far more likely, just because it represented 'more chances of having a life'? Would you then react similarly to still greater figures all the way up to infinity, concluding that it was infinitely likely (absolutely certain) that there would be infinitely many humans?

Suppose your religion convinced you that the figure had been settled by a divine coin tossed just once: heads for five trillion humans, tails for half a trillion. Would you say it was far more likely that the coin had landed heads? And if your faith next became that heads would have meant infinitely many humans, while tails still meant only half a trillion, would you think it absolutely certain that the coin had landed heads? Presumably not.

Notice that introducing temporal position isn't really relevant to the point which is in question here. A simpler version of the point would run as follows. Suppose all humans had to exist at the same time. Suppose you had no knowledge of whether there were any humans apart from yourself. You knew merely that God had decided to toss his coin *just once*, and that if it had landed heads then he would have created ninety million humans, while if it had landed tails then he would have created only a single human. Would you therefore think the odds ninety million to one that God's coin had landed heads?

As a variant, suppose that a toss of heads would have led to ninety million people, one of them named 'Dr Black', whereas a toss of tails would have led to only a single person, 'Dr Green'. Forgetting your name, but knowing you were created as a result of the toss, would you think it just as good a bet that you were Dr Black as that you were Dr Green? That sounds very wrong. Surely you ought instead to say to yourself that there is a half-chance that God's coin landed tails, making you Dr Green, whereas even if it had instead landed heads your chance of being Dr Black would still be as low as one in ninety million. Much wiser, there-fore, to bet that you are Dr Green.

In cases like these we must reject the intuition – it is danger-ously attractive because of the many other cases where it puts us on the right path – that to estimate probabilities we ought to ask what bets would maximize winnings when an experiment was repeated indefinitely many times. If God tosses his coin many trillion times, then it is virtually certain that only about one in ninety million of the resulting humans will have been created on a toss of tails. Correspondingly, any human created during the tosses ought to bet very confidently that he or she had been created on a toss of heads. But this is no good reason for betting that the toss was of heads, telling God to create ninety million people rather than one, if the coin was to be tossed *once only*.

Might it be objected that the moral I'm here trying to draw is flatly opposite to the one drawn in the cases of London and Little Puddle? There, didn't I say you would have special cause to believe you were in London because London was the larger? Indeed I did, but there is no inconsistency. Imagine an amnesiac knowing that London and Little Puddle *both exist* – which is like knowing that God tossed his coin once and created London *and then tossed it again* and created Little Puddle. The amnesiac knows he is in one of the two places, but doesn't know which. If he has no other relevant evidence, he should prefer to think himself in London because London is the larger. But what if, *not* knowing whether London exists, he discovers he's in Little Puddle? The discovery should strengthen his suspicion that London is a fiction – for if London were real then he could have expected to be in London instead, it being the larger.

It would be absurd of him to argue that he should prefer to believe in London's reality 'because this would put me in a bigger group of observers, the inhabitants of the region Little-Puddle-plus-London'. The slogan that 'you should prefer to think yourself in a spatial or temporal region containing more people' must be interpreted sensibly. (In trying to make it unremarkable that you find yourself pre-2150, don't comment that you inhabit the region *the-total-temporal-spread-of-the-human-race*, and that this region may well be heavily populated thanks to there being huge numbers of post-2150 humans!)

(IIIb) A larger human race offers the observer more chance of being human rather than, say, a five-eyed inhabitant of Andromeda.

This objection fails as well. As a first step towards seeing why, imagine that an urn contains ten balls marked 'Andromedan' and ten marked 'pre-2150 human'. A single ball is to be drawn. The ball could be drawn now or else after adding another thousand 'human' balls to the urn, the thousand all being marked 'human born after 2150'. Wouldn't adding those thousand balls greatly increase the likelihood that the drawn ball would be 'human' rather than 'Andromedan'? It certainly would. Nevertheless, the thousand additional 'humans' would have greatly *decreased* the likelihood that this particular ball would be marked 'pre-2150 human'. In fact, they would have decreased it exactly as much as if they'd been a thousand 'Andromedans' instead.

Similarly, the likelihood of an observer's being a human living before 2150 could never be increased, while it might well be greatly diminished, by any fact that the human race would, when it ended, have included many humans born after that date. Talk of its being 'in one respect increased because this gives the observer more chance of being human rather than non-human' is a blunder. Obviously, as was indicated in (IIIa), adding more and more post-2150 humans could only decrease the likelihood that *a human observer* would be in the class of pre-2150 humans. But we can now see as well that it would decrease the likelihood of *an observer's* being in that class – unless, that's to say, some magic principle meant that the number of observers had to be kept constant, so that adding a human had always to be 'paid for' by throwing out a non-human.

Still, mustn't we concede that if there were, say, ninety-six trillion trillion observers who were non-humans, then adding a few hundred billion post-2150 humans would *only slightly* decrease an observer's likelihood of being a pre-2150 human? We must indeed. (The ninety-six trillion trillion 'would be doing almost all the work'. The extra few hundred billion humans would make virtually no difference.) Yet this concession, together with everything the previous two paragraphs said about an observer's likely circumstances, could well be thought of only marginal interest. For the matter before us isn't whether the human race is large or small compared with the race of Andromedans, or with all non-human races lumped together. If this were at issue then non-humans could enter into one's calculations, the question being where *as an observer* one would be likely to find oneself (among humans? among Andromedans, Martians or chimpanzees?). But Carter asks something different. He asks how long the human race is likely to last. He is interested in such affairs as whether the humans before the year 2150 will have been many or few compared with the humans afterwards. Disregarding dinosaurs, dolphins and Fred Hoyle's intelligent interstellar clouds, he concentrates on how likely one would be to live before 2150 granted that one was *a human observer*.

Imagine you are asking what proportion of humans are brown-skinned. As a blind child, you have only a vague hunch about the matter – but if you next learn that you yourself are brown-skinned, then this may appreciably strengthen your grounds for believing that more than one in a million are. In being influenced by what you have learned, you don't first have to ask how many Andromedans exist.

(IIIc) Picturing several actual human races proves that Carter is wrong. 'Suppose', this objection might run, 'that there were many human races scattered through the universe: our own race and other races sufficiently similar to ours to count as human for present purposes. Suppose half the races were extremely long-lasting and galaxy-colonizing, made up of vastly many observers, while the rest were short-lasting. And let's say – to simplify things – that all the races originated at the same instant and had equal populations until the year 2150. Can't this scenario give us the right mathematical intuitions? Imagine we knew it was correct. How, in this case, could finding ourselves before 2150 provide any grounds for thinking that our race was short-lasting?'

I reply that in this very special case we could have no such grounds. The chances that you and I, who are pre-2150 humans, were early in a long-lasting race would be precisely equal to the chances of our being in a short-lasting one, because precisely half of all pre-2150 humans would be in long-lasting races. Ex hypothesi all this *would be known to us*, so that there would be nothing left to discuss. In this peculiar situation it really could make sense to talk of an exact balance between 'more numerous opportunities' of existing in one of the long-lasting human races and a correspondingly greater unlikelihood of finding oneself before 2150 if one were in such a race. If you lacked all evidence of your position in time, you would have excellent reasons for betting you were in a long-lasting race. Most humans – most *actual humans* rather than just most possible humans – would be in long-lasting races, and you would know it. In Bayesian terms, the prior probability of finding yourself in a long-lasting race would be very high. (The case is very unlike the one considered on p. 227 above where finding yourself alive gives no reason for suspecting that God's coin fell heads, so that five trillion humans were created, rather than that it fell tails, so that only half a trillion were. For that other case concerned mere possibilities only; it was a case of *either* five trillion *or else* half a trillion, and not of *fully five and a half trillion actually existing people*; for remember, God's coin was tossed *just once*.)

In fact, however, we of course *don't know* anything of the kind just now described – and furthermore, we have very forceful grounds for believing something altogether different. Even if there were nothing dubious about the idea of many actual human races, any suggestion that half the races were long-lasting and galaxy-colonizing would be very hard to reconcile with a truth familiar to you and me. For if half the races were like this, then where-abouts in time could a human expect to be? Answer: *after 2150*, because it would be there that the vast majority of humans would be. Yet it's a truth well known to you and me that we don't find ourselves there.

What if we had guessed too hastily, overlooking the relevance of this well-known truth? Our guess that, among many actual human races, fully half were long-lasting would then need to be revised – although it might, of course, survive without very strong revision if we had started off very confident in it. Any probability estimates associated with such an over-hasty guess, for instance the estimate that any human before 2150 had a half-chance of being in a long-lasting human race, would now need to be revised as well.

231

Here, as elsewhere, we must remember the difference between being perhaps misled by evidence and being misguided, silly, when tending to trust the evidence. Yes, *on the hypothesis that* half the human races discussed above are long-lasting and galaxy-colonizing, it follows that you yourself, a human alive before AD 2150, must be a person in an unusual temporal position, a person liable to be misled by your evidence. This doesn't mean, however, that your evidence gives you no cause to distrust the hypothesis in question. The Devil may know gleefully that it is misleading evidence, but you do not. Whenever some theory tells you that what you yourself see would be seen by some observers, but that they would be observers rare at, say, the one in a thousand level, or perhaps the one in a trillion trillion level, then you can have a right to prefer some alternative, not particularly unlikely theory: the theory, for instance, that you were wrong in your initial ideas about whether dogs hardly ever bite, or whether long-lasting races are common, or (a case which Chapter 6 will discuss) whether two dice have landed double-six.

The upshot is that we could happily agree with the point (suggested to me by Don Page) that if there existed many human races, half of them extremely long-lasting, then any human alive as early as you and me would face alternatives which were equally peculiar: (1) that he or she existed very, very unusually early in a long-lasting race, and (2) that he or she was one of the proportionately very, very few humans whose race was short-lasting. For there is in point of fact no need for us to choose between being in the first and being in the second of these two highly improbable positions. Instead we could, for instance, simply reject the idea of many actual human races – which, after all, would be easily done since our reasons for believing in extraterrestrials of any kind, let alone ones worth calling 'humans', are rather easy to challenge. Alternatively we could picture almost all human or humanlike races as becoming extinct soon after learning how to build nuclear bombs and to pollute everything.

232

Group IV

The objections of the fourth and most important group concern the fact that our world may well be indeterministic. These objections will be treated quickly here: for a more complete treatment, see Chapter 6.

(IVa) The contents of the urn haven't yet been settled.

The more attractive version of this objection runs as follows. There is always a firm fact of the matter, 'out there in the world' whether or not we can know it, of how many names there actually are in any given urn. But the world may be, perhaps for quantum-physical reasons, *a radically indeterministic world* in which there isn't yet any relevantly similar fact of how long the human race is going to last. However, the doomsday argument does need such a fact in order to run smoothly. ('The number of names in the urn may not have been settled by anything which has yet occurred.')

A second version of the objection says instead that any indeterminism would exclude any usable facts about *exactly who* would be doing any observing at later times. ('Precisely what the names are is something which may not have been settled by anything which has yet occurred.') But this version is fairly obviously faulty. If it were guaranteed that there would be a trillion trillion humans after me, then I would be a very unusually early human regardless of whether the precise identities of the trillion trillion had yet to be fixed.

The first version is genuinely strong, though. Still, it only reduces the power of the doomsday argument instead of destroying it.

By a world that is 'radically indeterministic' I mean one which would almost certainly develop differently from how it actually has done, if it could somehow be returned to exactly its initial state. I am not challenging the 'chaos theory' point that two worlds, although each entirely deterministic, could develop very differently if they started off even marginally different.

Again, we're not here concerned with the theory that the world would be one in which we could make useful efforts *only if* it were indeterministic. For present purposes it doesn't matter whether such a theory is right – although I myself would say that today's chess computers, operating in deterministic ways, can make 'useful efforts' to defeat human champions.

For present purposes the important point is instead this. If our world were indeterministic, there could well be no usable fact of how long the human race will last. Urn analogies might therefore work only rather poorly. They mightn't do much to weaken even the theory that the human race (or else it and the far more intelligent beings to which it would give rise over long ages, if one hesitated to call those beings 'human') has a half-chance of lasting for trillions of universe-colonizing years – a possibility which F. Dyson and S. Frautschi give reasons for taking seriously in the case of an infinitely expanding universe.[13] Whether it will last for trillions of years might depend almost entirely on what happens in the next few centuries, a period of extreme danger. Perhaps the matter will be decided by just one or two events. Perhaps these will be governed by marked quantum uncertainties.

Even so, the doomsday argument would retain considerable force against the theory that it is altogether probable that the human race will last for many hundred thousand years and colonize the galaxy – because to the believer in indeterminism the words 'altogether probable' signal that even indeterministic factors are unlikely to prevent this. On the hypothesis that, at such and such a date near the end of the twentieth century, it was 97 per cent (or 98.5 per cent, or 99.9 per cent) probable that the human race's temporal entirety would include several trillion people, of whom only a few tens of billions had been born by that date, would a human observer be at all likely to find that he or she had been born by then? Evidently not.

Again, Carter's reasoning can be forceful, even in an indeterministic world, if the indeterminism is judged of a sort unlikely to have much influence on how long the human race will last. Notice too that initially indeterministic factors influencing the affair might at this very moment be becoming deterministic or virtually deterministic, perhaps through human decisions which were irrevocable or virtually irrevocable. All humans born at later times would need to take account of this.

(IVb) The Shooting Room objection

This objection is that combining constant growth with indeterminism can generate unwarranted fears, as a story illustrates. Thrust into a room, you are assured that at least 90 per cent of those who enter it will be shot. Panic! But you then learn you will leave the room alive unless a double-six is thrown, first time, with two dice. How is this compatible with the assurance that at least 90 per cent will be shot? The answer is that successive batches of people thrust into the room are each of them ten times larger than the previous batch, so that the forecast 'At least 90 per cent will be shot' will be confirmed when a double-six is eventually thrown. If you know this, and know also that how the dice were going to fall would be utterly unpredictable even by a demon who knew everything about the situation when they were thrown, then shouldn't your panic vanish?

Paradoxical though this may be, I agree that your panic ought to vanish in the situation described, despite the fact that shooting would be the fate of most of the people who'd ever have been thrust into the room. However, the situation which forms the background for the doomsday argument is different in two chief respects.

The first is that we lack any assurance that the human race will end at a time decided utterly randomly, indeterministically, let alone that dice-like factors give it a known, constant probability of surviving beyond each new generation. We might actually rather confidently say that if the race gets through the next four centuries safely then it will survive for very many further centuries, but that it may well end by AD 2150 through, for instance, poisoning its environment.

The second is that the Carter–Leslie line of thought, while it does find population increase impressive, in no way depends on the idea that it is guaranteed (or highly likely) that human numbers will, like the numbers of those thrust into the Shooting Room, expand at a constant rate until such time as the human race becomes extinct. In order for this idea to be correct, the race would need to be guaranteed (or highly likely) to end fairly shortly, which would actually make the doomsday argument redundant; for if it instead continued to grow at the present rate, then in less than 1,500 years it would have a mass greater than the Earth's, while not too long afterwards it would be expanding at faster than the speed of light. But the doomsday argument can yield very disturbing risk-estimates even when it is assumed, rather, that population figures will remain at roughly late-twentieth-century levels until Doom.

Maybe they will instead crash irrevocably not to zero but to something like it. This prospect, too, could be found disturbing.

Don't too vividly imagine a scene of the far future, perhaps ten thousand centuries after rapid population growth has ended, in which comfortably secure people look back on Carter and Leslie as quaint characters who happened to live at an unusual time: a time when the vast majority of humans hadn't yet been born, and also a time of rapid population growth so that something like 10 per cent of those born up to that date were still living. For remember, you and I aren't those comfortably secure people. You and I lack their knowledge. And in a world which had been fairly sure to be like theirs, human observers could expect to find themselves as late as them or later – not near the end of the twentieth century, among signs suggestive of imminent disaster.

The normal reaction to the doomsday argument is that every point in human population history must be occupied by somebody, and that therefore there could be nothing disturbing in our finding ourselves where we do. Those who have this reaction typically think of it as very obviously correct. Alas, nothing is obvious here, whether or not our world is radically indeterministic. Yes, people existing near the end of the twentieth century would of course find themselves near the end of the twentieth century no matter how long humankind was going to survive. But finding yourself at such and such a position in space can be suggestive evidence against theories which would make you specially unlikely to find yourself there. Now, the same seems to be true of finding yourself at such and such a position in time.

The next chapter will develop this point with the help of thought experiments in which spatial and temporal positioning are repeatedly compared.

6

TESTING
THE ARGUMENT

—————•••—————

(1) This chapter looks again at various points made in Chapter 5, considering them with the help of thought experiments. These are designed for discovering whether there are crucial differences between position in space and position in time, particularly in the case of an indeterministic universe.

(2) The chapter also considers the doomsday argument's 'reference class'. Could beings of the far future, for instance, be counted as 'humans' despite being very different from you and me? Could the argument be applied to all intelligent beings in a series beginning with humans but ending with advanced computers? Thought experiments might once again give us our answers.

THE DOOMSDAY ARGUMENT:
RECAPITULATION, AND THEN
NEW COMMENTS

As this chapter,[1] like the others, is intended to be readable in isolation, it starts with a brief recapitulation. The doomsday argument, originated by B. Carter and then published and defended by J. Leslie, with variants by J. R. Gott and H. B. Nielsen, points out that you and I would be fairly unremarkable among human observers if the human race were to end shortly: perhaps 10 per cent of all humans born up to today are – because of the recent population explosion – living at this very instant. If, in contrast, the race were going to survive for many more millennia, perhaps colonizing the entire galaxy, then you and I would be very unusually early humans: humans who would eventually turn out to have been extremely near the beginning of time as measured by a Population Clock whose hand had advanced by one step whenever a new human was born. This can strengthen whatever reasons we have for suspecting that the human race will not survive long. People unwilling to accept this point will systematically underestimate the risks humanity runs from environmental destruction, germ warfare and other threats to its prolonged survival.

'Doomsday argument' can be a misleading label since all that is involved is a magnification of risk-estimates. Suppose, for example, that the 'total risk' of Doom Soon – the probability that the human race will, presumably through its dangerous behaviour, become extinct inside some fairly short period – is judged by you to be 10 per cent before you consider the argument. When you do come to consider it, this might lead you to a revised estimate of 80 per cent. But notice that the newly estimated 80 per cent risk of Doom Soon, besides being no excuse for utter despair, would have been arrived at against the background of dangerous ways in which the human race *was thought likely to behave*. Now what if, of the 10 per cent with which you started, 5 per cent represented the estimated risk connected with environmental destruction? After the 'total risk' had been re-evaluated as 80 per cent, the risk of Doom Soon from Environmental Destruction would have been re-evaluated as 40 per cent, presumably. (40 per cent is one-half of 80 per cent, just as 5 per cent is one-half of 10 per cent. There would seem to be no good reason to change the proportion from one-half into something else.) But whereas it might be impossible to do anything to counter certain other types of risk, for example the risk that some very distant but very violent cosmic phenomenon will suddenly pour its radiation at us, we could be frightened into doing something vigorous to reduce environmental destruction when we looked at that alarming figure of 40 per cent. Now, the Carter–Leslie reasoning is sensitive to new evidence of risk-reduction efforts because, for one thing, such evidence can lead us to revise the view that humans were likely to behave in dangerous ways. Any human who tries to stop environmental destruction is helping to cast doubt on that view.

In generations after successful efforts had been made to clean up the environment, people considering the doomsday argument would very obviously have a right to take account of those efforts. It's silly to think that human efforts could never increase the probability that doom would be long delayed. The doomsday argument says nothing of the sort. It is an argument which could retain some power for as long as the human race continued, but its capacity to frighten would be perpetually changing to take account of new evidence.

The doomsday argument is open to many objections. As the previous chapter made clear, I accept one of them, at any rate. If we live in a radically indeterministic world, there not yet being any usable 'fact of the matter' of how long the human race will last, then the argument may be considerably weakened – the extent of the weakening depending, naturally, on the degree to which humankind's future shares in the indeterminism. But whatever its weaknesses, the argument has a central point which simply cannot be wrong. It does supply grounds for increased reluctance to believe that you and I will turn out to have been very early in time as measured by the above-described Population Clock. In this chapter my main aim will be to support this firm statement with various thought experiments.

How does the current explosion in human numbers form the basis for an interesting doomsday argument? Note, for a start, that the situation today is in many ways radically new. The human race's former ability to survive from century to century may therefore give us little guidance about how much longer it is likely to survive. Carter argues for a shift in estimated probabilities – and even those who have severe doubts about his argument, so that their probability-estimates are hard to alter, may be less resistant to altering them when they are very unsure about them anyway.

A common reason for unwillingness to alter such estimates is this: that the human race is seen as facing, year by year, dangers which remain constant and which have no relation to population size. Supposedly, the situation is as if a Master of the Universe were throwing several dice together in each year, planning to put an end to humankind – perhaps with a gigantic asteroid – when all the dice landed as sixes. Now, if this were an appropriate story to tell oneself and if the dice in the story *were radically indeterministic* (an important qualification, to be discussed in due course), then the doomsday argument might look very unimpressive. We certainly cannot know that the story is appropriate, however. There are actually quite strong grounds for suspecting the reverse. Today's population explosion, besides being itself a source of new dangers, is the result of technological advances which are dangerous. The doomsday argument could help to convince us of this. In the face of novel and largely unknown risks, why remain confident that numerous humans will live after us?

What if the human race were going to end in the next hour? We should, of course, be very reluctant to believe this. Its initially estimated probability ought to be extremely low. The doomsday argument couldn't make it anything other than extremely low, not even if it led us to re-estimate it as a thousand times greater, because a figure such as 0.000000000000000000000001 per cent isn't going to yield anything very big even when multiplied by a thousand. What if it were true nevertheless? As noted earlier, it would then be true that something like one in ten humans who had ever been born would be alive when the race ended, so that you and I wouldn't be very surprisingly positioned among all humans ever. But what if humankind instead survived for at least another few centuries? Suppose that population figures stabilized at about ten billion in AD 2050. How many further centuries would pass before it could be said that roughly half the human race had lived at times later than you and me? *About two centuries only.* If galactic colonization then began, population once again doubling every fifty years as it has in recent times, then by about the year 3000 you and I would have been shown to have lived when at least 99.99 per cent of all humans hadn't yet been born.

Notice that the Carter–Leslie reasoning could be understood as strengthening either of two competing hypotheses in this area: the first, that the human race will end shortly, and the second, that galactic colonization would never be feasible, no matter how long the race lasted. (In fact, it could strengthen the two hypotheses simultaneously. Although they compete, their plausibilities could both be raised. Compare how Bob's absence from his usual desk can support both 'Bob has been promoted as he demanded' and 'Bob has carried out his threat to leave the firm.')

The human mind is ill suited to handling probabilities. On a throw of two fair dice together, Leibniz considered two sixes exactly as probable as a six and a five. An even worse error was made by d'Alembert, for whom the results to be expected from tossing the same coin three times differed from those of tossing three coins at once. And while Carter's doomsday argument certainly faces some interesting objections, it also meets with many others which are really very weak but which are stated with tremendous confidence by intelligent people. This one, for instance: that the argument fails at once since 'as everybody knows' nothing probabilistic can be concluded from a single case, and your own observed position in human population history is indeed a single case, while it would be a mere joke to try to widen your evidential base by asking your contemporaries what *their* positions were. In answering such an objection, a thought experiment can be useful. Imagine two urns each containing just one ball marked with your name. In the first urn there are a thousand balls altogether, bearing different names; in the second, only ten. Unsure that the left-hand urn contains the thousand, but thinking this 75 per cent probable, you draw a ball at random from it. Your name is on the ball. Of the perhaps ten and perhaps a thousand names in the urn, yours has been the very earliest to be drawn. Shouldn't this reduce your confidence that there are still another 999 names waiting to be drawn? It certainly should. A straightforward calculation suggests that you should shift to thinking it roughly 97 per cent probable that there are only nine names remaining. Now, while so simple a thought experiment cannot establish the doomsday argument's correctness, one point seems clear. You mustn't protest that because the experiment involves drawing just a single name, and because 'as everybody knows' probabilities cannot be determined from single cases, it follows that the early drawing of your name could show nothing whatever.

Disregard all the books which thunder that no probability should ever be derived from a single test. Those books are in error. Imagine two urns. One contains a million black balls and one white; the other, a million white balls and one black. Not having a clue as to which urn is which, you pick one of them with the

241

help of a tossed coin. You draw a ball, and it is white. What are the odds that it came from the urn containing the million white balls? Answer: a million to one in favour. To arrive at this answer, simply consider the million and one equally probable ways in which a white ball could have been drawn. A million of them involve draws from the urn with the million white. Only one involves a draw from the other.

Odds of a million to one in favour of some hypothesis are rather good odds. There is no magical unreliability attaching to results just because they are results of single trials. Consider the hypothesis that a coin is double-headed, arrived at when seventeen tosses yield seventeen heads. The odds against this occurring with a fair coin are much less impressive than a million to one. (Repeating the urn experiment several times, in each case choosing the same urn after replacing the drawn ball and shaking vigorously, can in some sense 'greatly improve' the reliability of the judgement that the urn contains the million white. But this only means that after, say, three successive whites have been drawn, the odds favouring this judgement are increased to a million million million to one. In another sense, those odds are no great improvement: the first odds were already overwhelmingly good.)

Thought experiments can often be replaced by actual experiments. Suppose you meet a sceptic who persists in thinking that 'because, of course, you cannot establish probabilities by single trials' a single draw of a white ball couldn't in the least strengthen the theory that the urn was the one with the million white. (I have met two such sceptics, a philosopher and a physicist. They had no doubts about their rightness.) Filling urns with hundreds of thousands of balls may be overly time-consuming, yet you can readily set up an experiment with two urns each containing twenty balls: nineteen black and one white in the first case, nineteen white and one black in the second. Invite the sceptic to choose an urn and to draw just one ball from it. In advance of the choosing and the drawing, he or she must please make an even bet, a dollar against your dollar, that the remaining balls in the urn will be black if the drawn ball is white, and vice versa. You will almost certainly win the bet. Repeat again and again with different urns and different balls, and expect to win almost always.

In what follows, though, we shall be making thought experiments which could only with immense difficulty be replaced by actual experiments. What's more, there will actually be a case where it would seem right for you to bet in a way which would cause most people in your circumstances to lose their money.

Before beginning the thought experiments we need to consider one last point. When wondering what degrees of probability we ought to attach ('subjectively'?) to various untidy real-life matters, we often rightly ask what the probabilities would ('objectively'?) be of getting various outcomes in tidy trials involving dice, coins, or balls pulled from urns. If past experience gives you equal reasons for thinking that Jones *will* and *will not* be in town tomorrow, and if the same applies to Smith and to Brown, and if past experience also indicates that the movements of all three are uncorrelated, then what should be your estimate of the probability that Jones, Smith and Brown will all be in town? It is as if 'Jones' were scratched on one face of a first coin, 'Smith' on one face of a second, 'Brown' on one face of a third, the issue being how likely you'd be to see all three names after tossing the coins. Saying this isn't 'confusing subjective and objective probabilities'. It is just using common sense.

The distinction between 'subjective' and 'objective' can be hard to draw, anyhow, because (a) there are often strong excuses for declaring that probabilities are simply 'subjective' expressions of ignorance, while on the other hand (b) it can be considered 'objective' that all persons having such and such evidence ought to view various matters as probable to exactly such and such degrees. Even when a series of events is ultimately deterministic, so that what we call its uncertainties are really only blindnesses in ourselves, we can succeed in modelling it with coins and dice – which should cause no surprise, surely, when nobody really knows whether the behaviour of coins and dice is ultimately indeterministic, a matter of probabilities 'out there in the world', 'objective in the fullest sense'.

Now for the experiments. Since they will be thought experiments only, let us say that the experimenter is always God or else the Devil. All the people involved are created specially for experimental purposes.

243

THE SMALL ROOM AND THE LARGE

This thought experiment introduces variants, some of them in-volving indeterminism in a radical way, on Chapter 5's 'London and Little Puddle' theme. You find yourself in a room crammed with as many humans as will have been born in the real world before AD 2150. (Specify, if you like, that you're in a corner filled by as many humans, perhaps a twelfth of those in the room, as were born at roughly the same time as your real-world self. The moral to be drawn from the experiment is unaffected by this refinement.[2]) Although impressive in size, the room is tiny by comparison with a second room, a room large enough to contain ninety thousand times more people. Its ever actually containing them was to depend on God's throw of two dice, thrown only once. Just if the dice fell appropriately, God would create all those hugely many other people too. Given all this, how would you most reasonably picture God's dice as having fallen? You need further information, obviously. There are two main cases to consider:

The case where the total number to be created was settled in advance

Suppose you further know (1) that the dice behaved in a radically indeterministic manner, so that there had been no possibility of being sure in advance how they would fall; (2) that you've strong initial reasons to suspect the dice were loaded (which nicely reflects our frequent sense of insecurity when estimating probabilities); (3) that the large room was to be filled unless the throw was a double-six; and (4) that the throw was made *before God created any people at all*, while immediately after it he created the small-room people plus any large-room people that the dice told him to create.

In view of all the above, wouldn't you have grounds for thinking the dice had in fact landed double-six, i.e. in the 'small-room people only' way? Although with those strong initial reasons for suspecting God's dice of being loaded, let's say you thought them no more likely to be loaded in the one than in the other of the two possible styles, i.e. *for* and *against* sixes. Well, what if you had been created blindfolded? You'd have had interesting prima facie grounds for expecting that they *had not* landed double-six. On the hypothesis that the dice are fair, the chances of their landing in some other fashion would have been fully thirty-five to one. Yet if they had landed in some other fashion, then, of the people God had created, many more would be in the large room than in the small: not just thirty-five times more, but ninety thousand times more. Waiting for the blindfold to be removed, it is in the large room that you'd very greatly have expected to be, had you known that it was in fact full of people. The small room would certainly contain some persons, but you could very greatly have expected that none of them would be *you*. It's in the small room that you actually find yourself, however. All things considered, therefore, it would seem that God's dice had probably landed in a way ensuring that nothing but the small room would be seen by anybody.

The intended moral is as follows. If one found one had been born into the human race at a time earlier than AD 2150 then one ought to view this as counting against the theory that it had been settled *from before the time of one's birth*, by divine dice or in some more plausible fashion, that the vast majority of all humans would be born after AD 2150.

Probability theory being so controversial an area, the road I have just taken to reach this moral is strewn with possible objections, as Chapter 5 showed. But let's assume for the moment that in the story as told above you would have attractive grounds for concluding that God had thrown a double-six, 'small-room people only'. The interesting question now is whether the same conclusion could be drawn if the story were altered in various ways.

What if God had instead planned that, after he had thrown the dice, all the small-room people would be created in such and such a year, while creation of the large-room people, if the dice said that there should be any, *would be deferred until some later year*? Should this alteration make any difference to your reluctance, on finding yourself in the small room, to believe in large-room people? In particular, should it make a difference if you knew that the year fixed for the possible creation of any large-room people *hadn't yet arrived*? I cannot see why, provided that 'reluctance to believe in large-room people' just means reluctance to believe that they'll have been created some day if they haven't been created already.

Whether any time fixed for the possible filling of the large room was a time before, after, or exactly simultaneous with the filling of the small room wouldn't make the slightest difference so long as whether the large room would be filled *had been settled before* the filling of the small one, the room in which you find yourself.

Is that correct, though? Isn't there perhaps some force in the protest that *so long as the large-room people aren't alive yet* there can be no possibility of finding oneself among them? I think not. The protest just expresses a triviality: that nobody is alive except at times when he or she is alive. Nothing so trivial can stop us drawing probabilistic conclusions from our observed temporal positions. Imagine that God had decided to create two batches of people, the one of just three people and the other of fifty-seven trillion. He would create the tiny batch, wait until all its members had died, and then create the huge batch. When, therefore, those in the tiny batch were considering the affair, nobody of the huge batch would yet have been created. As a person created in this experiment and knowing these facts, but blindfolded and waiting for your eyes to be freed, should you much expect to find yourself among the fifty-seven trillion? Surely you should. For imagine that you instead said to yourself that if the fifty-seven trillion *weren't alive YET* then you couldn't possibly be among them. Imagine that you therefore accepted an even bet, a dollar against a dollar, that you were in the group of just three. Suppose that all the other people created during the experiment were similarly blindfolded and said the same thing to themselves, all of them then betting in your way. There would be fifty-seven trillion losers and only three winners. This would seem good enough grounds for rejecting such a way of betting. (Similarly if you knew you were in the later batch, but didn't know whether God's plan had specified that it would be the bigger of the two. It would be unwise to say to yourself: 'If the bigger batch had in fact been created earlier, then none of its members *would be alive STILL*, so I couldn't be among them; hence there's fully a half-chance that my batch is the small one.')

What if the hair and eye colours of each possible large-room person hadn't yet been fixed when the people in the small room were created? What if God hadn't yet decided whether any large-room people would be all men, all women, or equal numbers of men and women? What if God had specified nothing at all about their various identities, except that they'd all be human? This too would make no difference. For the central point is that if it had been settled, before the small-room people were brought into existence, that vastly many large-room people would exist as well, whether simultaneously or later, then you'd have expected to find yourself as a large-room person. Blindfolded and waiting for your eyes to be freed, it's on that basis that you would need to bet.

It would again make no difference if God had decreed that the large-room people, if there were to be any, would be generated by the small-room people in the usual way, instead of deciding to create them himself. The central point would be unaffected. It would remain unaffected even if people were always born with 'Small room, early in time' or 'Large room, late' appropriately stamped on their foreheads.

In short: various things said in Chapter 5 would seem to have been right. Thought experiments seemingly confirm that, as a ground for rejecting Carter's general way of reasoning, the point that any observations made in the future *aren't yet being made* is as worthless as the more specific point that everybody *now* wondering whether to use such reasoning must be wondering it neither earlier nor later than *exactly now*. (Please distinguish these worthless points from the quite different one, to be considered in just a moment, that whether there would be any future people, and if so, then how many there would be, *mightn't yet have been settled* by God or by deterministic natural factors.)

Why discuss the case where the filling or non-filling of the large room is settled even before any small-room people are created? A main reason for discussing it is this. The real world might perhaps be *fully deterministic*, a world whose entire future had been settled by the fine details of the situation at the beginning of time. When the total number of people to be created *is settled before the creation of anyone at all*, this corresponds to the situation in a real world of that type, one in which (as thought experiments seem to have confirmed) the doomsday argument runs smoothly.

However, the idea that the real world is fully deterministic is rather unpopular nowadays. Let's therefore next vary our thought experiments.

247

The case corresponding to an indeterministic world

How can our thought experiments be made to mirror an indeterministic world? The solution is simple enough. We can vary them by placing God's throw of the dice *at a time later than* the creation of the small-room people.

Once again you find yourself in the small room. Can you conclude anything about the fall of the dice? Let's specify, just as before, that God's dice are radically indeterministic. How they would fall couldn't have been settled by the situation at any earlier time. Let's say you know this, adding that you even know for sure that the dice are utterly fair, unloaded. You further know, as before, that only a double-six could prevent the creation of the large-room people. Finally, you know that the dice have yet to be thrown. (In fact this final point is needlessly specific. All that's essential is that the dice-throwing occur *after the time of your own creation*. It cannot then matter whether the throwing is before or after you get around to considering any argument analogous to Carter's doomsday argument. Still, the extra specificity can help to make it obvious how you should reason.) Can finding yourself in the small room give you any grounds for picturing the dice as landing double-six?

The answer is that it cannot. The dice are fair and thoroughly unpredictable. They haven't yet been thrown. The probability that they will land double-six is therefore exactly one in thirty-six. End of argument.

An objection to this might be that on the B-theory of Time[3] – the theory (favoured by Einstein) that being past, being present, being future are affairs just as relative as *being over there* and *being here* – there always is an actual 'fact of the matter' about how dice are about to fall. They can be looked on as falling in some definite way 'a little further along the fourth dimension'. It is *true now* that they will fall in such and such a way, despite our having no ordinary means of telling what the way will be. And if this is so, then mightn't reasoning like Carter's give us a non-ordinary method of telling it, or at least of gaining some strong indication of it?

The answer is No. The objection fails, regardless of whether the B-theory is correct. Even if it had been true from the beginning of time that the universe would develop in exactly such and such a manner, the human race stretching temporally for precisely such and such a number of years, all this would be fully compatible with the radical *indeterminism* of everything – the building up of later events *from* earlier events in ways which are fixed by the shapes which those earlier events just do happen to take, among very many shapes which they could have taken. Radical indeterminism would mean that any firm but ordinarily unknowable facts about future population figures wouldn't be facts to which reasoning like Carter's could properly appeal. Carter's reasoning mustn't work in one way if the world's temporal career comes into existence bit by bit, as is maintained by what philosophers call the A-theory of Time, and in an altogether different way if the successive stages of that career are 'all there together' in B-theory fashion so that the world has what Einstein once described as 'a four-dimensional existence'. If we could know that the fall of two fair, radically indeterministic dice, still waiting to be thrown, would be what settled whether the human race survived beyond AD 2150, and also that only a double-six could prevent its survival, then the chances of its surviving beyond AD 2150 would have to be estimated as exactly thirty-five out of thirty-six, and that would be that. That would be that, regardless of whether it was already unknowably true that those indeterministic dice were going to land in a particular fashion, so that the human race's future was going to be such and such.[4]

Does this destroy the doomsday argument? Unfortunately it only weakens it. In the world as it actually is, we could have no assurance that the probability that the human race would survive for this or that number of years was ever precisely such and such. We could have nothing near to firm knowledge of dice-like factors giving the race a high probability of surviving for very many further centuries. True enough, the world might be radically indeterministic. The fact that our births had occurred at these or those times, and on Earth, could in this case do little to oppose the notion that they had occurred when there was, say, a 12 or a 20 per cent likelihood that humans would spread right across the galaxy during numerous further years, making us among perhaps the earliest billionth of all humans. On the other hand, it could do a great deal to oppose the notion that this had been really very likely:

roughly 97 per cent likely, for instance. You and I could reasonably be very reluctant to believe in cosmic dice, so to speak, dice which hadn't yet been thrown at the time when we were born, which gave thirty-five chances out of thirty-six (a probability of roughly 97 per cent) that humankind's temporal entirety would contain about a billion times more humans than had been born up to that time. Unless forced to believe it by firm knowledge of the dice, why should we believe we had been born when it was *virtually determined* that the human race would continue onwards for so long that we'd have been among the earliest billionth of all humans?

Notice that the closer some situation approached to being 100 per cent probable, the more justifiably we could say that it was indeed *virtually determined* – that any indeterminism in the factors controlling it was virtually certain to be unimportant. Even supposing the world to be indeterministic, Carter's reasoning could act very powerfully against the theory that when we were born the human race had been virtually sure to survive for very many more centuries. Correspondingly, it could work fairly powerfully against the theory that there had been a 72 per cent likelihood of this, or a 65 per cent likelihood of it.

Besides, the world might be entirely deterministic. If it is, then it's just a mistake to think that Carter's argument is weakened by 'the undetermined nature of the future' – by 'the fact that whether we'd turn out to have been extraordinarily early humans could be settled only by indeterministic cosmic dice thrown *after* we'd come into existence'. Although people nowadays very often think of quantum theory as showing that the world is radically indeterministic, there are expert physicists who think differently, as Chapter 3 discussed. While it seems plain enough that quantum chanciness is somehow 'out there in the world', we must bear in mind that even the chanciness which characterizes dice-throwing is 'out there' in a fairly important sense – a sense which is, however, compatible with the notion that a demon who knew enough about the world's states at any moment could predict how all its dice would fall.

250

The Shooting Room

The Shooting Room thought experiment was considered briefly in Chapter 5. It is time to look at it in detail. Imagine that the Devil creates people in a room, in a batch or several batches. Successive batches would be of 10 people, then 100, then 1,000, then 10,000, then 100,000, and so forth: each batch ten times as large as its predecessor. You find yourself in one such batch. At every stage in the experiment, whether there will be any later batches is decided by the Devil's two dice, thrown together. The people in any batch watch the dice as they fall. So long as they don't fall double-six, the batch will exit from the room safely. If they fall double-six everybody in the batch is to be shot, the experiment then ending. How confident should you be of leaving the room safely?

Once again, we start by specifying that the dice are fair and also radically indeterministic. There are no ordinary means whereby you could know how they were going to fall. Still, mightn't there be an unordinary method of telling that they would probably fall double-six? Imagine that all people in the experiment betted they would see the dice falling double-six so that they would be shot. At least 90 per cent of them would be right. If the dice fell double-six on the first possible occasion, 100 per cent of them would be right: there would be just one batch of ten people, all of whom would be shot. If they fell double-six on the next possible occasion, one hundred people would be shot, out of the 110 who would ever have been in the Shooting Room. That amounts to about 91 per cent. If they fell double-six on the third possible occasion then the proportion of victims would be close to 90 per cent, a figure which would be approached more and more closely as the experiment continued – if it did continue instead of ending. Hence most or all who entered the room would win their bets, if they betted that shooting would be their fate. As B. van Fraassen remarked, an insurance agent eager to insure all of them, reasoning that each batch had thirty-five out of thirty-six chances of leaving the room safely, would be making a costly mistake. (Suppose that double-six was going to arrive after fifty throws of the dice. What would then happen 'usually'? Well, *on almost all occasions* – i.e., on fully forty-nine out of fifty occasions

– batches entering the room would exit from it safely; but *most people* entering the room would not.) Oughtn't you to expect a bullet, therefore?

In the story as I've so far been telling it the Devil can continue creating people indefinitely and has no difficulty in fitting them into the room, no matter how long the throwing of a double-six is delayed. In other words, the room is infinitely large. Wouldn't the story deliver much the same moral, though, even if the room were merely gigantic enough to make it almost completely certain that a double-six would have fallen before its capacity became strained? This is somewhat controversial. There would always be a feeble probability of everyone's surviving even a trillion trillion trillion trillion trillion dice throws, or absolutely any larger but finite number of throws. What if one assumed that when a batch exiting safely was the very largest which could be fitted into the room, the experiment would have to end? Taking account of the hugeness of the last possible batch, some people might argue that this would more than compensate for the tininess of the chance that it would be attained, 'the average possible person entering the room' having fully thirty-five chances out of thirty-six of exiting safely. Other people would say, as I would, that *possible persons* leaving the room safely after even a figure as 'low' as a trillion trillion trillion trillion throws should simply be disregarded: all that's important is that shooting is immensely likely to happen earlier, bringing death to most or all *actual persons* who have entered the room. But let us by-pass this dispute by specifying that the room is indeed infinitely large, so that sooner or later there is bound to be some last batch which suffers shooting. What should the story's moral then be?

The right moral would seem to be that you should expect to get out of the room alive. True, this is in a way wildly paradoxical, given that at least 90 per cent of those who betted they would get out alive would lose their bets. It can nevertheless seem fairly plain that you personally should expect the dice not to fall double-six – if you do know for sure that they are fair, radically indeterministic dice. For there the dice are, resting in the Devil's hand; they haven't yet been thrown; and there is either no 'fact of the matter' of how they are going to fall, or else (see the discussion earlier in this chapter of the irrelevance of the B-theory of Time) *no fact of the matter to which you can properly appeal.* All you can say is that you have thirty-five chances out of thirty-six of leaving the room safely. End of argument, I think. Still, the affair is so paradoxical that it's hard to feel completely sure. For whatever reasoning you use to convince yourself that you really must expect to leave the room safely – the reasoning, for instance, that those with the bad luck to be shot 'will exist in their over-whelming numbers *only because* my own batch wasn't shot'[5] – there is always the difficulty that of all the people who'd ever actually have been in the room, people all with exactly the same grounds as you for trusting this reasoning, at least 90 per cent would get bullets. (J.-P. Delahaye, a mathematician strongly supporting the doomsday argument after spending many days trying to refute it, introduced a slight variant on the Shooting Room Paradox in *Pour la science*.[6] He underlined its paradoxical nature by heading his discussion 'Neuf chances sur dix de gagner et de perdre' – 'A 90 per cent probability both of winning and of losing.')

Does the Shooting Room Paradox show the doomsday argument's wrongness? The answer would seem to be that – like the second version of the story of the small and large rooms, the version in which the dice are thrown *after* the small-room people are created – it only weakens Carter's reasoning instead of ruining it.

For one thing, there's no chance that population will continue to grow at the present rate for very long: the human race would soon be expanding at above the speed of light. It seems, even, that we might expect at least a temporary halt, perhaps through famine, towards the middle of the twenty-first century. At that stage human numbers will have climbed, if doomsday or a severe population crash hasn't arrived earlier, to something like ten billion. Now, suppose we said to ourselves that during any period of rapid population growth the doomsday argument was likely to deliver the wrong moral, a moral like the one mistakenly drawn by anybody who expected to be shot in the above-described situation. Suppose we told ourselves that the human race could be assumed to get to AD 2050 and a population size of ten billion with no difficulty, and that any possible later growth caused by galactic colonization should simply be disregarded. Even granted all of this, which is a great deal to grant, Carter's reasoning could remain disturbingly strong. For remember, the human race would only have to last for *about two centuries* beyond the year 2050, at a population size of ten billion, for it to be true that *roughly half* the race had lived at times later than you and me. And if the race continued onwards at the same size, then people as early as you and me would be in a very tiny minority after a few thousand years.

Besides, we can return to the points made about the small and large rooms. We haven't, so to speak, examined the dice with great care to see whether the chances of their landing disastrously are truly very small, so that the future number of humans is virtually determined to be enormous. Even prior to considering Carter's reasoning, we might have quite powerful grounds for suspecting that the probability that there will be humans after the next few centuries is considerably less than the probability that two fair dice will avoid falling double-six over the course of the next few throws. And we may go so far as to suspect that how long humankind will survive has long been virtually settled, or that the factors most likely to influence the affair are very unlike dice thrown repeatedly. We may actually suspect that the world is entirely deterministic, despite what so many people have written about quantum indeterminism.

How would full determinism affect matters? Suppose the Devil had decided to let each batch leave the Shooting Room safely until successive digits of pi (the ratio of a circle's circumference to its diameter, whose first digits are 3.14159 . . .) yielded a double-six. After the seven millionth digit (a point which the Devil, no mathematician, chose without knowing what this digit would be and which digits would come next), successive digits were to be taken two by two: just two new digits whenever a new batch was in the room. You find yourself in the room. The Devil's computer is calculating what the next two digits will be. Should you expect them to be 6 and 6? You should indeed. For now there's no need for you to accept the paradoxical conclusion which seemed forced on you in the indeterministic version of the experiment. You cannot say that, when you arrived in the room, whether you'd exit from it safely hadn't yet been fixed by factors working deterministically. There is nothing indeterministic in the successive digits of pi. Admittedly, examining the previous digits calculated by the computer gives you no guidance about what the next two will be: your mastery of mathematics is insufficient. But you must expect disaster. Disaster is what will come to over 90 per cent of those who will ever have been in your situation.

In this completely deterministic case it would be silly to argue that doom – shooting – 'oughtn't to be expected since *at most points in time* the people who expected it would be wrong'. For, given determinism, what's crucial is that if everybody expected it, then *most people* who expected it would be right.

Human decisions affecting batch sizes ('population sizes') could be brought into variants of the tale. Imagine, for example, that the Devil had been indifferent about the numbers in any batches after the first. He had left it to Joan to decide this, Joan being somebody in the first batch. I now find myself in some later batch. Whether I'm to be shot will depend, as before, on whether the computer generates a double-six. Joan had no freedom to influence the computer. None the less, whether I should expect to be shot would depend on what I learned about Joan's decision. What if she'd decided that the numbers in any later batches would be held constant? I should then expect to leave the room alive, obviously. If, on the other hand, she'd decided that any later batch would be a hundred times larger than the batch before it, then I should expect to be shot. There's no real paradox here. Yes, there would be nothing worth calling 'the real risk of being shot, a risk out there in the world', which was in any way influenced by Joan's decision, but *my estimate of the risk of being shot* ought to depend on what I knew about her decision. It would certainly be important if Joan had set up a situation which, *evolving deterministically from before the time that I was born*, would lead to the shooting of the vast majority of all who had ever entered the room.

Imagine instead that I'm with Joan in the first batch. I hear the Devil telling her that there may be later batches, and that if so, whether they will be the same size as the first, or smaller, or up to a hundred times larger, is for her to decide. Joan decides that any new batch would be a hundred times larger than the one before. She and I then learn that any given batch will leave the room safely unless the computer generates a double-six. If it does generate a double-six then the batch will be shot, the experiment then ending. Now, suppose I'm firmly convinced that all events, human decisions included, are ultimately deterministic: the human brain is 'a decision-making machine' and what Joan was going to decide about the sizes of any later batches had been settled before she and I came into existence. Should I expect to be shot? Indeed I should. Once again, it would make no sense to say that something called 'the real risk of being shot' could somehow have been influenced by Joan's decision; but once again, too, *my estimate of the risk of being shot* could very reasonably depend on what I knew about her decision. It could certainly be relevant that, thanks to Joan's decision, if there were *even one* later batch then I'd be a person from a tiny group, a person among the earliest 1 per cent of all who'd ever have entered the room. I ought to be reluctant to believe I was in so tiny a group, if firmly persuaded that the sizes of any batches had been settled deterministically before I came into existence. If, on the other hand, I thought of Joan's decision as indeterministic, then I could have excellent hopes of leaving the room safely despite the fact that shooting would be the fate of most who had ever entered it. There's nothing too paradoxical in any of this.

JUST WHO SHOULD COUNT AS BEING HUMAN?

Now, what about the doomsday argument's 'reference class'? Who ought to be considered 'humans' for its purposes? Looking towards the past, at what date shall we say that humans first diverged from the manlike apes? Imagining the future, should we still call a race 'human' when it had undergone great evolutionary changes?

With respect to the past, an initial reaction might be that it would scarcely matter where we drew the line between humans and non-humans. The numbers involved would be much the same whether we counted, say, only the members of *homo sapiens sapiens*, thought to have arisen about a hundred thousand years ago, or whether we instead counted all of *homo sapiens*, a group which includes the Neanderthals and stretches back for perhaps six hundred thousand years – or even whether we included everyone since the split away from the line which led to modern chimpanzees, a split occurring perhaps five million years ago. Population figures at all early dates were tiny compared with those today. In generating the rough estimates given earlier in this chapter, I assumed that the first humans appeared some half a million years ago, yet looking backwards twice as far would have made little difference.

When we look to the future, in contrast, a great deal might seem to depend on whether descendants of all the greatly altered types imagined by O. Stapledon in his *Last and First Men*[7] – let alone members of the 'humanity that has become completely etherialized, becoming masses of atoms in space communicating by radiation, and ultimately perhaps resolving itself entirely into light' of the British crystallographer J. D. Bernal's *The World, the Flesh, and the Devil*[8] – were to be counted as 'humans'. One could imagine, too, many degrees of fusion between our descendants and computers to which their brains were permanently linked. Should they all be called humans? Again, the cosmologist P. C. W. Davies has written to me that, while finding the doomsday argument 'generally convincing',[9] he still wonders whether it may not suggest only that the human race will soon be entirely replaced by computers. Yet, particularly if they had been designed to think very much as we do, mightn't the computers themselves be 'humans' for the doomsday argument's purposes? Some would say that computers, no matter how intelligent, would for ever lack consciousness and so couldn't be true observers. It isn't at all clear, however, that they would be right.

While all of this could lead to some interesting discussions, perhaps nothing too much hangs on it. What I have tried to show is that Carter's line of reasoning contains a warning for us. It tells us that we ought to make very sure of our facts before dismissing any dangers confronting the human race. Carter and I argue for a shift in the direction of reduced confidence. No doubt the shift would be greater if today's humans could perhaps have descendants continuing onwards for many million years, not just a few thousand years, and if these could all be counted as 'humans'. Maybe, too, the tragedy that humankind had ended after a few thousand years would be smaller if it had ended only through being replaced by computer-based intelligent systems – provided, of course, that those systems truly were conscious beings. Yet such matters aren't really crucial. The really crucial issue is whether Carter's argument works at all. If it does, then it can give us an important warning even if we confine our attention to the human race's chances of surviving for the next few centuries. All the signs are that these centuries would be very heavily populated if the race met with no disaster, and they are centuries during which there would presumably be little chance of transferring human thought-processes to machines in a way which would encourage people to call the machines 'human'. Furthermore, if the doomsday argument pointed towards the replacement of ordinary humans by intelligent machines, then this would itself be something rather interesting, and possibly rather frightening.

All the same, it would be good to have a technique for testing various suggested answers to the 'reference-class' questions I have just been raising. And such a technique is available, I think. It involves looking at an urn analogy.

Imagine you are trying to estimate how many balls of a particular class an urn contains. Suppose it's the class of *red balls*, and that you know the urn has just red balls, green balls and yellow balls. Here you can use Bayesian reasoning. Such reasoning, I argued, applies well to the type of situation in which the doomsday argument is strongest: the situation in which the world is either (a) fully deterministic or else (b) with indeterminisms of a type unlikely to have much effect on how long humankind will survive. In a situation of this type 'the number of names in the urn' – the total number of humans who will ever have lived – has already been settled, or virtually settled. Now, what light can Bayesian reasoning throw on reference-class puzzles?

Well, suppose you know that the urn has a thousand balls. What if you get a red ball on your very first draw? This could much increase your reluctance to believe that there had been only one red ball, or only ten red balls. To find how much your reluctance should be increased, you could use Bayes's Rule as given in Chapter 5. It shows how big a shift your probability-estimates should undergo.

Next, imagine that what interests you is instead how many of the balls fall into the class of *balls either red or green*. Drawing a red ball in the first draw, you should once again be influenced in your probability-estimates. For instance, the observed red ball could lead to a vigorous Bayesian shift away from an estimate that, with a probability of 99 per cent, only three out of the thousand balls had been in the red-or-green 'reference class'.

The thing to note is that the red ball can be treated either just as a red ball or else as a red-or-green ball. Bayes's Rule applies in both cases. When we're interested in how many red balls there are in the urn, we need to treat the ball just as a red ball. The 'prior probabilities' entering into our Bayesian calculation are then probabilities for such and such numbers of red balls. When, in contrast, what interests us is how many red-or-green balls the urn contains, then we have to treat the red ball as red-or-green. Correspondingly, the prior probabilities entering into the calculation are the prior probabilities of various numbers of balls in the red-or-green-ball class.

Entirely as you'd expect, Bayesian calculations using exactly the same evidence, the evidence that a red ball has been drawn, result in *different shifts* in the cases of estimates of the two different kinds: estimates of the probabilities that the urn contains various numbers of red balls, and estimates of the probabilities that it contains various numbers of balls which are either red or green.

All this evidently continues to apply when being-red-or-green is replaced by being-red-or-pink, or by being-red-or-reddish. But you will, of course, have to make up your mind about just how similar a ball must be to a bright red one for you to be willing to call it 'reddish'. Count dark violet balls as reddish, if you want. Just be clear about what you are doing, and adjust your prior probabilities accordingly.

Suppose all the balls in the urn are numbered. A ball is drawn. It turns out to be bright red. Note that it is not only a bright red ball whose number has been drawn *at random* from the numbers of all the *bright red* balls in the urn, but also a red-or-reddish ball whose number has been drawn *at random* from the numbers of all the *red-or-reddish* balls in the urn. So the doomsday argument, which treats the observer as if drawn from an urn randomly, is untroubled by the point that a typical human – 'the sort of human you could expect to get on a random draw' – could well be thought of as an untypical mammal, 'typicality' in one reference class threatening always to turn into extreme unusualness when the reference class is slightly revised. (Red balls aren't typical green balls, obviously, yet one and the same ball can have been drawn randomly both from the class of red balls and from the class of red-or-greens. And although the dark red balls in an urn may be no more typical of its red balls than humans are typical of mammals, a randomly drawn ball which turns out to be dark red really was a ball drawn randomly from all the dark red balls in the urn; we do not have to worry about whether it is perhaps 'a random red ball instead of a random dark red one'.)

The moral could seem to be that one's reference class might be made more or less what one liked for doomsday argument purposes. What if we wanted to count our much-modified descendants, perhaps with three arms or with godlike intelligence, as 'genuinely human'? There would be nothing wrong in this. Yet if we were instead interested in the future only of two-armed humans, or of humans with intelligence much like that of humans today, then there would be nothing wrong in refusing to count any others.

Reference-class changes were introduced earlier in this book. In connection with Fermi's famous question, 'Where are they?', it was said that we could treat ourselves, if we liked, as *members of a technologically advanced species*, then using this when considering the probability that our universe would come to contain numerous such species. But, it was pointed out, we might choose instead to treat ourselves just as *members of the human race*, then developing a doomsday argument concerning the future of humankind. And it was later emphasized that an observer could well disregard various of his or her features – for instance being male or being female, or having eyes or hair coloured in one way or in another – if they were irrelevant to the question at hand: the question, for instance, of whether any people (no matter what their sexes, eye colours, etc.) had been created in a large room. In contrast, learning about your skin colour could become important if you were a blind child trying to guess how many humans were brown-skinned.

Is it right, though, to think that the doomsday argument's reference class can be varied very much as we please?

Widenings of reference classes can easily be taken too far. For example, we ought to think twice before accepting any widening which counted as 'observers' even primitive forms of animal life. These might well not be conscious at all. Furthermore it could be held that full consciousness involves introspective ability of a kind which even chimpanzees haven't yet acquired. The psychologist Julian Jaynes has gone so far as to maintain that humans themselves only recently acquired it.[10] Once, arguing heatedly with a Reader in Animal Behaviour who claimed that lions weren't really conscious, I suddenly saw that his theory had much to be said for it. The concept of consciousness is very far from being a clear one. Freud's 'unconscious mind' is supposedly capable of very complex information processing. Our unconscious processing of visual information is known to be extremely intricate, something of which no modern computer is capable, although it takes place in a flash.

Again, some ways of *narrowing* a reference class might perhaps seem inappropriate. For instance, you personally are particularly early in the class of all humans born on or after the actual day on which you were born. This surely mustn't be allowed to yield a doomsday argument of a type particularly threatening to people born exactly when you were.

Should the common ancestors of humans and Neanderthals enter into doomsday argument calculations? It might perhaps be complained that making the reference class into humans-after-splitting-away-from-Neanderthals would be coming too near to imitating the man who makes his reference class into people-born-as-late-as-himself-or-later, or at least to some other man who counts nobody born more than a century earlier than himself. The doomsday argument might therefore need to go quite far back when seeking what it was willing to count as humans. Yet although, as Chapter 5 said, we can reject the idea that the argument's Population Clock could start to operate only when humans became able to pass exams in probability theory, we might still want its tickings to begin only on the arrival of beings who could observe their positions in time in a fairly sophisticated way: one which no chimpanzee, for instance, can manage. Chimpanzees may know it's suppertime, yet presumably they can form no concept of being at a particular point in the history of the chimpanzee species. Now, the same would no doubt have been true of the common ancestors of humans and Neanderthals. In this case, mightn't the doomsday argument simply disregard them?

The following consideration turns out to be the crucial one. Granted that one needed to take account of those common ancestors, this wouldn't in fact prove it was wrong to operate with the

reference class humans-after-splitting-away-from-Neanderthals. For
as Carter pointed out to me, 'taking account of them' could take
the following form. We could say that the fact that the humans,
or almost-humans, who had existed before the split *had propagated
their kind successfully for thousands of centuries* suggested that
humans after the split weren't likely to be few. The successful
survival of the earlier humans or almost-humans for greatly many
years would, of course, have some tendency to show that their
descendants, too, would survive long. A user of Bayes's Rule could
therefore take those earlier beings into consideration when estimating prior probabilities for various possible numbers of future
beings in a reference class – 'humans' – which was itself defined
sufficiently narrowly to exclude them.

A little further thought shows that the same kind of thing can
be done even in the case of narrowing the reference class down
to humans-born-as-late-as-you-or-later. No inappropriately frightening doomsday argument will result from narrowing your
reference class down to this, provided you adjust your prior
probabilities accordingly. Imagine you'd been born knowing all
about Bayesian calculations and about human history. The prior
probability of the human race ending *in the very week you were
born* ought presumably to have struck you as extremely tiny.
And that's quite enough to allow us to say the following: that
although, if the human race had been going to last for another
century, people born in the week in question would have been
exceptionally early in the class of those-born-either-in-that-week-
or-in-the-following-century, this would have been a poor reason
for you to expect the race to end in that week, instead of lasting
for another century.

How much widening of the reference class is appropriate when
we look towards the future? There are strong grounds for widening
it to include our evolutionarily much-altered descendants, three-
armed or otherwise, as 'humans' for doomsday argument purposes
– granted, that's to say, that their intelligence would remain well
above the chimpanzee level. For remember, we aren't just trying
to estimate how many of those descendants will fall into a particular
group, such as the group of the two-armed. What we are trying
to say is whether the human race is likely to meet with disaster
shortly, giving us very few descendants of any type. Three-armed

descendants, five-eyed descendants, descendants able to sense radio waves or solve immensely complicated equations at a glance would surely all need to be counted as humans; for the arrival of third arms, sensitivity to radio waves, tremendous intelligence could hardly be 'doomsday' in any interesting sense. Moreover, I feel inclined to say that highly intelligent machines with humanlike thought-processes, or even ones with thought-processes very different from those of humans, should also count for doomsday argument purposes, so long as they were 'descended from' us in the sense that they all ultimately owed their existence to the fact that intelligent life had once arisen on Earth in human form.

When, therefore, we try to predict whether we shall have descendants after the next few centuries, we may need to bear in mind that our descendants could include vastly many intelligent machines, perhaps much better fitted than humans to colonize the galaxy. Now, the prospect of having vastly many descendants, if the human race gets through the next few centuries safely, is precisely what the doomsday argument gives as a ground – not, let me stress for one last time, a crushing, despair-justifying ground, but *some* ground none the less – for increased fear that the race *won't* get through those centuries safely.

POSTSCRIPT

Andrei Linde has suggested to me that the doomsday argument fails for the following curious reason. The universe is such, he thinks, that it is technologically feasible for the human race to continue for infinitely long. Humans could well take advantage of this. It would follow that no matter how many years separated a human from the start of human history, this human would be (in a readily understandable sense of these words) *'infinitely early'* in the total lifetime of the human race.

Linde hasn't convinced me. Suppose that, instead of dismissing it outright, you started off rather liking Linde's theory of an infinitely prolonged future for the human race. Were the theory true, your actual temporal position would indeed be, as Linde has noticed, in some sense *exactly as early* (that is 'infinitely early') regardless of when you existed, and therefore never more surprisingly early in one case than in another. The doomsday argument would fail. However, there is no need for the argument's supporters to assume that Linde's theory is true, and then try to compare various possible temporal positions for their degrees of surprisingness. Instead they should start by comparing how early their own positions would be if Linde's theory *weren't true* with how early they would be if it *were*. In the second case, their positions would be in a sense infinitely early; in the first case, not. Now, this gives superbly strong probabilistic grounds for rejecting the theory.

ADDITIONAL NOTE FOR PHYSICISTS

A variant on the doomsday argument appears to destroy many-worlds quantum theory.[11] Or at least, it would seem to destroy those variants of many-worlds quantum theory in which, as was fairly plainly intended by the theory's first inventor, H. Everett, every observer splits at each successive moment into vastly more 'versions' of himself or herself: one version for each possible set of observations which the laws of quantum physics allow to flow from the situation at the previous moment.[12] If they believed that such repeated splitting really took place, people should expect to die very soon, virtually regardless of how much evidence there seemed to be against this, because there would be so vastly many more observer-versions at later minutes than at earlier ones, right up to the arrival of death: the overwhelming majority of all observer-versions would therefore find themselves within a few minutes of dying. Since, as was argued in this and in the previous chapter, one cannot escape that kind of conclusion by protesting that observations to be made at future minutes 'aren't yet being made', and since it would be absurd for everybody to expect to die very soon, the idea of splitting will apparently have to be abandoned.

In effect, one's seeming position in one's lifetime – far away from imminent death – would appear to refute Everett unless his theory is on other grounds immensely likely to be right, which it surely isn't. For suppose one could be certain of Everett's correctness. One would then face two alternatives, each wildly implausible: first, that one was a very exceptionally early version of an observer who would have vastly many more later versions, and second, that one's observations were being made just before death arrived. But there is in fact no need to choose between these strange alternatives. Instead one can simply reject Everett's position.

Notice that it can further be argued that on Everett's theory there would be not only very many more observer-*versions* at later than at earlier times, but also very many more *observers*: so very many more that this would itself throw very strong doubt on the theory. The difficulty for Everett is that the repeated branchings of his cosmos cram it with more and more branches in which observers might be born. Looking further and further back in time, either through the history of living intelligence or through the stages of one's own life history, one sees ever earlier observers or ever earlier stages which would have ever higher quantum amplitudes in the wavefunction of Everett's universe. They would be branches of a tree which branched constantly as it rose. Earlier branches, with higher quantum amplitudes, could appropriately be described as 'weightier' because the sub-branches, sub-sub-branches, etc. to which they would eventually give birth, would be far more numerous than those which would be born from branches splitting off at later times. In Everett's world-picture, this idea of having a greater number of 'offshoots' replaces the ordinary notion that higher quantum amplitudes correspond to greater probabilities of being real, because according to Everett absolutely all branches, sub-branches, etc. are equally real: he interprets probabilities as frequencies rather than as 'propensities to become real'. But the pleasures and pains felt at the points where the branches are much weightier surely oughtn't to be thought of as being correspondingly much more vivid or vigorous: the toothache of today isn't many trillion trillion times weaker than the toothache of last week, is it? Nor, I suggest, should they be thought of as being felt somehow 'more numerously' or 'as if more numerously' – which, Carter pointed out to me, could ruin my argument against Everett, which he saw as decisive in other respects. That's to say: any observation occurring where a branch is weighty ought, I think, to be treated as indeed a single observation, not as if it were many trillion trillion identical observations being made, at different points across the thickness of the branch, by different observer-versions all blessed with identical experiences.

Note, though, that D. Deutsch recommends supplementing Everett's position by an axiom that there exists a continuously infinite-measured set of universes, divided into disjoint subsets, and that each subset consists of a continuous infinity of identical universes which become partitioned by measurement.[13] Although many people find infinities of identical universes very hard to accept, Deutsch's 'Everett-type' theory does at least have the advantage that imminent death would no longer be predicted.

7

PRISONER'S DILEMMA AND
NUCLEAR REVENGE

——— •◆• ———

> To give the human race much chance of survival, consid-
> erable co-operation may be needed. When dealing with
> selfish people, one way of encouraging co-operation is to
> point to the benefits they could expect from it. Another is
> to use threats. Both ways involve problems in decision
> theory, perhaps best illustrated by the case of trying to
> prevent nuclear war. (This will be a very brief chapter,
> avoiding a host of technicalities.)[1]

Suppose two nations seem to be moving towards nuclear war. Each
might see much reason to strike first, so as to destroy many enemy
missiles before they could be launched.

A ground for not striking first is the hope of remaining in the
situation in which no nuclear bombs are exploded by anyone. Yet
this can raise 'prisoner's dilemma' problems.

A ground for not striking second is that one's nation may have
been so nearly annihilated that there remain no benefits to be had
by striking. This raises problems of whether it can be right to carry
out acts of revenge.

NOT STRIKING FIRST: CO-OPERATION
AND PRISONER'S DILEMMA

Say that two superpowers – call them Oceania and Eurasia – have
constructed huge nuclear arsenals. For the two of them taken

267

together, the best outcome would be that nuclear war never broke out. For Oceania taken singly, however, it would be better if it made a first strike that destroyed most of Eurasia's nuclear missiles. It would then have removed a very dangerous rival and might come to control the globe. Eurasia's remaining missiles might be lauched in revenge, yet because of Oceania's 'Star Wars' shield only one or two would reach their targets. On the other hand it would be terrible if Eurasia ever struck first. So no matter what Eurasia's present plans are, Oceania will do better by attacking.

Eurasia, which has built its own Star Wars shield ('to make the world a safer place', the same excuse as Oceania used), has similar reasons for attacking. Each nation is in what is called a prisoner's dilemma. Although continued peace would be best for the pair of them, each has selfish grounds for starting a war. And nations often are selfish. A supposed duty to be selfish may actually be built into the oaths their Presidents are required to take. If Oceania and Eurasia are indeed selfish, then their situation resembles that of two selfish prisoners, Oliver and Edward, each invited to betray the other by a prison governor whose threats and offers of reward make betrayal the rational policy. ('Rational' is a word with no agreed meaning, but, following a common practice, I'm making it function in such a way that what's rational for you depends on what your aims happen to be. Unselfish people can act with rational unselfishness, but in Oliver's case rationality lies in what will benefit Oliver.) The prison governor believes a warder has been murdered by the two prisoners jointly. If neither of them confesses, then the crime will go unpunished. The governor separates the prisoners. Each is now told that if he confesses while the other remains silent, then he will be freed at once, his partner getting ten additional years in prison. If both confess, they will get five additional years apiece. Oliver and Edward will thus each do better by confessing, no matter what the other does.

All this has a great deal of force, but, I'll be arguing, rather less than most philosophers believe. For suppose the parties in a prisoner's dilemma are appreciably alike. This should affect any calculation of the benefits to be expected from 'ratting' – confessing, betraying trust, starting a nuclear war, or whatever. The result, I suggest, is that ratting will often not be rational, not even for the entirely selfish. That could be very important because prisoner's dilemmas are deplorably common. They occur with alarming frequency when people ask themselves whether to aim at co-operation. They can arise, for instance, when boats are chasing dwindling supplies of fish. Suppose each captain appeals to the others not to catch more than the officially permitted tonnage. A captain who breaks the rules can be an analogue of a prisoner who confesses.

My argument can be helped along by a story. Walking up to what looks like a gigantic mirror, I find myself pressing against flesh instead of glass. The universe, I conclude, must be fully symmetrical. The flesh belongs to my double – left–right reversed, but in all other respects a perfect replica.

The universe must also be fully deterministic, its events dictated in all their details by the laws of nature, for otherwise it would be a miracle that my double's movements exactly mirrored mine. This may not trouble me, however. I needn't spring to the conclusion that all freedom of choice is illusory. Yes, in a deterministic universe my brain would be 'just a decision-making machine' in a fairly strong sense. All the same, it could genuinely make decisions. It could select actions from a great many which my body could carry out, instead of merely seeming to select them. As well as being what I thought with, my brain cells could be what I chose with. I wouldn't have to wait and see whether my legs carried me away from a hungry lion. I could instead freely decide to run.

Don't I have twice as much power as I earlier believed? Besides governing my own hands and legs, don't I govern my double's too? Can't I make him run, wave or clap whenever I want? Can't I choose to throw two stones instead of just one: the stone I throw to kill a bird, and the second stone which must fly from my double's hand simultaneously? If ever I controlled what my image did in a mirror, why deny that I control what my double does? Well, grounds for denying it are easy to find. In crucial respects, I and my double are independent. I do not genuinely cause him to run whenever I run myself. You might equally well declare that *he* causes *me* to run, which he surely doesn't. My decision to run is generated by my own brain cells, not his. None the less, by choosing to run I can *ensure* that my double runs. Without causing him to throw stones, I can *see to it* or *make it certain* that he throws them. All I need do is throw stones myself.

Imagine that, seeing a bird in the other half of the universe, I want it to die. It's no use my hurling a rock towards it. On reaching the place where the universe-halves joined, the rock would simply collide with the other rock which my double had hurled simultaneously. Yet what if a rock of mine kills the precisely similar bird in my half of the universe? The bird I want dead will inevitably be killed as well.

Clumsy though it may sound, let's talk of my 'quasi-causing' various events in the other half of the universe: my double's sudden decision to run round in circles, or the death of the bird that he kills, or whatever. *Quasi-causation*, although it of course isn't genuine causation, can be every bit as good for seeing to it that things get done. In fact, it can often be a lot better. Suppose that, just by pleading with my double, I try to cause him to kill his bird with his rock. I shall get nowhere until I decide to kill my bird with mine. If I want him to struggle out of bed and vote Democrat, I must struggle out of bed and vote Democrat myself. Nothing else will do, granted that we are perfect replicas of each other.

Although cosmologists have sometimes toyed with the idea that ours is a fully symmetrical universe, this seems improbable. What relevance, then, can the story of me and my double have to real life, let alone to any prisoner's dilemma? The answer is suggested by D. Lewis.[2] While perfect replication may be a fiction, people often are pretty good replicas of one another. Drop a rock on my foot, and how am I likely to react? Presumably much as you would if I dropped a rock on yours.

Don't products of military academies often say and do quite ludicrously similar things? Isn't the same true of those with British public-school educations? Of inmates of prisons, or of convents? Of people who were born to riches? Of the poor and the oppressed? In fact, take any two adults at random and place them in similar circumstances. Aren't they liable to show quite marked behavioural likenesses?

The quasi-causation in my story could be called *perfect*. Absolutely always when I throw a stone, my double throws one too. If he loses his temper as a rock hits his foot, I am 100 per cent sure to be losing mine. But while real life may offer nothing quite so dramatic, it clearly includes a great deal of *imperfect* quasi-causation. Ways of behaving may never be exactly replicated, but there are often impressive correlations. People do things which are predictably alike because their natures are similar, just as two balls bounce in the same fashion because their construction is much the same. You cannot deny this, no matter what you think about freedom of the will. Over years of decision-making, humans really can build up nice or nasty natures for themselves, so that they act with characteristic unselfishness or characteristic selfishness.

Well, imperfect quasi-causation is something we can exploit. We can exploit it rather as the perfect quasi-causation of my story was exploited for bird-killing. In the prisoner's dilemmas typically discussed, the prisoners (or prisoner-analogues) are in identical circumstances. There is nothing wrong in this. When you hope to shed light on a philosophical, mathematical or scientific point, then it is often best to discuss tidy, idealized cases. But what one tends to overlook is that just a little more idealization would give us prisoners who were known to be alike in all respects, their brains being decision-making machines which reacted to threats and offers identically. And in that case the standard conclusion to prisoner's-dilemma discussions, namely that it makes sense for selfish people to confess or betray or start nuclear wars etc., would be nonsense. There can be no such thing as your *selfishly striving to do better than* somebody who is facing exactly similar prospects of punishment and reward, and who is (to your firm knowledge) bound to behave exactly as you do. On the other hand, you have every reason to be confident that this somebody won't 'rat' if you don't.

It follows that you have every reason to choose what will be best for the pair of you. The idea of 'getting greater benefits for yourself no matter what your fellow prisoner does' fails entirely when his or her behaviour is sure to mirror yours. What's more, it begins to fail long before perfect mirroring is achieved. To the varying extents that various people are replicas of one another, they can be said to have varying degrees of 'quasi-causal grip' on one another: when one of them acts trustingly, for instance, then this will have some quasi-causal tendency towards ensuring that the others do likewise. Admittedly the tendency will often be very slight. At other times it could be strong, though. Not strong *causally*, since quasi-causation isn't causation, but strong none the less.

The phenomenon of quasi-causation is definitely real, and exploitable. The world doesn't work by magic, yet only magic could bring it about that *perfect replication* could be exploited while *imperfect replication* couldn't. Still, clever folk will disagree over just how important quasi-causation is. The matter calls for considerable research.

Unimportantly or importantly – I'm inclined to say 'very importantly' when I read various nuclear warfare studies – the reality of quasi-causation reinforces all the more commonly recognized points in favour of trusting others and acting co-operatively. This point, for example: that people tend to react well when they are trusted. Or this one: that selfish lives are often scarcely worth living.

NOT STRIKING SECOND:
THE RIGHTS AND WRONGS OF
NUCLEAR REVENGE

When a nation has carried out a nuclear first strike with thousands of bombs, what could be the point of retaliating? As a utilitarian I see moral point in actions only when they stand a chance of doing some good. Those who follow Kant might well have little difficulty in viewing nuclear revenge as 'avenging justice'. Kant speaks of the need to execute murderers even though the heavens fall. But I don't admire Kant's approach. How could you have a duty to do something which would harm some people without bringing benefits to others? How could it be *right* to perform acts which made the world *worse*? No doubt these are just rhetorical questions because, as discussed in Chapter 4, there is no way of proving that maximizing benefits is what we ought to strive for. 'It's right to try to maximize benefits' isn't in the least like 'Bachelors are wifeless.' Still, I'll be assuming that the only really interesting issue is whether *threatening retaliation* could be right on grounds, roughly speaking, of getting the largest expected benefits in return for the least risks, and whether it would then follow, as D. Gauthier has argued,[3] that *actual retaliation* could be called for when one's threats had failed.

Nuclear revenge might, of course, act deterrently. It could teach people that nuclear bombs should never again be dropped, because retaliation could be expected. But let's concentrate on whether nuclear revenge could be appropriate even when no deterrent purpose could possibly be served. Imagine that such revenge would be certain to destroy all that was left of the human race. Could it still somehow be right? Could a moral and rational person be forced into it by the fact that he or she had been right to threaten revenge? Gauthier would answer Yes.

To see the attractions of Gauthier's position, consider the case of a world which still contains thousands of nuclear weapons long after the Soviet Union's collapse. Nuclear warfare, it seems, is almost sure to annihilate the human race unless people can be persuaded never to resort to it. ('Limited nuclear war' is probably nonsense. Warring peoples quickly lose their tempers, then doing as much killing as they can.) A nation's thoroughly moral leader therefore gives orders for building a doomsday machine. This means, of course, a large group of machines, a complex and fully autonomous system of sensors and computers. If nuclear bombs are exploded anywhere, then this will be detected automatically, a central computer then triggering sufficiently many further bombs to destroy the entire human race.

Building the doomsday machine might be moral because it offered the best chance that the human race *wouldn't* be destroyed. In the absence of such a machine, nations could be tempted to initiate nuclear warfare. Common sense might say that the likely outcome would be annihilation for everybody, yet since when have nations been eager to consult common sense? The best policy could be to build the machine and invite people to inspect it thoroughly. Then even the blindest would see no point in dropping nuclear bombs.

Let's grant that the moral leader has good grounds for ordering the machine to be built. But suppose now that (as in the United States) some constitutional clause prevents handing over full control of nuclear weapons to machinery. The doomsday system can therefore operate only if the leader presses a button 'in agreement' when the central computer 'wants' to trigger the bombs. The leader might go to a hypnotist or a brain surgeon, saying 'Make me a reliable component of the doomsday threat. Ensure that I'd never hesitate to press the button. Then tell everybody what you've done.' Couldn't this be ethically required? So that a threat retained its credibility, couldn't some truly moral person ensure that he or she really would take nuclear revenge, even if taking it freely would be an immoral use of freedom? For deterrent purposes, mightn't it be a duty to 'zombiefy' oneself.

Let's agree that the answer is Yes. Somebody could have superb moral grounds for *freely ensuring that he or she would act revengefully* if threats failed, even if *actually acting revengefully* could only be done immorally by any free person. There's nothing too paradoxical here. Guarantees of revenge can be good when they minimize the risk that the human race will be destroyed. This can be true despite how the revenge would destroy the human race.

But now, what if other constitutional clauses prevent the zombiefication? What if the leader's only recourse is to state firmly, 'I really will press the button and annihilate everybody if nuclear war breaks out'? Although a thoroughly moral person, couldn't the leader make a threat of this type, inviting the psychologists of other nations to check with lie detectors (which, let's say, were completely reliable) that the threat really was firm, i.e. would almost certainly be carried out in response to any nuclear attack? Gauthier would say so. Let us now prove him wrong.

As the point to be made against him will be a purely logical one, it can be developed with the help of a fantastic hypothesis. Fantasticality doesn't affect the logic of the affair. Imagine, then, that in return for ten billion dollars I've told the Devil he can have my soul, to torment for ever and ever, if you flip a coin and it falls heads. I know that you know this, and that you have quite a liking for me. Unfortunately it turns out that you nevertheless feel tempted to flip the coin: the Devil is offering you fifty billion dollars for doing so. What am I to do? Suppose the Devil suggests the following. He'll carry off both our souls to damnation – endless years of torment – whenever I give the word. Assuming I know you to be rational, can't I now reasonably threaten you with damnation if you flip the coin? To be absolutely sure of avoiding the Devil's clutches, couldn't I make a solemn declaration that if

274

you flip it then I'll automatically demand damnation for you and me? Couldn't I next invite you to use a completely reliable lie detector on me, while I repeat the declaration?

The answer is No. Unless I were crazy, the lie detector would reveal that I had no plan to send our two souls to damnation if you flipped the coin. And even were I mad enough to have formed such a plan, accompanied by much gritting of teeth and pushing forward of the jaw, I'd have to be still more mad to act on it while the coin was still in the air or after it had landed tails. Unless insanely revengeful, I'd never actually whizz myself off to an infinity of torture just as soon as you'd dared to coin-flip. True, if able to rely on your rationality and your knowledge of all the facts, I could zombiefy myself – make myself irrational – so that the threat to have us damned became sure to be effective. You'd then know that flipping the coin would lead to your damnation, and therefore wouldn't flip it. But the threat could never work if it were known that I'd remain rational. No rational person would carry out such a threat.

Well, this is an area where being fully and consistently *moral* behaves just like being fully and consistently *rational*. Faced with the choice of whether to take a form of revenge which involved the deaths of all human beings, the moral leader would decide not to take it.

Still, it could be right to have threatened revenge. After all, onlookers couldn't be sure about the absence of insanely revengeful tendencies. It might be rather a good thing that many present-day leaders have them. And during the Cold War the nuclear peace may have been kept only because each superpower suspected the other of having them.

NOTES

INTRODUCTION

1 The Introduction's treatment of the doomsday argument is based largely on Leslie 1989e, 1990b and 1992a and e. For much more about the argument, see Chapters 5 and 6.

2 As J. J. C. Smart writes, even a very low probability, when 'multiplied by a macro disaster', would be something having 'macro disvalue', a point immensely important when we consider 'the millions of years of possible evolution of the human race that lie ahead if we do not destroy ourselves' (Smart 1984, p. 140).

3 McCrea 1975; Begelman and Rees 1976.

4 Peterson 1993.

5 Leslie 1993c and d, for instance.

6 Heilbroner 1975.

7 See Tipler 1982, Tipler 1994, chapter 2, and Wesson 1990.

8 Gott 1993, p. 16.

9 See also Gott 1994 for replies to other critics.

10 I believe it needs a firm fact of this type, a fact theoretically predictable, even if – as on some views about the nature of time – all things which will ever be true about the future must be true already, regardless of whether the world is indeterministic. The point is controversial, and Chapter 6 will return to it.

1 WAR, POLLUTION, DISEASE

1 Putnam 1979, p. 114.

2 C. Sagan, 1980, p. 266.

3 Kiernan 1994a, p. 15.

4 Adamson 1990, pp. 171–3.

5 C. Sagan 1980, p. 267.

NOTES

6 Turco et al. 1983; Greene et al. 1985; Schneider and Thompson 1988; Nelson 1989; Chapman and Morrison 1989, chapter 8.
7 R. Kennedy 1968, p. 110.
8 For a detailed analysis of the crisis, see Gottfried and Blair 1988, pp. 169–98.
9 Kissinger 1979, p. 622.
10 Schelling 1960, chapter 8.
11 McNamara 1985, as reprinted on p. 140 of Bethe 1991.
12 MacKenzie 1990.
13 McNamara 1985, p. 144. See also Bethe et al. 1984; Tirman 1984; Broad 1985; Franklin 1988, pp. 199–203, including the intriguing reminder that in 1940 Reagan starred in a film about a ray machine destined to 'make America invincible' and so to be 'the greatest force for world peace ever discovered'; and Casti 1990, pp. 313–18, on mathematical investigations of SDI's tendency to produce an offensive arms race.
14 Kiernan 1994b.
15 Carnesale et al. 1983.
16 Blair 1993a, chapter 6.
17 ibid., p. 339.
18 Perera 1994.
19 Blair and Kendall 1990, p. 53.
20 Blair 1993a, p. 273.
21 Britten 1986, p. 154.
22 Blair and Kendall 1990, p. 57. See also Blair 1993a, p. 214, citing A. Gorokhov, Pravda, February 21, 1990.
23 Britten 1986, p. 156.
24 C. Sagan 1980, p. 271. For much more on the topic see S. D. Sagan 1993: for example pp. 99–100 on the bear which set off sabotage alarms during the Cuban Missile Crisis -- but at one base the Klaxon went off instead so that pilots, firmly believing that hostilities had begun, started their nuclear-armed interceptors down the runway. Other pages are particularly disturbing in their illustrations of how additional safety systems can themselves lead to new possibilities of accidental nuclear war.
25 Blair and Kendall 1990, p. 55.
26 Britten 1986, p. 152.
27 Hart and Goldwater 1980.
28 Blair and Kendall 1990, p. 55.
29 ibid., p. 53.
30 ibid., p. 58.
31 Blair 1993a, pp. 192–3.

32 Blair 1993b.
33 Blair and Kendall 1990, p. 54.
34 ibid., p. 54.
35 ibid., p. 54; Blair 1993b.
36 Keegan 1987, pp. 341–3.
37 Blair and Kendall 1990, p. 57.
38 Britten 1986, p. 156. See also Ballard 1986, and S. D. Sagan 1993, pp. 254–5.
39 Blair and Kendall 1990, p. 58.
40 See, for example, Burrows and Windrem 1994.
41 Perera 1994.
42 Hassard 1992.
43 Edwards 1995.
44 Harris and Paxman 1982, p. 239.
45 Piller and Yamamoto 1988, p. 25.
46 ibid., p. 191; cf. Wheale and McNally 1988, p. 203.
47 Geissler 1986, p. 8.
48 Murphy et al. 1984, p. 28.
49 Harris and Paxman 1982, pp. 129–30.
50 Murphy et al. 1984, pp. 28–30.
51 Harris and Paxman 1982, pp. 103, 160.
52 Murphy et al. 1984, p. 32.
53 Piller and Yamamoto 1988, p. 35.
54 Geissler 1986, p. 10 of editor's introduction.
55 Harris and Paxman 1982, p. 221.
56 ibid., pp. 161–7.
57 ibid., pp. 162–3.
58 ibid., pp. 155–9.
59 Horgan 1994.
60 Geissler 1986, p. 3.
61 Piller and Yamamoto 1988, p. 98.
62 ibid., p. 107.
63 ibid., p. 100.
64 ibid., pp. 24, 105.
65 ibid., pp. 98, 112.
66 Watson-Watt 1961, pp. 177, 213.
67 Meadows et al. 1992, p. 85.
68 Goldsmith and Hildyard 1992, p. 130.
69 Mosey 1990, pp. 81–94, and above all pp. 94–6 on the accident's 'institutional dimension'.
70 Barnaby 1988, p. 119, and Cook 1989, p. 112.
71 Goldsmith and Hildyard 1992, p. 116.

72   Beardsley 1994b.
73   Graedel and Crutzen 1989, pp. 58, 64, 66.
74   Lovelock 1979, p. 132.
75   Myers 1984, p. 100.
76   Meadows et al. 1992, p. 65.
77   Blaustein and Wake 1995.
78   Rennie 1993.
79   Lovelock 1986, p. 28.
80   Morone and Woodhouse 1986, p. 6, citing Doll and Peto 1981.
81   Kates 1994, p. 119.
82   Pearce 1990, p. 60.
83   Meadows et al. 1992, p. 83.
84   J. Brown 1994.
85   Weiner 1990, pp. 139, 277.
86   Holmes 1995.
87   Lovelock 1986, p. 28.
88   Lovelock 1979, p. 39.
89   Meadows et al. 1992, p. 96.
90   Rind 1995.
91   Davis 1990, p. 9.
92   Gribbin and Kelly 1989, p. 52.
93   Kaplan 1994, p. 75.
94   Charlson and Wigley, 1994.
95   Horgan 1990.
96   Palmer 1989; Bell 1994.
97   Pearce 1994b.
98   Burgess 1982; Chapman and Morrison 1989, pp. 216–20.
99   Lovelock 1979, p. 45.
100 Chapman and Morrison 1989, p. 220.
101 Schneider 1989, p. 73.
102 Myers 1991, p. 33.
103 Leggett 1992.
104 ibid., p. 41.
105 Charles 1990.
106 Brennan 1990, p. 95.
107 Chapman and Morrison 1989, pp. 236–7.
108 Lovelock 1985, pp. 53–4.
109 Sylvan 1990, p. 39.
110 Wignall 1992, p. 55.
111 White 1990, p. 43.
112 Pearce 1994a.
113 Adamson 1990; French 1994.

114 Morone and Woodhouse 1986, p. 113; Schneider 1989, p. 77.
115 Mackenzie 1994.
116 Kaplan 1994, p. 75.
117 Holmes 1994.
118 Harris and Paxman 1982, p. 137.
119 Hardin 1968.
120 Hardin 1981, p. 226.
121 Meadows et al. 1992, pp. 136–7.
122 Goldsmith and Hildyard 1992, pp. 125–6.
123 Durrell 1986, p. 34; cf. Barney 1989, p. 37, suggesting extinction of '15 to 20 percent of all species' in the final two decades of the twentieth century, 'mainly because of loss of wild habitat'.
124 Myers 1984, p. 156.
125 Cherfas 1994.
126 Wilson 1989, p. 110.
127 Barrow and Tipler 1986, p. 583.
128 Herbert 1988, pp. 11–12.
129 L. Brown, 1992.
130 Piel 1994.
131 *A Blueprint for Survival*, whose conclusions were very similar, appeared from the pens of E. Goldsmith and R. Allen in the same year. J. Maddox then rushed out *The Doomsday Syndrome*, a violent attack on Goldsmith and Allen (Meadows et al. 1972; Goldsmith and Allen 1972; Maddox 1972).
132 Meadows et al. 1992, pp. 18–19. *The Global 2000 Report to the President* (1980; see Barney 1989), commissioned by President Carter, had reached similarly disturbing conclusions about the interaction between growing population, diminishing resources and a deteriorating environment. Simon and Kahn 1984 contains responses from optimists.
133 Meadows et al. 1992, p. 101, quoting the economist L. Thurow.
134 Homer-Dixon 1994.
135 Lovelock 1979, p. 140.
136 Kaplan 1994, pp. 54–9.
137 Ross 1994, p. 241.
138 Mitchison 1993, p. 144.
139 P. Brown 1994.
140 Bader and Dorozynski 1993, p. 68.
141 Myers 1991, p. 132.

2 OTHER DANGERS

1 Close 1988, p. 37.
2 Davies 1994, pp. 1, 3.
3 Alvarez et al. 1980, 1992; N. Swinburne, 1993.
4 Courtillot 1990.
5 Alper 1994, pp. 47–51.
6 Wignall 1992; Erwin 1993; Alper 1994.
7 J.V. Smith 1986; Levasseur-Regourd 1992.
8 Close 1988, pp. 52, 61.
9 Muller 1988.
10 Henbest 1992; *The Economist* (unsigned) 1993, pp. 81–4.
11 Close 1988, pp. 56–9.
12 Chapman and Morrison 1989, pp. 276–9.
13 *The Economist* (unsigned) 1993, p. 13.
14 ibid., p. 83.
15 Matthews 1992; Lewin 1992.
16 Close 1988, p. 209.
17 Tucker 1981.
18 Ellis and Schramm 1995.
19 Oort 1977.
20 Clark et al. 1978.
21 Townes and Genzel 1990.
22 Reid et al. 1978; Wolfendale 1978.
23 Hawking 1993, p. 110.
24 Schilling 1992.
25 Croswell 1995.
26 Narlikar 1984, pp. 175–6.
27 Markov 1989, p. 17.
28 Davies 1994, p. 6.
29 Zimmerman 1984, p. 150.
30 See, for instance, Wheale and McNally 1988, pp. 60–4, 74–6. Krimsky 1982 gives a very open-minded discussion of such suggestions.
31 Wheale and McNally 1988, p. 42.
32 Piller and Yamamoto 1988, p. 183; cf. Wheale and McNally 1988, pp. 64–8.
33 Piller and Yamamoto 1988, p. 189.
34 Beardsley 1994a, p. 29. For much more on these lines see Chapter 4, 'Jumping genes', of Wheale and McNally 1988.
35 W. Brown 1994.
36 Coghlan 1993.

37 Bain et al. 1992.
38 Wheale and McNally 1988, p. 184; see also pp. 68–76, 155–7, 179–87, 233–4, for more discussion of the difficulties of risk assessment.
39 Moravec 1988, pp. 134–5.
40 Littlewood and Strigini 1992, pp. 64–5.
41 G. Smith 1992.
42 Cross 1995.
43 Moravec 1988, p. 135.
44 ibid., pp. 135–6.
45 Strauss 1990.
46 MacGowan and Ordway 1966, p. 233.
47 ibid., pp. 234–5.
48 Drexler 1986, pp. 174–6.
49 MacGowan and Ordway 1966, pp. 230–3.
50 Moravec 1989, pp. 167–9.
51 Moravec 1988, pp. 4, 59–78, 74, 100.
52 Jackson 1982; R. Swinburne 1986, pp. 186–92.
53 Searle 1984 and 1990, for instance.
54 R. Swinburne 1986, p. 158.
55 Leslie 1979, pp. 12–13, 171–7.
56 Cf. ibid., p. 173.
57 Bohm 1990.
58 Bohm and Hiley 1993, pp. 382–3.
59 Penrose 1987, p. 274.
60 Penrose 1989, p. 399.
61 Marshall 1989.
62 Lockwood 1989, particularly chapter 14. See also Hodgson 1991, pp. 110–11, 383–8, 401–20; Herbert 1993, chapter 10; and Penrose 1994, particularly chapter 7.
63 Feynman 1960.
64 Amabilino and Stoddart 1994.
65 von Neumann 1966.
66 Drexler 1986, p. 19.
67 Drexler 1992. See also Schneiker 1989; Moravec 1988, pp. 72–4; Stix 1991 and 1992.
68 Ettinger 1964.
69 Drexler 1986, pp. 172–4.
70 Drexler 1989, pp. 507–16.
71 Drexler et al. 1991.
72 Drexler 1986, pp. 182–7, 194.
73 Murray 1989; Peterson 1993.

74   Hawking 1993, p. 144.
75   Chapman and Morrison 1989, p. 150.
76   Zeeman 1992.
77   Casti 1990, pp. 307–18.
78   Mehta and Barker 1991.
79   Bak and Chen 1991.
80   Bak, Flyvbjerg and Sneppen 1994.
81   Cherfas 1994, pp. 39–40.
82   Coleman and De Luccia 1980.
83   Turner and Wilczek 1982.
84   Hut and Rees 1983.
85   Coleman and De Luccia 1980, p. 3314.
86   Lederman and Schramm 1989, p. 232.
87   Dawson 1989.
88   Weinberg 1993, pp. 187–8.
89   Burgess and Hutchinson 1993.
90   W. O'Neill 1993.
91   Crum and Roy 1994; Putterman 1995.
92   Dawson 1989.
93   Herman 1990, p. 179.
94   N. Brown 1990, p. 85.
95   Burgess and Hutchinson 1993, pp. 31–2.
96   Winston 1991.
97   Burgess and Hutchinson 1993, p. 33.
98   Ellis, Linde and Sher 1990, pp. 203–5.
99   Demaret and Lambert 1994, p. 165.
100   Flores and Sher 1983, p. 1682.
101   Sher 1989, pp. 335–6.
102   Veltman 1986, p. 78.
103   't Hooft 1980; Quigg 1985; Jackson et al. 1986, pp. 70–3; Veltman 1986; Leslie 1989a, pp. 54, 76–7.
104   See also Carr and Rees 1979; Davies 1982; Leslie 1982, 1983a and c, 1985, 1986a and b, 1987, 1988a and b, 1990a, 1992f, 1993d, 1994c and e, 1995a 'Cosmology' and 1996; Barrow and Tipler 1986; Polkinghorne 1986.
105   Weinberg 1989, pp. 6–9.
106   See, for instance, Linde 1985, and pp. 10, 26, 68–9 and 152–8 of Linde 1990; or Rozental 1988, pp. 66–124.
107   Linde 1990, p. 26.
108   Weinberg 1993: see especially pp. 177–82.
109   Leslie 1989a, chapters 7 and 8; R. Swinburne 1990.
110   Ruthen 1993.

111 Rhodes 1986, p. 418.
112 Reprinted in Bethe 1991, pp. 30–3.
113 Koonin and Nauenberg, 1989.
114 Gupta and Westfall 1993, p. 35.
115 Ruthen 1993.
116 Lee and Wick 1974.
117 Farhi and Jaffe 1984, pp. 2389–90.
118 ibid., p. 2380.
119 Ruthen 1993.
120 Hut and Rees 1983, p. 508.
121 McCusker 1991, p. 23.
122 Close 1988, p. 187.
123 Shaw, Shin, Dalitz and Desai 1989.
124 Desai and Shaw 1991, p. 210.
125 Guth 1981 and 1989; Guth and Steinhardt 1984; Linde 1985 and 1990.
126 Guth 1989, p. 136.
127 Linde 1985, p. 17.
128 Linde 1994, p. 53.
129 Farhi and Guth 1987, p. 149.
130 Farhi, Guth and Guven 1990.
131 Blau, Guendelman and Guth 1987.
132 Starobinsky and Zeldovich 1992, pp. 105–6.
133 Farhi and Guth 1987, p. 150.
134 Blau, Guendelman and Guth 1987, p. 1759.
135 Linde 1992, p. 439.
136 This is accepted even by E. P. Tryon, the physicist who first made the suggestion that our universe might be a quantum vacuum fluctuation with zero total energy (see Tryon 1973). He writes (Tryon 1984, p. 15) that the suggestion 'is not rigorous, and cannot be made so: the net energy of a universe defies precise definition'.

3 JUDGING THE RISKS

1 Morgan 1993.
2 Dyson 1979a, or see chapter 6 of Dyson 1988 for something less technical; Frautschi 1982; Linde 1988.
3 Islam 1983; Barrow and Tipler 1986, chapter 10; Tipler 1994, reviewed in Leslie 1995b; Davies 1994.
4 G. O'Neill 1977.

5   Barrow and Tipler 1986, chapter 9; Brand 1977; Close 1988, pp. 209–15; Davoust 1991, chapter 4; Dyson 1979b, chapter 21, and 1988, chapter 9; McDonough 1987, chapter 13; Rood and Trefil 1981, chapters 13 and 14; Sagan 1980, chapter 8; Shklovskii and Sagan 1966, chapters 32 and 34; Sullivan 1993, chapter 16; Tipler on pp. 155–73 of Rothman et al. 1985.

6   Drexler 1986, pp. 260–1. One might replace the passenger vehicles by much lighter spacecraft carrying frozen human ova, together with mothering and teaching machines.

7   Dyson 1968.

8   Matloff and Mallove 1981.

9   Dyson 1968; Finney and Jones 1985; Forward 1986.

10   Dyson 1966.

11   Tipler 1994, p. 55.

12   Barrow and Tipler 1986: see Leslie 1992f for the relevant quotations.

13   Hart 1982.

14   Brin 1983.

15   Nielsen 1989, p. 452.

16   Moravec 1988, p. 188.

17   Brin 1983, p. 302.

18   Moravec 1988, pp. 136–9.

19   Brin 1983, pp. 296–8.

20   'Unless you can point your finger at the man who was responsible when something goes wrong then you have never had anyone really responsible': Admiral H. Rickover, principal architect of the US Navy's nuclear propulsion programme, as cited during D. Mosey's important discussion of 'institutional failure' (Mosey 1990, p. 105).

21   P. Kennedy, 1993.

22   Wallich 1995.

23   Myers 1991, p. 20.

24   Rhodes 1986, p. 511.

25   The first committee member prefers A to B, and B to C; the second prefers B to C, and C to A; the third prefers C to A, and A to B. So there are two votes for A's being better than B, and two for B's being better than C, and two for C's being better than A.

26   Brin 1983, p. 299.

27   They are discussed on pp. 84–9 of Leslie 1979.

28   Hume 1748, section VIII; Mill 1867; Mackie 1977, chapter 9; Odegard 1984; Tipton 1988.

29   von Neumann 1955.

30   Salmon 1975, p. 356.

31   Bohm and Hiley 1993, pp. 157–8, 285; Hiley and Peat 1987, p. 13 of editors' introduction.
32   Albert 1994, p. 67; Leslie 1994a.
33   Boyer 1975 and 1985; Puthoff 1989 and 1990; see also Haisch, Rueda and Puthoff 1994.
34   Puthoff 1990, p. 54.

4   WHY PROLONG HUMAN HISTORY?

1   Putnam 1979, pp. 122–3.
2   For something on a larger scale, see Leslie 1972, 1979, chapter 12 and 1986c.
3   Mackie 1977.
4   Mackie 1982.
5   Above all in Leslie 1972 and 1979.
6   Leslie 1970, 1978b, 1979, 1980, 1986c, 1989a, chapter 8 and 1993c and d.
7   Particularly Leslie 1983b and d, and 1989c.
8   Rawls 1971.
9   Black 1967, p. 467.
10   Narveson 1967.
11   Bennett 1978, pp. 64–5.
12   Parsons 1980.
13   Bennett 1978, p. 62.
14   Pp. 44–7 of Sikora and Barry 1978.
15   Parfit 1984, p. 489.
16   Kneale 1950, p. 153.
17   See, for instance, the articles in part 5 of Smart 1987.
18   Anscombe 1958, p. 17.
19   Parfit 1984.
20   Examples of all this are scattered through Partridge 1981.
21   Once again see Partridge 1981; or consult Sikora and Barry 1978.
22   Glover 1977, p. 70.
23   Partridge 1981, p. 201.
24   ibid., p. 283.

5 THE DOOMSDAY ARGUMENT

1 This chapter is based largely on Leslie 1992d, 'Time and the anthropic principle'.
2 Carter 1974, p. 291.
3 Dicke 1961.
4 Wheeler 1973, for instance.
5 Hawking and Israel 1979, p. 19 of editors' introduction.
6 Particularly Leslie 1989e and 1990b, but see also p. 214 of 1989a.
7 Nielsen 1989, particularly pp. 454–9.
8 Carter 1983, p. 363.
9 Nielsen 1989.
10 Leslie 1990b.
11 See Leslie 1989a.
12 Marochnik 1983.
13 Dyson 1979a; Frautschi 1982.

6 TESTING THE ARGUMENT

1 The chapter is based largely on Leslie 1993b and 1994b.
2 Admittedly it's 'more difficult' – less probable – to find yourself in the corner of the room, rather than just somewhere or other inside it. But the additional difficulty is equally important regardless of whether you might instead be outside the room entirely. Bayesian calculation shows that the refinement has no effect.
3 The B-theory is defended in Leslie 1976, and in chapter 9 of Leslie 1979.
4 The strength of my conviction that the B-theory is irrelevant depends in part on my further conviction that the competing theory, the A-theory, has at least a logical possibility of being right (which some people would deny).
5 Compare the case of an Exchanging Envelopes Paradox where one envelope – but you don't know which – contains twice the dollars of another. Here you could offer the following argument against eagerness to swop envelopes: that while a swop does give a half chance of doubling your money, you'd double it *only because* you'd started with the smaller of the amounts in the two envelopes, whereas halving it would mean you'd started with the larger. Therefore, if you call the amount in your envelope x, it's a blunder to think of the other envelope as worth more, viz. half *x-doubled*

plus half *x-halved*. [I am grateful to David Lewis for this comparison, and for correspondence leading to the Shooting Room Paradox.]

6 Delahaye 1994, p. 106.
7 Stapledon 1930.
8 Bernal 1969, p. 47.
9 Reactions of this kind are more common among cosmologists and philosophers of science than among scientists and philosophers generally. W. Israel and M. J. Rees of the cosmologists and M. Lockwood and J. J. C. Smart of the philosophers of science are among those who react in some such way. Familiarity with the B-theory of Time seems an important factor here. Smart, a leading defender of the B-theory, tentatively agrees with me that whether you are a B-theorist ought not to affect the doomsday argument. However – I'm here simply reporting how minds work – it does in practice influence reactions to the argument. It helps people to treat observed positions in time rather as they would treat observed positions in space, for Carter's purposes. Now, the B-theory is particularly popular with philosophers of science and cosmologists. (Let me mention as well the remarkable finding that women tend to think the doomsday argument obviously strong, whereas men tend to dismiss it. Is it that women are happy to believe that men have messed up the world, or are they less hostile towards new ideas, or what?)
10 Jaynes 1976.
11 Earlier, I had taken this theory fairly seriously: see pp. 84–91 of Leslie 1989a and pp. 145–6 of Leslie 1982.
12 See the papers by Everett, DeWitt and J. Wheeler in DeWitt and Graham 1973.
13 Deutsch 1985, especially p. 20.

7 PRISONER'S DILEMMA AND NUCLEAR REVENGE

1 Some of the technicalities get lengthy treatment in Leslie 1991, 'Ensuring two bird deaths with one throw'.
2 Lewis 1979. I am not saying that Lewis would follow me in all the conclusions I draw from the suggestion.
3 Gauthier 1990.

BIBLIOGRAPHY

Adamson, D. (1990) *Defending the World*, London: Tauris.

Albert, D. Z. (1994) 'Bohm's alternative to quantum mechanics', *Scientific American*, May, 58–67.

Alper, J. (1994) 'Earth's near-death experience', *Earth*, January, 42–51.

Alvarez, L. W., Alvarez, W., Asaro, F. and Michel, H. (1980) 'Extraterrestrial cause for the Cretaceous-Tertiary extinction', *Science*, June 6, 1095–1108.

Alvarez, W. and Asaro, F. (1992) 'The extinction of the dinosaurs', pp. 28–56 of J. Bourriau (ed.) *Understanding Catastrophe*, Cambridge: Cambridge University Press.

Amabilino, D. and Stoddart, F. (1994) 'Molecules that build themselves', *New Scientist*, February 19, 25–9.

Anscombe, G. E. M. (1958) 'Modern moral philosophy', *Philosophy*, January, 1–19.

Bader, J. and Dorozynski, A. (1993) 'La Grande Offensive des virus', *Science et Vie*, February, 63–70.

Bain, J. D., Switzer, C., Chamberlain, A. R. and Benner, S. A. (1992) 'Ribosome-mediated incorporation of a non-standard amino acid into a peptide through expansion of the genetic code', *Nature*, April 9, 537–9.

Bak, P. and Chen, K. (1991) 'Self-organized criticality', *Scientific American*, January, 46–53.

Bak, P., Flyvbjerg, H. and Sneppen, K. (1994) 'Can we model Darwin?', *New Scientist*, March 13, 36–9.

Ballard, M. (1986) 'Drug abuse in the military and its contribution to accidents', pp. 46–55 of I. Fenton (ed.) *The Psychology of Nuclear Conflict*, London: Coventure.

Barnaby, F. (ed.) (1988) *The Gaia Peace Atlas*, New York: Doubleday.

Barney, G. O. (ed.) (1989) *The Global 2000 Report to the President*, Cabin John, Md.: Seven Locks Press (revised edition of Vol. I of the three-volume report of the same name, Washington, D. C.: US Government Printing Office, 1980).

289

Barrow, J. D. and Tipler, F. J. (1986) *The Anthropic Cosmological Principle*, Oxford: Clarendon Press.

Beardsley, T. (1994a) 'La Ronde', *Scientific American*, June, 26–9.

—— (1994b) 'Lethal legacy: Soviet reactor sites menace Eurasia', *Scientific American*, July, 20–2.

Begelman, M. C. and Rees, M. J. (1976) 'Can cosmic clouds cause climatic catastrophes?', *Nature*, May 27, 298–9.

Bell, M. (1994) 'Is our climate unstable?', *Earth*, January, 24–31.

Bennett, J. (1978) 'On maximizing happiness', pp. 61–73 of Sikora and Barry 1978.

Bernal, J. D. (1969) *The World, the Flesh, and the Devil*, Bloomington: Indiana University Press.

Bethe, H. A. (1991) *The Road from Los Alamos*, New York: American Institute of Physics.

Bethe, H. A., Garwin, R. L., Gottfried, K., and Kendall, H. W. (1984) 'Space-based ballistic-missile defense', *Scientific American*, October; reprinted as pp. 113–31 of Bethe 1991.

Black, M. (1967) 'Probability', pp. 464–79 of P. Edwards (ed.) *The Encyclopedia of Philosophy*, New York: Macmillan.

Blair, B. G. (1993a) *The Logic of Accidental Nuclear War*, Washington, D.C. : Brookings Institution.

—— (1993b) 'Cold War relics: old risks from Russian and US doomsday machines', *The Globe and Mail*, Toronto, 11 October.

Blair, B. G. and Kendall, H. W. (1990) 'Accidental nuclear war', *Scientific American*, December, 53–8.

Blau, S. K., Guendelman, E. I. and Guth, A. H. (1987) 'Dynamics of false-vacuum bubbles', *Physical Review D*, March 15, 1746–66.

Blaustein, A. R. and Wake, D. B. (1995) 'The puzzle of declining amphibian populations', *Scientific American*, April, 52–7.

Bohm, D. (1990) 'A new theory of the relationship of mind and matter', *Philosophical Psychology* 3: 271–86.

Bohm, D. and Hiley, B. J. (1993) *The Undivided Universe*, London and New York: Routledge.

Boyer, T. (1975) 'Random electrodynamics: the theory of classical electrodynamics with classical electromagnetic zero-point radiation', *Physical Review*, February 15, 790–808.

—— (1985) 'The classical vacuum', *Scientific American*, August, 70–9.

Brand, S. (ed.) (1977) *Space Colonies*, Harmondsworth: Penguin.

Brennan, R. P. (1990) *Levitating Trains and Kamikaze Genes*, New York: Wiley.

Brin, G. D. (1983) 'The "Great Silence": the controversy concerning extraterrestrial intelligent life', *Quarterly Journal of the Royal Astronomical Society* 24: 283–309.

Britten, S. (1986) 'The invisible event', pp. 132–77 of I. Fenton (ed.) *The Psychology of Nuclear Conflict*, London: Coventure.

Broad, W. J. (1985) *Star Warriors*, New York: Simon & Schuster.

Brown, J. (1994) 'Antarctic ozone going fast', *New Scientist*, September 10, 11.

Brown, L. (1992) 'Ten years to save the world', *New Scientist*, February 22, 8.

Brown, N. (1990) *New Strategy Through Space*, Leicester: Leicester University Press.

Brown, P. (1994) 'Mystery virus linked to asbestos cancer', *New Scientist*, May 21, 4.

Brown, W. (1994) 'Disabled "cancer genes" still pose a risk', *New Scientist*, February 12, 4.

Burgess, D. and Hutchinson, H. (1993) 'Stronger than atoms', *New Scientist*, November 20, 28–33.

Burgess, E. (1982) 'Venus: the twin that went wrong', *New Scientist*, June 17, 786–8.

Burrows, W. E. and Windrem, R. (1994) *Critical Mass: The Dangerous Race for Superweapons in a Fragmenting World*, New York: Simon & Schuster.

Carnesale, A., Doty, P., Hoffmann, S., Huntington, S. P., Nye, J. S. and Sagan, S. D. (1983) *Living with Nuclear Weapons*, New York: Bantam Books.

Carr, B. J. and Rees, M. J. (1979) 'The anthropic principle and the structure of the physical world', *Nature*, April 12, 605–12.

Carter, B. (1974) 'Large number coincidences and the anthropic principle in cosmology', pp. 291–8 of M. S. Longair (ed.) *Confrontation of Cosmological Theories with Observational Data*, Dordrecht: Reidel. Reprinted in Leslie 1990a, pp. 125–33.

—— (1983) 'The anthropic principle and its implications for biological evolution', *Philosophical Transactions of the Royal Society of London* A 310, 346–63.

—— (1989) 'The anthropic selection principle and the ultra-Darwinian synthesis', pp. 33–63 of F. Bertola and U. Curi (eds) *The Anthropic Principle*, Cambridge: Cambridge University Press.

Casti, J. L. (1990) *Searching for Certainty*, New York: William Morrow.

Chapman, C. R. and Morrison, D. (1989) *Cosmic Catastrophes*, New York: Plenum Press.

Charles, D. (1990) 'The sea's forgotten carbon enters climate debate', *New Scientist*, December 15, 10.

BIBLIOGRAPHY

Charlson, R. J. and Wigley, T. M. L. (1994) 'Sulfate aerosol and climatic change', *Scientific American*, February, 48–50.

Cherfas, J. (1994) 'How many species do we need?', *New Scientist*, August 6, 37–40.

Clark, D., Hunt, G. and McCrea, W. (1978) 'Celestial chaos and terrestrial catastrophes', *New Scientist*, December 14, 861–3.

Close, F. (1988) *End*, Harmondsworth: Penguin.

Coghlan, A. (1993) 'Bacteria hold the key to genetic pollution', *New Scientist*, August 7, 14.

Coleman, S. and De Luccia, F. (1980) 'Gravitational effects on and of vacuum decay', *Physical Review D* 21, June 15, 3305–15.

Cook, J. (1989) *An Accident Waiting to Happen*, London: Unwin Hyman.

Courtillot, V. E. (1990) 'A volcanic eruption', *Scientific American*, October, 85–92.

Cross, M. (1995) 'The night clocks go back 100 years', *New Scientist*, April 15, 6.

Croswell, K. (1995) 'Gamma rays signal death knell', *New Scientist*, March 25, 19.

Crum, L. A. and Roy, R. A. (1994) 'Sonoluminescence', *Science*, October 14, 233–4.

Davies, P. C. W. (1982) *The Accidental Universe*, Cambridge: Cambridge University Press.

—— (1994) *The Last Three Minutes*, New York: Basic Books.

—— (1995) *About Time: Einstein's Unfinished Revolution*, New York: Simon & Schuster.

Davis, C. (1990) *Science for Good or Ill*, Santa Barbara: Nuclear Age Peace Foundation.

Davoust, E. (1991) *The Cosmic Water Hole*, Cambridge, Mass.: MIT Press.

Dawson, J. M. (1989) 'Plasma particle accelerators', *Scientific American*, March, 54–61.

Delahaye, J.-P. (1993) 'Machines, prédictions et fin du monde', *Pour la science*, September, 96–103.

—— (1994) 'Désespérante espérance', *Pour la science*, November, 102–6.

Demaret, J. and Lambert, D. (1994) *Le Principe anthropique*, Paris: Armand Colin.

Desai, M. S. and Shaw, G. L. (1991) 'Technological implications of stable strange quark matter', *Nuclear Physics B* Proc. Suppl. 24B, 207–10.

Deutsch, D. (1985) 'Quantum theory as a universal physical theory', *International Journal of Theoretical Physics* 24: 1–41.

DeWitt, B. S. and Graham, N. (eds) (1973) *The Many-Worlds Interpretation of Quantum Mechanics*, Princeton: Princeton University Press.

BIBLIOGRAPHY

Dicke, R. H. (1961) 'Dirac's Cosmology and Mach's principle', *Nature*, November 4, 440–1. Reprinted as pp. 121–34 of Leslie 1990a.

Doll, R. and Peto, R. (1981) *The Causes of Cancer: Quantitative Estimates of Avoidable Risks of Cancer in the United States Today*, New York: Oxford University Press.

Drexler, K. E. (1986) *Engines of Creation*, New York: Doubleday.

—— (1989) 'Biological and nanomechanical systems: contrasts in evolutionary capacity', pp. 501–19 of C. G. Langton (ed.) *Artificial Life*, Redwood City: Addison-Wesley.

—— (1992) *Nanosystems*, New York: John Wiley & Sons.

Drexler, K. E., Peterson, C. and Pergamit, G. (1991) *Unbounding the Future: the Nanotechnological Revolution*, New York: Morrow.

Durrell, L. (1986) *State of the Arc*, New York: Doubleday.

Dyson, F. (1966) 'The search for extraterrestrial technology', pp. 641–55 of R. E. Marshak (ed.) *Perspectives in Modern Physics*, New York: Wiley-Interscience.

—— (1968) 'Interstellar transport', *Physics Today*, October, 41–5.

—— (1979a) 'Time without end: physics and biology in an open universe', *Reviews of Modern Physics*, July, 447–60.

—— (1979b) *Disturbing the Universe*, New York: Harper & Row.

—— (1988) *Infinite in All Directions*, New York: Harper & Row.

Edwards, R. (1995) 'Cherry red and very dangerous', *New Scientist*, April 29, 4–5.

Ehrlich, P. (1968) *The Population Bomb*, New York: Ballantine.

—— (1990) *The Population Explosion*, New York: Ballantine.

Ellis, J. and Schramm, D. N. (1995) 'Could a nearby supernova explosion have caused a mass extinction?', *Proceedings of the National Academy of Sciences, USA*, January, 235–8.

Ellis, J., Linde, A. and Sher, M. (1990) 'Vacuum stability, wormholes, cosmic rays and the cosmological bounds on m_t and m_h', *Physics Letters B*, December 13, 203–11.

Erwin, D. H. (1993) *The Great Palaeozoic Crisis*, New York: Columbia University Press.

Ettinger, R. C. W. (1964) *The Prospect of Immortality*, New York: Doubleday.

Farhi, E. and Guth, A. H. (1987) 'An obstacle to creating a universe in the laboratory', *Physics Letters B*, January 8, 149–55.

Farhi, E., Guth, A. H. and Guven, J. (1990) 'Is it possible to create a universe in the laboratory by quantum tunneling?', *Nuclear Physics B*, July 30, 417–90.

Farhi, E. and Jaffe, R. L. (1984) 'Strange matter', *Physical Review D*, December 1, 2379–90.

Feynman, R. P. (1960) 'There's plenty of room at the bottom', *Engineering and Science*, February, 22–36.

Finney, B. R. and Jones, E. M. (eds) (1985) *Interstellar Migration and the Human Experience*, Berkeley: University of California Press.

Flores, R. A. and Sher, M. (1983) 'Upper limits to fermion masses in the Glashow-Weinberg-Salam model', *Physical Review D*, April 1, 1679–82.

Forward, R. L. (1986) 'Feasibility of interstellar travel: a review', *Journal of the British Interplanetary Society* 39: 379–86.

Franklin, H. B. (1988) *War Stars*, New York: Oxford University Press.

Frautschi, S. (1982) 'Entropy in an expanding universe', *Science*, August 13, 593–9.

French, H. F. (1994) 'Making environmental treaties work', *Scientific American*, December, 94–7.

Gauthier, D. (1990) 'Deterrence, maximization and rationality', pp. 298–321 of *Moral Dealing*, Ithaca: Cornell University Press.

Geissler, E. (ed.) (1986) *Biological and Toxin Weapons Today*, Oxford: Oxford University Press.

Glover, J. (1977) *Causing Death and Saving Lives*, Harmondsworth: Penguin.

Goldsmith, E. and Allen, R. (1972) *A Blueprint for Survival*, London: Penguin.

Goldsmith, E. and Hildyard, N. (eds) (1992) *The Earth Report 3*, London: Mitchell Beazley.

Gott, J. R. (1993) 'Implications of the Copernican principle for our future prospects', *Nature*, May 27, 315–19.

—— (1994) 'Future prospects discussed: Gott replies', *Nature*, March 10, 108.

Gottfried, K. and Blair, B. G. (eds)(1988) *Crisis Stability and Nuclear War*, New York: Oxford University Press.

Graedel, T. E. and Crutzen, P. J. (1989) 'The changing atmosphere', *Scientific American*, September, 58–68.

Greene, O., Percival, I. and Ridge, I. (1985) *Nuclear Winter*, Cambridge: Polity Press.

Gribbin, J. and Kelly, M. (1989) *Winds of Change*, Sevenoaks: Hodder & Stoughton.

Gupta, S. D. and Westfall, G. D. (1993) 'Probing dense nuclear matter in the laboratory', *Physics Today*, May, 34–40.

Guth, A. H. (1981) 'Inflationary universe: a possible solution to the horizon and flatness problems', *Physical Review D*, January 15, 347–56.

—— (1989) 'Starting the universe: the Big Bang and cosmic inflation', pp. 105–46 of J. Cornell (ed.) *Bubbles, Voids, and Bumps in Time*, Cambridge: Cambridge University Press.

Guth, A. H. and Steinhardt, P. J. (1984) 'The inflationary universe', *Scientific American*, May, 116–28.

Haisch, B., Rueda, A. and Puthoff, H. E. (1994) 'Inertia as a zero-point-field Lorentz force', *Physical Review A*, February, 678–94.

Hardin, G. (1968) 'The Tragedy of the Commons', *Science*, December 13, 1243–8.

—— (1981) 'Who cares for posterity?', pp. 221–34 of Partridge 1981.

Harris, R. and Paxman, J. (1982) *A Higher Form of Killing: The Secret History of Chemical and Biological Warfare*, New York: Hill & Wang.

Hart, G. and Goldwater, B. (1980) *Recent False Alerts from the Nation's Attack Warning System: Report to the Senate Committee on Armed Services*, October 9, Washington, D. C.: US Government Printing Office.

Hart, M. H. (1982) 'Atmospheric evolution, the Drake equation, and DNA: sparse life in an infinite universe', pp. 154–66 of M. H. Hart and B. Zuckerman (eds) *Extraterrestrials: Where Are They?*, New York: Pergamon Press. Reprinted as pp. 256–66 of Leslie 1990a.

Hassard, J. (1992) 'Arms and the ban', *New Scientist*, November 28, 38–41.

Hawking, S. W. (1993) *Black Holes and Baby Universes*, London: Bantam Press.

Hawking, S. W. and Israel, W. (eds) (1979) *General Relativity*, Cambridge: Cambridge University Press.

Heilbroner, R. L. (1975) 'What has posterity ever done for me?', *New York Times*, 19 January. Reprinted as pp. 191–4 of Partridge 1981.

Henbest, N. (1992) 'The "planet" that came in from the cold', *New Scientist*, November 14, 24–5.

Herbert, N. (1988) *Faster Than Light*, New York: New American Library.

—— (1993) *Elemental Mind*, New York: Dutton.

Herman, R. (1990) *Fusion*, Cambridge: Cambridge University Press.

Hiley, B. J. and Peat, F. D. (eds) (1987) *Quantum Implications*, London: Routledge & Kegan Paul.

Hodgson, D. (1991) *The Mind Matters*, Oxford: Clarendon Press.

Holmes, B. (1994) 'Super rice extends limits to growth', *New Scientist*, October 29, 4.

—— (1995) 'Arizona fights for the right to stay cool', *New Scientist*, April 29, 7.

Homer-Dixon, T. (1994) 'Is anarchy coming? A response to the optimists', *The Globe and Mail*, Toronto, May 10, A22.

't Hooft, G. (1980) 'Gauge theories of the forces between elementary particles', *Scientific American*, June, 104–38.

Horgan, J. (1990) 'Vapor trail', *Scientific American*, March, 24–6.

—— (1994) 'Biowarfare wars', *Scientific American*, January, 22.

Hume, D. (1748) *Enquiry concerning Human Understanding*, London.

Hut, P. and Rees, M. J. (1983) 'How stable is our vacuum?', *Nature*, April 7, 508–9.

Islam, J. N. (1983) *The Ultimate Fate of the Universe*, Cambridge: Cambridge University Press.

Jackson, F. C. (1982) 'Epiphenomenal qualia', *Philosophical Quarterly*, April, 127–36.

Jackson, J. D., Tigner, M. and Wojcicki, S. (1986) 'The superconducting supercollider', *Scientific American*, March, 66–77.

Jaynes, J. (1976) *The Origin of Consciousness in the Breakdown of the Bicameral Mind*, Boston: Houghton Mifflin.

Kaplan, R. D. (1994) 'The coming anarchy', *Atlantic Monthly*, February, 44–76.

Kates, R. W. (1994) 'Sustaining life on Earth', *Scientific American*, October, 114–22.

Keegan, J. (1987) *The Mask of Command*, New York: Viking Penguin.

Kennedy, P. (1993) *Preparing for the Twenty-First Century*, New York: Random House.

Kennedy, R. (1968) *13 Days*, London: Macmillan.

Kiernan, V. (1994a) 'A bomb waiting to explode', *New Scientist*, February 26, 14–15.

—— (1994b) 'Star Wars lives on in a Jumbo jet', *New Scientist*, June 18, 4.

Kissinger, H. (1979) *White House Years*, Toronto: Little, Brown.

Kneale, W. C. (1950) 'Objectivity in morals', *Philosophy*, April, 149–66.

Koonin, S. and Nauenberg, M. (1989) 'Calculated fusion rates in isotopic hydrogen molecules', *Nature*, June 29, 690–1.

Krimsky, S. (1982) *Genetic Alchemy: The Social History of the Recombinant DNA Controversy*, Cambridge, Mass.: MIT Press.

Lederman, L. M. and Schramm, D. N. (1989) *From Quarks to the Cosmos*, New York: W. H. Freeman.

Lee, T. D. and Wick, G. C. (1974) 'Vacuum stability and vacuum excitation in a spin-0 field theory', *Physical Review D*, April 15, 2291–316.

Leggett, J. (1992) 'Running down to Rio', *New Scientist*, May 2, 38–42.

Leslie, J. (1970) 'The theory that the world exists because it should', *American Philosophical Quarterly*, October, 286–98.

—— (1972) 'Ethically required existence', *American Philosophical Quarterly*, July, 215–24.

—— (1976) 'The value of time', *American Philosophical Quarterly*, April, 109–21.

—— (1978a) 'God and scientific verifiability', *Philosophy*, January, 71–9.

—— (1978b) 'Efforts to explain all existence', *Mind*, April, 181–94.

—— (1979) *Value and Existence*, Oxford: Basil Blackwell.

—— (1980) 'The world's necessary existence', *International Journal for Philosophy of Religion*, Winter, 207–23.

—— (1982) 'Anthropic principle, world ensemble, design', *American Philosophical Quarterly*, April, 141–51.

—— (1983a) 'Cosmology, probability and the need to explain life', pp. 53–82 of N. Rescher (ed.) *Scientific Explanation and Understanding*, Lanham and London: Center for Philosophy of Science and University Press of America.

—— (1983b) 'Why not let life become extinct?', *Philosophy*, July, 329–38.

—— (1983c) 'Observership in cosmology: the anthropic principle', *Mind*, July, 573–9.

—— (1983d) Review of E. Partridge (ed.) (1981), *Social Indicators Research* 12: 323–6.

—— (1985) 'Modern cosmology and the creation of life', pp. 91–120 of E. McMullin (ed.) *Evolution and Creation*, Notre Dame: University of Notre Dame Press.

—— (1986a) 'The scientific weight of anthropic and teleological principles', pp. 111–19 of N. Rescher (ed.) *Current Issues in Teleology*, Lanham and London: Center for Philosophy of Science and University Press of America.

—— (1986b) 'Anthropic explanations in cosmology', pp. 87–95 of A. Fine and P. Machamer (eds) *PSA 1986: Volume One*, Ann Arbor: Edwards Brothers (Proceedings of the 1986 Biennial Meeting of the Philosophy of Science Association).

—— (1986c) 'Mackie on neoplatonism's "replacement for God"', *Religious Studies*, September/December, 325–42 (A reply to chapter 13 of J. L. Mackie's *The Miracle of Theism*, Oxford: Clarendon Press, 1982, a chapter reacting to Leslie 1979).

—— (1987) 'Probabilistic phase transitions and the anthropic principle', pp. 439–44 of J. Demaret (ed.) *Origin and Early History of the Universe*, Liège: Presses of the University of Liège.

—— (1988a) 'No inverse gambler's fallacy in cosmology', *Mind*, April, 269–72.

—— (1988b) 'The prerequisites of life in our universe', pp. 229–58 of G. V. Coyne, M. Heller and J. Zycinski (eds) *Newton and the New Direction in Science*, Citta del Vaticano: Vatican Observatory.

—— (1988c) 'How to draw conclusions from a fine-tuned universe', pp. 297–311 of R. J. Russell, W. R. Stoeger and G. V. Coyne (eds) *Physics, Philosophy and Theology*, Citta del Vaticano: Vatican Observatory (Proceedings of the papal Newton Tercentenary workshop at Castel

Gandolfo; distributed by University of Notre Dame Press).

—— (1989a) *Universes*, London and New York: Routledge.

—— (1989b) 'The Leibnizian richness of our universe', pp. 139–46 of N. Rescher (ed.) *Leibnizian Inquiries*, Lanham and London: Center for Philosophy of Science and University Press of America.

—— (1989c) 'The need to generate happy people', *Philosophia*, May, 29–33.

—— (1989d) 'Demons, vats and the cosmos', *Philosophical Papers*, September, 169–88.

—— (1989e) 'Risking the world's end', *Bulletin of the Canadian Nuclear Society*, May, 10–15. Reprinted in *Interchange* (1990) 21, 1: 49–58.

—— (ed.) (1990a) *Physical Cosmology and Philosophy*, New York: Macmillan.

—— (1990b) 'Is the end of the world nigh?', *Philosophical Quarterly*, January, 65–72.

—— (1991) 'Ensuring two bird deaths with one throw', *Mind*, January, 73–86.

—— (1992a) 'Doomsday revisited', *Philosophical Quarterly*, January, 85–9.

—— (1992c) 'The doomsday argument', *Mathematical Intelligencer* 14, 2: 48–51.

—— (1992d) 'Time and the anthropic principle', *Mind*, July, 521–40.

—— (1992e) 'Bayes, urns and doomsday', *Interchange* 23, 3: 289–95.

—— (1992f) 'Design and the anthropic principle', *Biology and Philosophy*, July, 349–54.

—— (1993a) 'Is it all quite simple?' (review of S. Weinberg, *Dreams of a Final Theory*, London: Hutchinson, 1993, and P. W. Atkins, *Creation Revisited*, Oxford: Freeman, 1992), *The Times Literary Supplement*, 29 January, 3–4.

—— (1993b) 'Doom and probabilities', *Mind*, July, 489–91.

—— (1993c) 'A Spinozistic vision of God', *Religious Studies* 29, September, 277–86.

—— (1993d) 'Creation stories, religious and atheistic', *International Journal for Philosophy of Religion*, October, 65–77. Reprinted as pp. 337–51 of R. Varghese and C. Matthews (eds) *Cosmic Beginnings and Human Ends*, Chicago: Open Court, 1995.

—— (1993e) 'More about Doom', *Mathematical Intelligencer* 15, 3: 5–7.

—— (1994a) 'The absolute now' (review of D. Bohm and B. J. Hiley, *The Undivided Universe*, London: Routledge, 1993, and S. W. Hawking, *Black Holes and Baby Universes*, London: Bantam Press, 1993), *London Review of Books*, May 12, 15–16.

—— (1994b) 'Testing the doomsday argument', *Journal of Applied Philosophy* 11, 1: 31–44.

—— (1994c) 'Anthropic prediction', *Philosophia*, July, 117–44.

—— (1994d) 'Fine tuning can be important', *Australasian Journal of Philosophy*, September, 383.

—— (1994e) 'Cosmology: a philosophical survey', *Philosophia*, December, 3–27.

—— (1995a) 'Cosmology', 'Cosmos', 'Finite/infinite', 'World', 'Why there is something', in J. Kim and E. Sosa (eds) *A Companion to Metaphysics*, Oxford: Basil Blackwell.

—— (1995b) 'Anyone for eternity?' (review of F. J. Tipler, *The Physics of Immortality*, London: Macmillan, 1995), *London Review of Books*, March 23, 7–8.

—— (1996) 'The anthropic principle today', in R. Hassing (ed.) *Final Causality in Nature and Human Affairs*, Washington, D. C.: Catholic University Press.

Levasseur-Regourd, A. (1992) '26 septembre 2000: la collision?', *Sciences et avenir*, October, 50–5.

Lewin, R. (1992) 'How to destroy the doomsday asteroid', *New Scientist*, June 6, 12–13.

Lewis, D. (1979) 'Prisoners' dilemma is a Newcomb problem', *Philosophy and Public Affairs*, Spring, 235–40.

Linde, A. D. (1985) 'The universe: inflation out of chaos', *New Scientist*, March 7, 14–18. Reprinted in Leslie 1990a, pp. 239–47.

—— (1988) 'Life after inflation', *Physics Letters B*, August 25, 29–31.

—— (1990) *Inflation and quantum cosmology*, San Diego and London: Academic Press.

—— (1992) 'Stochastic approach to tunneling and baby universe formation', *Nuclear Physics B*, March 16, 421–42.

—— (1994) 'The self-reproducing inflationary universe', *Scientific American*, November, 48–55.

Littlewood, B. and Strigini, L. (1992) 'The risks of software', *Scientific American*, November, 62–75.

Lockwood, M. (1989) *Mind, Brain and the Quantum*, Oxford: Blackwell.

Lovelock, J. E. (1979) *Gaia*, New York: Oxford University Press.

—— (1985) 'Are we destabilising world climate?', *The Ecologist* 15: 52–5.

—— (1986) 'Gaia: the world as living organism', *New Scientist*, December 18, 25–8.

McCrea, W. H. (1975) 'Ice ages and the galaxy', *Nature*, June 19, 607–9.

McCusker, B. (1991) 'The quarks that fell to Earth', *New Scientist*, July 20, 22–5.

McDonough, T. R. (1987) *The search for extraterrestrial intelligence*, New York: Wiley.

MacGowan, R. A. and Ordway, F. I. (1966) *Intelligence in the Universe*,

Englewood Cliffs: Prentice-Hall.

Mackenzie, Deborah (1994) 'Will tomorrow's children starve?', *New Scientist*, September 3, 24–9.

MacKenzie, Donald (1990) *Inventing Accurary: A Historical Sociology of Nuclear Missile Guidance*, Boston: MIT Press.

Mackie, J. L. (1977) *Ethics: Inventing Right and Wrong*, Harmondsworth: Penguin.

—— (1982) *The Miracle of Theism*, Oxford: Clarendon Press.

McNamara, R. (1985) 'Reducing the risk of nuclear war', *Atlantic Monthly*, July, reprinted as pp. 138–50 of Bethe 1991.

Maddox, J. (1972) *The Doomsday Syndrome*, London: Macmillan.

Markov, M. A. (1989) *The Past and the Future of the Universe*, Moscow: Nauka.

Marochnik, L. S. (1983) 'On the origin of the Solar System and the exceptional position of the sun in the galaxy', *Astrophysics and Space Science* 89: 61–75.

Marshall, I. N. (1989) 'Consciousness and Bose–Einstein condensates', *New Ideas in Psychology* 7: 73–83.

Matloff, G. L. and Mallove, E. (1981) 'Solar sail starships: the clipper ships of the galaxy', *Journal of the British Interplanetary Society* 34: 371–80.

Matthews, R. (1992) 'Enemy from space replaces red menace', *New Scientist*, November 14, 4.

Meadows, D. H., Meadows, D. L., Randers, J. and Behrens, W. H. (1972) *The Limits to Growth*, New York: New American Library.

Meadows, D. H., Meadows, D. L. and Randers, J. (1992) *Beyond the Limits*, Post Mills: Chelsea Green.

Mehta, A. and Barker, G. (1991) 'The self-organising sand pile', *New Scientist*, June 15, 40–3.

Mill, J. S. (1867) Chapter 26 of *An Examination of Sir William Hamilton's Philosophy*, London: Longmans, Green & Co.

Mitchison, A. (1993) 'Will we survive? (As host and pathogen evolve together, will the immune system retain the upper hand?)', *Scientific American*, September, 136–44.

Moravec, H. P. (1988) *Mind Children: The Future of Robot and Human Intelligence*, Cambridge, Mass.: Harvard University Press.

—— (1989) 'Human culture: a genetic takeover underway', pp. 167–99 of C. G. Langton (ed.) *Artificial Life*, Redwood City: Addison-Wesley.

Morgan, M. G. (1993) 'Risk analysis and management', *Scientific American*, July, 32–41.

Morone, J. G. and Woodhouse, E. J. (1986) *Averting Catastrophe*, Berkeley: University of California Press.

Mosey, D. (1990) *Reactor Accidents: Nuclear Safety and the Role of Institutional Failure*, Sutton: Nuclear Engineering International Special Publications and Butterworth Scientific.

Muller, R. (1988) *Nemesis*, New York: Weidenfeld & Nicolson.

Murphy, S., Hay, A. and Rose, S. (1984) *No Fire, No Thunder: The Threat of Chemical and Biological Weapons*, New York: Monthly Review Press.

Murray, C. (1989) 'Is the Solar System stable?', *New Scientist*, November 25, 60–3.

Myers, N. (ed.) (1984) *Gaia: An Atlas of Planet Management*, New York: Doubleday.

—— (1991) *The Gaia Atlas of Future Worlds*, New York: Doubleday.

Narlikar, J. (1984) *Violent Phenomena in the Universe*, Oxford and New York: Oxford University Press.

Narveson, J. (1967) 'Utilitarianism and new generations', *Mind*, January, 62–72.

Nelson, J. (1989) 'Fractility of soot smoke: implications for the severity of nuclear winter', *Nature*, June 22, 611–13.

Neumann, J., von (1955) *The Mathematical Foundations of Quantum Theory*, Princeton: Princeton University Press.

—— (1966) *Theory of Self-Reproducing Automata* (edited and completed by A. W. Burks), Urbana: University of Illinois Press.

Nielsen, H. B. (1989) 'Random dynamics and relations between the number of fermion generations and the fine structure constants', *Acta Physica Polonica B*, May, 427–68.

Odegard, D. (1984) 'Analytical approaches to determinism', *Dialogue*, June, 271–80.

O'Neill, G. (1977) *The High Frontier*, New York: William Morrow.

O'Neill, W. (1993) 'Fusion at a pinch', *New Scientist*, February 6, 24–5.

Oort, J. H. (1977) 'The galactic center – structure and radiation characteristics', *Annual Review of Astronomy and Astrophysics* 15: 295–362.

Palmer, T. (1989) 'A weather eye on unpredictability', *New Scientist*, November 11, 56–9.

Parfit, D. (1984) *Reasons and Persons*, Oxford: Clarendon Press.

Parsons, T. (1980) *Nonexistent Objects*, New Haven: Yale University Press.

Partridge, E. (ed.) (1981) *Responsibilities to Future Generations*, Buffalo: Prometheus.

Pearce, F. (1990) 'Whatever happened to acid rain?', *New Scientist*, September 15, 57–60.

—— (1994a) 'All gas and guesswork', *New Scientist*, September 14, 14–15.

—— (1994b) 'Will global warming plunge Europe into an ice age?', *New Scientist*, November 11, 20–1.

301

Penrose, R. (1987) 'Minds, machines and mathematics', pp. 259–76 of C. Blakemore and S. Greenfield (eds) *Mindwaves*, Oxford: Basil Blackwell.

—— (1989) *The Emperor's New Mind*, Oxford: Oxford University Press.

—— (1994) *Shadows of the Mind*, Oxford: Oxford University Press.

Perera, J. (1994) 'Can anyone control nuclear weapons?', *New Scientist*, April 2, 35.

Peterson, I. (1993) *Newton's Clock: Chaos in the Solar System*, New York: W. H. Freeman.

Piel, G. (1994) 'AIDS and population "control"', *Scientific American*, February, 124.

Piller, C. and Yamamoto, K. R. (1988) *Gene Wars: Military Control over the New Genetic Technologies*, New York: William Morrow.

Polkinghorne, J. C. (1986) *One World: The Interaction of Science and Theology*, London: SPCK.

Puthoff, H. (1989) 'Source of vacuum electromagnetic zero-point energy', *Physical Review A*, November 1, 4857–62.

—— (1990) 'Everything for nothing', *New Scientist*, July 28, 52–5.

Putnam, H. (1979) 'The place of facts in a world of values', pp. 113–40 of D. Huff and O. Prewett (eds) *The Nature of the Physical Universe*, New York: John Wiley.

Putterman, S. J. (1995) 'Sonoluminescence: sound into light', *Scientific American*, February, 46–51.

Quigg, C. (1985) 'Elementary particles and forces', *Scientific American*, April, 84–95.

Rawls, J. (1971) *A Theory of Justice*, Cambridge, Mass.: Harvard University Press.

Reid, G. C., McAfee, J. R. and Crutzen, P. J. (1978) 'Effects of intense stratospheric ionisation events', *Nature*, October 12, 489–92.

Rennie, J. (1993) 'Malignant mimicry: false estrogens may cause cancer and lower sperm counts', *Scientific American*, September, 34–8.

Rhodes, R. (1986) *The Making of the Atomic Bomb*, New York: Simon & Schuster.

Rind, D. (1995) 'Drying out the tropics', *New Scientist*, May 6, 36–40.

Rood, R. T. and Trefil, J. S. (1981) *Are We Alone?*, New York: Scribners'.

Ross, P. E. (1994) 'A new Black Death?', *Forbes*, September 12, 240–50.

Rothman, T. et al. (1985) *Frontiers of Modern Physics*, New York: Dover.

Rozental, I. L. (1988) *Big Bang, Big Bounce*, New York: Springer-Verlag.

Ruthen, R. (1993) 'Strange matters: can advanced accelerators initiate runaway reactions?', *Scientific American*, August, 17.

Sagan, C. (1980) *Cosmos*, New York: Random House.

BIBLIOGRAPHY

Sagan, S. D. (1993) *The Limits of Safety: Organizations, Accidents, and Nuclear Weapons*, Princeton: Princeton University Press.

Salmon, W. C. (1975) 'Determinism and indeterminism in modern science', pp. 351–67 of J. Feinberg (ed.) *Reason and Responsibility*, 3rd edition, Encimo: Dickenson.

Schelling, T. C. (1960) *The Strategy of Conflict*, London: Oxford University Press.

Schilling, G. (1992) 'Black holes by the million litter the galaxy', *New Scientist*, July 11, 16.

Schneider, S. H. (1989) 'The changing climate', *Scientific American*, September, 70–9.

Schneider, S. and Thompson, S. (1988) 'Simulating the climatic effects of nuclear war', *Nature*, May 19, 221–7.

Schneiker, C. (1989) 'Nanotechnology with Feynman machines: scanning tunneling engineering and artificial life', pp. 443–500 of C. G. Langton (ed.) *Artificial Life*, Redwood City: Addison-Wesley.

Searle, J. R. (1984) *Minds, Brains and Science*, Cambridge, Mass. : Harvard University Press.

—— (1990) 'Is the brain's mind a computer program?', *Scientific American*, January, 26–31.

Shaw, G. L., Shin, M., Dalitz, R. H. and Desai, M. (1989) 'Growing drops of strange matter', *Nature*, February 2, 436–9.

Sher, M. (1989) 'Electroweak Higgs potentials and vacuum stability', *Physics Reports* 5 and 6: 273–418.

Shklovskii, I. S. and Sagan, C. (1966) *Intelligent Life in the Universe*, New York: Dell.

Sikora, R. I. and Barry, B. (eds) (1978) *Obligations to Future Generations*, Philadelphia: Temple University Press.

Simon, J. L. and Kahn, H. (eds) (1984) *The Resourceful Earth*, Oxford: Basil Blackwell.

Smart, J. J. C. (1984) *Ethics, Persuasion and Truth*, London: Routledge & Kegan Paul.

—— (1987) *Essays Metaphysical and Moral*, Oxford: Basil Blackwell.

Smith, G. (1992) 'Running out of time', *New Scientist*, February 29, 54.

Smith, J. V. (1986) 'The defence of the Earth', *New Scientist*, April 17, 40–4.

Stapledon, O. (1930) *Last and First Men*, London: Penguin.

Starobinsky, A. A. and Zeldovich, Y. B. (1992) 'The spontaneous creation of the universe', pp. 97–133 of Y. B. Zeldovich and M. V. Sazhin (eds) *My Universe*, Chur: Harwood Academic Publishers.

Stix, G. (1991) 'Golden screws: micromechanical devices edge towards commercial uses', *Scientific American*, September, 166–9.

—— (1992) 'Micron machinations', *Scientific American*, November, 106–17.

Strauss, S. (1990) 'Artificial life', *The Globe and Mail*, Toronto, April 28, D1 and D4.

Sullivan, W. (1993) *We Are Not Alone* (revised edition), New York: Dutton.

Swinburne, N. (1993) 'It came from outer space', *New Scientist*, February 20, 28–32.

Swinburne, R. (1986) *The Evolution of the Soul*, Oxford: Clarendon Press.

—— (1990) 'Argument from the fine-tuning of the universe', pp. 154–73 of Leslie 1990a.

Sylvan, R. (1990) *Universal Purpose, Terrestrial Greenhouse and Biological Evolution*, Research Series in Unfashionable Philosophy, Research School of Social Sciences, Australian National University, Canberra.

The Economist (unsigned) (1993) 'The threat from space' (pp. 13–14) and 'The hard rain' (pp. 81–4), September 11.

Tipler, F. J. (1982) 'We are alone in our galaxy', *New Scientist*, October 7, 33–7.

—— (1994) *The Physics of Immortality*, New York: Doubleday.

Tipton, I. (1988) 'Freedom of the will', pp. 489–510 of G. H. R. Parkinson (ed.) *An Encyclopaedia of Philosophy*, London: Routledge.

Tirman, J. (ed.) (1984) *The Fallacy of Star Wars*, New York: Vintage.

Townes, C. H. and Genzel, R. (1990) 'What is happening in the center of our galaxy?', *Scientific American*, April, 46–55.

Tryon, E. P. (1973) 'Is the universe a vacuum fluctuation?', *Nature*, December 14, pp. 396–7. Reprinted as pp. 216–19 of Leslie 1990a.

—— (1984) 'What made the world?', *New Scientist*, March 8, 14–16.

Tucker, W. H. (1981) 'Astrophysical crises in the evolution of life in the galaxy', pp. 287–96 of J. Billingham (ed.) *Life in the Universe*, Cambridge, Mass.: MIT Press.

Turco, R., Toon, O. B., Ackerman, T. P., Pollack, J. B. and Sagan, C. (1983) 'Nuclear winter: global consequences of multiple nuclear explosions', *Science*, 23 December, 1283–92.

Turner, M. S. and Wilczek, F. (1982) 'Is our vacuum metastable?', *Nature*, August 12, 633–4.

Veltman, M. J. G. (1986) 'The Higgs boson', *Scientific American*, November, 76–84.

Wallich, P. (1995) 'Derivatives: not the real thing', *Scientific American*, January, 28.

Watson-Watt, R. (1961) *Man's Means to his End*, Toronto: McClelland and Stewart.

Weinberg, S. (1989) 'The cosmological constant problem', *Reviews of Modern Physics*, January, 1–23.

—— (1993) *Dreams of a Final Theory*, London: Hutchinson.

Weiner, J. (1990) *The Next One Hundred Years*, New York: Bantam.

Wesson, P. S. (1990) 'Cosmology, extraterrestrial intelligence, and a resolution of the Fermi–Hart Paradox', *Quarterly Journal of the Royal Astronomical Society* 31: 161–70.

Wheale, P. R. and McNally, R. M. (1988) *Genetic Engineering*, New York: St Martin's Press.

Wheeler, J. A. (1973) 'Beyond the end of time', pp. 1196–1217 of C. W. Misner, K. S. Thorne and J. A. Wheeler, *Gravitation*, San Francisco: W. H. Freeman. Reprinted as pp. 207–15 of Leslie 1990a.

White, R. M. (1990) 'The great climate debate', *Scientific American*, July, 36–43.

Wignall, P. (1992) 'The day the world nearly died', *New Scientist*, January 25, 51–5.

Wilson, E. O. (1989) 'Threats to biodiversity', *Scientific American*, September, 108–16.

Winston, R. (1991) 'Nonimaging optics', *Scientific American*, March, 76–81.

Wolfendale, A. (1978) 'Cosmic rays and ancient catastrophes', *New Scientist*, August 31, 634–6.

Zeeman, C. (1992) 'Evolution and catastrophe theory', pp. 83–101 of J. Bourriau (ed.) *Understanding Catastrophe*, Cambridge: Cambridge University Press.

Zimmerman, B. K. (1984) *Biofuture*, New York: Plenum Press.

INDEX